DISCARD

HORITY

Journalistic Authority

Legitimating News in the Digital Era

Matt Carlson

Columbia University Press   New York

Columbia University Press
Publishers Since 1893
New York   Chichester, West Sussex
cup.columbia.edu

Copyright © 2017 Columbia University Press
All rights reserved

Library of Congress Cataloging-in-Publication Data

Names: Carlson, Matt, 1977– author.
Title: Journalistic authority : legitimating news in the digital era / Matt Carlson.
Description: New York : Columbia University Press, 2017. | Includes bibliographical
    references and index.
Identifiers: LCCN 2016053747 | ISBN 9780231174442 (cloth : alk. paper) |
    ISBN 9780231174459 (pbk. : alk. paper) | ISBN 9780231543095 (e-book)
Subjects: LCSH: Journalism—Objectivity—United States. | Journalistic ethics—
    United States. | Journalism—United States—History—21st century. | Digital media—
    United States.
Classification: LCC PN4888.O25 .C35 2017 | DDC 071/.3—dc23
LC record available at https://lccn.loc.gov/2016053747

∞

Columbia University Press books are printed on permanent and durable acid-free paper.
Printed in the United States of America

Cover design: Diane Luger

To Barbie Zelizer, my teacher

Contents

Acknowledgments

For a book that takes a relational approach to journalistic authority, it seems fitting to salute all the relationships that made this work possible. I have had the good fortune to be surrounded by so many talented journalism scholars, and their fingerprints are all over this book. In particular, I want to thank Chris Anderson, Dan Berkowitz, Marcel Broersma, Rasmus Kleis Nielsen, Chris Peters, David Ryfe, Michael Schudson, Linda Steiner, Nikki Usher, and Tim Vos for their feedback on this project in its various stages. A special thanks goes to Sue Robinson and Seth Lewis for their early help in thinking through what this book could look like and for their constant support. Marcel Broersma and Chris Peters provided an opportunity to think out loud at the "Rethinking Journalism II" conference at the University of Groningen in January 2014.

My greatest debt is to my graduate advisor, Barbie Zelizer, who inspired my interest in this topic with her own work. This book is dedicated to her.

I also want to thank my institution, Saint Louis University, for its support, particularly with the yearlong sabbatical that provided the time to make this work possible. As I was writing the book, my research assistants—Samir Adrissi, Meilin Shen, Carolyn Jackson, and Nik Fischer—offered invaluable help from first steps to last. All along the process, April Trees has been a supportive department chair.

At Columbia University Press, Philip Leventhal saw the potential of this book and helped shepherd it through, ultimately making it the best book it can be.

Finally, I express my gratitude to my wife Curtis and my daughters, Lizzie and Claire, for making our home such a pleasant—and endlessly entertaining—place to write a book.

JOURNALISTIC AUTHORITY

Introduction

The Many Relationships of Journalism

"Of all the arguments under way these days at the noisy crossroads of the news business, none is quite so basic as the debate over journalistic authority—who has it, and what it is worth."[1] With these words, then *New York Times* executive editor Bill Keller opened his review of Alan Brinkley's 2010 biography, *Henry Luce and His American Century.* The book chronicles Luce's rise from Yale University dropout to creator of a unique journalistic form: the weekly news magazine. *Time* and later *Life* would become not merely influential news sources but part of the collective culture—magazines whose pictures and prose captured the collective attention of a nation. Visible in homes, newsstands, waiting rooms, buses, and trains, they came to symbolize the force of mass communication.

Although the story of Luce's ascension atop the pinnacle of twentieth-century journalism is fascinating on its own, the book review offered Keller the opportunity to opine on the state of journalism in the opening years of the twenty-first century—a time when many observers of the press seemed ready to shrug off mass communication as a quaint notion connected to a bygone century. Keller stood at the helm of one of the world's most venerated news organizations in an ocean of digital icebergs. Beset by an ethos esteeming the flat configuration of networked participation, Keller clung to a vision of journalism as a hierarchical public service, encompassed in a "conviction that a significant population of serious people feel the need for someone with training, experience and standards—reporters and editors—to help them dig up and sort through the news, identify what's important and make sense of it." In Keller's argument, journalists work on behalf of audiences to structure the world into a coherent and believable news product—a responsibility best reserved for legitimate professionals. This ideology has been clearly expressed each day for more than a century in the upper right-hand corner of the newspaper Keller edited: "All the news that's fit to print."

On any given day, the hundreds of journalists working at the *Times* churn out an incredible array of stories created in accordance with this vision. Below the iconic Gothic letters, either printed in ink or rendered in pixels, readers encounter stories ranging from on-the-ground accounts of battles in the Middle East to a review of the latest Broadway play. The newspaper assembles what is important or interesting at any moment, at least as selected by its hierarchically arranged staff. The *New York Times* delivers the news of the day. It is joined in this endeavor by the cacophony of Twitter, the microtargeting of a neighborhood blog, BuzzFeed listicles, an endless stream of commentary on cable television, the vast reservoir of formally secret documents housed by WikiLeaks, and a multitude of other sites that also tell us the news of the day. In this media environment, audiences confront a bewildering array of news stories claiming to represent or explain the world.

Journalistic authority has increasingly become a topic of concern, due in no small part to the transformation of all media, from the scarcity of the analog age to the abundance of the digital era. Keller's review provides a glimpse into how the head of a venerated news organization struggles with the ways in which digital media alter the availability of news, its economic structures, and the relationship between journalists and their audiences. Digital media have brought new potentialities and new players. Google News, Facebook, and Twitter are relatively new services, yet all three have become indelible parts of the news ecosystem. The advertising dollars that propped up traditional journalism outlets continue to migrate online, often away from news. A surplus of new digital sites for news, including those with particular political viewpoints, fragments the collective attention once commanded by newspapers and television networks. Even more recently, the rise of automated journalism in which computer programs author news stories without the intervention of humans further introduces new questions about what makes news legitimate. Taken together, the strains of digital media cannot be confined to just the technical, organizational, or economic realms. Instead, the central question has become how all these different aspects coalesce to spark a more fundamental rethinking of what news *is*. Where does journalism derive its authority?

Journalists are joined in this pondering by scholars who are also making sense of a changing news landscape. Several in the latter group have followed Keller's emphasis on journalistic authority as a means to conceptualize larger shifts taking place across the news.[2] Their studies shed valuable light on the variability of journalism. They expose how the introduction of new technologies and the forms they produce lead to a clash of paradigms as the technical restrictions governing who may create media dissipate. Long-entrenched understandings of news as a professional product run up against new experiments and experiences based on different normative foundations that accentuate participation and transparency.[3]

As journalistic authority becomes an area of concern both within the industry and among scholars, there is an urgent need to delve deeper into the term to pinpoint its meaning. Too often references to journalistic authority get made without any depth or explanation. Such usage assumes that the term contains sufficient innate meaning to do the necessary analytical labor it is required to do. This is just not the case.

On the surface, journalistic authority seems to have an intuitive meaning as some form of trust or credibility to be possessed, coveted, or lost. This may be how the term is employed familiarly, but this usage inhibits a fuller understanding of the concept and how it functions. Simplistic invocations of journalistic authority as a stand-in for trust or as an implied characteristic end up not being able to explain much about authority or journalism. At best, they hint at the underlying complexity of news. More often, this lack of a fleshed-out concept of journalistic authority disconnects journalism from its context, leaving its entanglement in webs of social relations unexplored. The lack of comprehensive theorizing on this issue comes right at the moment it is most needed to help grasp what is happening to journalism—and how to study it.

This book enters the conversation by asking a basic question at the heart of authority: How is it that journalism comes to possess a right to be listened to?[4] Answering this question requires explaining the particular modes and networks necessary for the news to be believed and legitimated in any place or time. It rests on sensitivity to context, including how the changing technology of news connects to changes in how news is thought about. Above all, it obliges the need to look at the relations that make authority possible.

WHY JOURNALISTIC AUTHORITY?

The argument for why authority should be a privileged concept for understanding journalism begins with recognizing the term to be enmeshed in a paradox. Although conceptually authority is quite hazy and underdeveloped, it is routinely said to be in crisis. Legacy news organizations have suffered enough declines in audiences, revenues, and credibility to raise questions about the continued viability of the basic paradigm of mass communication in which professional journalists create a news product to be consumed by large audiences. Many journalists have expressed deep anxiety over what Alex S. Jones, director of Harvard's Shorenstein Center on Media, Politics, and Public Policy, calls "a crisis of diminishing quantity and quality, of morale and sense of mission, of values and leadership."[5] Looking across such claims, Todd Gitlin dissects this crisis into several domains, one of them being the "elusive crisis of authority" that has deepened from concerns over credibility to something graver involving the very legitimacy of the predominant model of objective journalism.[6] To anyone following the news industry closely, Gitlin's claims do not seem controversial or exaggerated but indicative of changes occurring across journalism. Assessing what these changes mean for journalistic authority requires addressing the first part of the paradox: our lack of understanding regarding what kind of authority journalists have.

To begin to theorize about journalistic authority, a starting point is Barbie Zelizer's comprehensive treatment of the topic in her account of how American journalists, especially within the nascent realm of television news, wove their coverage of the 1963 assassination of President John F. Kennedy into lasting narratives supporting their authority. Zelizer's definition of journalistic authority as "the ability of journalists to promote themselves as authoritative and credible spokespersons of 'real-life' events"[7] contributes much to this book. In tracking how journalists construct narratives about the value of their work, she reaffirms that journalists' claims to being "authoritative chroniclers" are never automatically granted but the product of continuous effort.[8] Zelizer's pioneering work provides a foundation for exploring the workings of journalistic authority.[9]

This book picks up from there by arguing that authority is the central element that makes journalism work. Some readers may cringe at this declaration for its normative agnosticism or its whiff of bland functionalism. The heart of journalism, many practitioners and academics hold, lies in its democratic purpose. This view has been crystallized by Bill Kovach and Tom Rosenstiel in their well-known book *The Elements of Journalism*.[10] After lengthy consultations with journalists and journalism scholars, the authors arrive at the following foundational premise for journalism: "The primary purpose of journalism is to provide citizens with the information they need to be free and self-governing," achieved through commitments to particular elements of journalism, including verification, independence, engagement, and providing a public forum.[11] This is a respectable mission that expresses why journalism is important by assigning it a central role in democratic life. Journalists provide valuable information that would otherwise be offered by self-interested institutional actors. From this vantage point, privileging authority errs by eschewing journalism's innate social value.

A critique of authority's privileged status made on these grounds misses the point. However nobly expressed, we cannot stop at the pronouncement of journalism's principles to understand the complex social relations through which it comes to have authority. Explaining the creation, maintenance, defense, and contestation of journalistic authority requires a broader vision of journalistic practices, news forms, underlying technologies, organizational structures, and the wider context in which news is produced and consumed. Within this context, the normative commitments and self-definitions journalists choose to endorse do matter a great deal. Yet norms and practices change over time. In the history of US journalism, the party press of the 1800s, the objective press of the 1900s, and newer digital forms emerging in the 2000s may appear unrecognizable to each other as legitimate news. Likewise, norms and practices differ across geopolitical contexts, across different media, and across outlets within a medium. In any time and place, journalists constantly make and remake the arguments undergirding journalistic authority[12]—that is, arguments for why journalists should be listened to at all.

To appreciate the variability of news while building a coherent theory of journalistic authority, this book moves beyond norms to begin with the most foundational question possible: what are the necessary conditions for any news story to be accepted as a legitimate account of an event? With little fanfare, audiences take in the news, adding to their stock of knowledge even while perhaps questioning or rejecting what's being communicated. This tacitness indicates the degree to which this question is as much about shared assumptions as it is about practices. To begin to answer it requires a conception of journalism as, at its core, a sociotechnical accomplishment involving an array of actors, organizational structures, communication technologies, and cultural practices. Much of the attention in journalism studies has focused on organizational aspects and the adoption of technological and procedural processes, but authority cannot be understood without viewing journalism as a cultural accomplishment as well.[13]

While culture is a complex term conjuring an array of meanings, its use here implies the need to connect practice and meaning within a shared context. An emphasis on culture moves beyond individualized examinations of news texts or the organizational characteristics through which they are produced to engage in a more holistic evaluation of the production and circulation of news. The value of this broad approach is bolstered by the difficulty of journalism as a referent. It refers at once to a set of practices, a material output, and an institution of public life. But more than this, journalism cannot be reduced to only the practitioners that create it. Conceptualizations of journalism must also encompass the technologies that facilitate it, the sources that contribute to it, the advertisers that fund it, the corporations that run it, the audiences that consume it, the policymakers that shape it, and the critics that critique it. In short, journalism is not merely a form of information transfer or a set of insulated professional communicators. It marks an entire social *context* that far exceeds the isolated news text. Actors make cultures through action, and like any other cultural form, journalism is malleable and contested, shaped from within and from the outside. Approaching the study of journalism culturally involves stressing connections between action and meaning and emphasizing a systemic vision incorporating the relations among diverse actors.

This leads to the central claim in this book: To encounter news, whether through seeking it out or having it pushed on us, is to enter into a relationship. Even the mundane act of reading, watching, or listening to the news, like any relationship, comes with a slew of expectations. Journalists are supposed to relay, record, and interpret events in the world, the vast majority of which take place outside or beyond the scope of the audience's daily experience. Audiences expect journalists to know and to communicate their knowing. And the news is expected to be a quality product, comprehensive and truthful and vital to public life. And we anticipate it will be either free or highly subsidized by someone else—advertisers, foundations, the state. This is a lot to ask—but ask we do.

We place many expectations on journalism. But if journalism is to be a watchdog working on our behalf, the fourth estate holding government accountable, a communal glue, an enabler of deliberative democracy, a diffuser of new scientific and technical knowledge, a judge of the arts, if it is to provide an accounting of the day's news, the first draft of history, an exchange of ideas, a space for disparate voices, a place where society makes sense of itself, if it is to be any of these things, it *must* have authority. But what kind of authority do journalists have? Who lays claim to it? How is it changing? And what does this mean for society? These are the question this book sets out to answer. The argument I put forward holds that journalistic authority can be understood relationally only as an understanding formed through the interactions among all the actors necessary for journalism to exist. This is a holistic perspective, and the chapters in this book break down the components of journalistic authority while probing contemporary struggles over what authoritative journalism should be. But before venturing into the question of what makes *journalism* authoritative, the place to begin is a wider view clarifying what makes *anything* authoritative.

BEING AN AUTHORITY

Media scholars have given scant attention to the tangled literature on authority spread out across political philosophy, sociology, science and technology studies, rhetoric, law, and theology. Generations of scholars have wrestled with the meaning of authority, a concept religious historian Bruce Lincoln has called "extraordinarily complex, hopelessly elusive, and almost as badly misconstrued in most scholarly discussions as it is in popular parlance."[14] This confusion owes something to authority's broad use across different domains, as well as the political question surrounding the role—or lack of a role, as Hannah Arendt argues[15]—of authority in modern life. To speak of authority is both to describe a hierarchical social arrangement and to engage in a normative deliberation regarding such an arrangement.[16]

The modern study of authority owes much to the work of Max Weber. The advancement of modern bureaucratic organizations in the nineteenth century was not merely about efficiently managing increasingly larger groups but transforming legitimacy away from its charismatic and traditional modes to privilege rational-legal authority.[17] Authority shifts from specific persons to an abstracted quality associated with delineated institutional roles. The legitimacy of bureaucracy—or of the bureaucrat—owes to the rules that govern that position. Obedience to authority develops out of a belief that the system itself—its "impersonal order"[18]—is legitimate and that the persons occupying positions within the bureaucracy adhere to these rules (or risk removal). Weber's perspective encompasses both actions performed by those seeking authority and the voluntary obedience of those being acted upon to this authority.

The sections below build off these fundamental properties to advance five key premises arising in the literature on authority. But first, a stark division must be made between being *in* authority and being *an* authority.[19] Actors said to be *in* authority possess a set of enforcement mechanisms and legitimating practices that those who are *an* authority do not have. Because we can hardly speak of journalists as being in authority in the same sense that police officers, judges, elected officials are all authorities, this book restricts its focus to journalism as *an* authority. As such, being *an* authority means, at its most basic, that one's "views or utterances are entitled to be believed."[20] The following five premises explore the core of what it means to create authoritative knowledge about the world to be believed by others.

The first premise of what it means to be an authority is possessing "a right to be listened to."[21] This meaning of authority has become muddled in modern English. Too often, power and authority are used interchangeably; to say one "has power over" or "has authority over" is largely to say the same thing. Returning to authority's Latin origins remedies the collapsing of these terms and the vacating of their nuances. The ancient Romans differentiated among three distinct words, each with its own nuance: *auctoritas*, *potestas*, and *potentia*.[22] The latter two relate etymologically to the English word *power*, although from different directions.[23] By contrast, *auctoritas* is a trickier term that has shed much of its original gist in its journey to becoming the modern word *authority*. Its distinction from other forms of power offers a good starting place for thinking about what makes journalism authoritative.

One way to define *auctoritas* is as a form of communicative authority that entitles those who possess it to speak and be heard. Political theorist H. M. Höpfl explains how the conflation of speakers and institutions gives rise to the qualities supporting claims to authority: "experience, knowledge, understanding, judgement, prudence, skill, decisiveness, gravity, a track-record of achievement and a lineage of eximious predecessors are all decisive for *auctoritas*."[24] This sense can be understood by translating the Latin word *auctor* not as its modern counterpart "author" but in its Latin usage of "founder" with its roots of authority in memory and tradition as well as defined social roles.[25] The communicative authority embedded in *auctoritas* has been translated in different ways. Höpfl defines it as the "capacity to initiate and to inspire respect"—granting its possessors *moral* authority over the world in contrast to coercive or legal power.[26] Authority cannot be reduced to coercion or persuasion but lies in between as a distinct form of influence. Bruce Lincoln views *auctoritas* through a communicative lens as "the capacity to make a consequential pronouncement," albeit within specific circumstances.[27] *Auctoritas* is context-bound. In certain situations, speakers in possession of *auctoritas* are in a position to be heard as authorities. But by whom?

The second premise is that authority is not an intrinsic quality of a person or institution but an asymmetrical relationship between those who have authority and those who recognize this authority. R. B. Friedman signals this relational understanding of authority by describing *auctoritas* as a "dependence on the 'account' of another person" on the condition that authority "always involves differentiated access."[28] The classic case is that of the clergy, who, through their authoritative position, possess a unique relationship with God exceeding that of lay worshippers.

By being ordained, both spiritually and institutionally, to lead the congregation through rituals and scriptures, the priest mediates the relationship between God and the lay community. In this example, authority is both relational and asymmetrical (and also contextual, as noncongregants reside outside this relationship). This general dynamic is a familiar part of contemporary society in which complex knowledge structures give rise to dependence on a wide variety of experts. We depend upon doctors, lawyers, scientists, accountants, cooking show hosts, and so on, to be authorities because of inequalities of access to knowledge, institutions, and technologies. Authority is always asymmetrical.

Although a degree of inequality is fundamental to authority, the asymmetry endemic to authority relations should be understood as acquiescent rather than coerced. This dynamic is nicely encapsulated in Richard Sennett's definition of authority as "a bond between people who are unequal."[29] Rather than victims of a one-sided dominance, participants who deem certain knowledge providers to be authoritative reaffirm inequality through a "mutually recognized normative relationship."[30] To argue for the right to be listened to is predicated on providing a service to others. As sociologist Frank Furedi argues, "Authority always derives its status from something outside itself."[31] Claims to authority invoke the greater good.

Having recovered authority's Latin roots and clarified its relational character, the question becomes what authority looks like. This brings up a third premise: authority is performed through discourse. Treating authority as some sort of material to be possessed, gained, or lost would be a mistake—even if it is often described this way colloquially. For Sennett, "authority is not a thing. It is an interpretive process which seeks for itself the solidity of a thing."[32] Language reifies authority by treating it as an object, but we cannot point to authority, only to the understanding of certain relationships as authoritative. Legal scholar James Boyd White defends this discursive view when he argues that "the object of authority is not an 'object' at all but a way of talking and thinking, an activity of mind and imagination and art."[33] Authority cannot be reduced to disconnected texts, individuals, organizations, or institutions but instead is continuously enacted through discourse. It is performative, bound up in exchanges between one laying claim to authority and one recognizing its legitimacy. Whether through such means as a sermon, a legal brief, or, as will be examined below, a news report, speakers constantly perform their authority through communicative conventions particular to the setting. In this view, one does not *have* authority as much as one *performs* authoritatively.

Bruce Lincoln extends this performative understanding of authority to encompass both the performer and the audience: "discursive authority is not so much an entity as it is (1) an effect; (2) the capacity for producing that effect; and (3) the commonly shared opinion that a given actor has the capacity for producing that effect."[34] The last part again signals the importance of considering authority from a relational perspective that does not treat authorities as speaking to no one in particular. Instead, a speaker in a specific context calls attention to her position to make pronouncements while inviting recognition of this authoritative position from the audience.

The fourth premise is that being an authority involves institutional control over knowledge within a bounded domain that is recognized as authoritative by others. This process forms the crux of Paul Starr's work on the professionalization of medicine.[35] Through the acquisition of technical knowledge about the body and the establishment of set procedures, doctors established themselves as the legitimate arbiters of health and medicine we depend on for our wellness. But doctors are not an authority in the sense given above (what Starr calls "social authority"). They possess "cultural authority," or "the probability that particular definitions of reality and judgments of meaning and value will prevail as valid and true."[36] As authorized knowers, doctors are listened to in matters of health; those of us outside the medical community defer to this judgment.

The close linkage between authority and knowledge production has long been a central concern within the sociology of the professions.[37] Professions set themselves apart through control over specific domains of knowledge. Andrew Abbott labels this type of authority "jurisdictional control" or "legitimate control of a particular kind of work."[38] For a professional group, the rewards of attaining jurisdictional control are many, including "the right to perform the work as it wishes, . . . to exclude other workers as deemed necessary, to dominate public definitions of the tasks concerned, and . . . to impose professional definitions of the tasks on competing professions."[39] Abbott highlights the rewards to be gained from possessing authority over knowledge production in particular areas—autonomy, external influence, and material benefits.

The final premise for thinking about authority is that it is always open to contestation and change. The preceding paragraphs have treated authority as stable and discrete, but this clearly is not the case. Looking across examples given so far, the Roman Senate lost its influence to increasingly autocratic emperors, the authority of Christian clergy has been questioned since the Reformation, the authority of medical doctors has been challenged by purveyors of Eastern medicine and antivaccination advocates, the authority of scientists faces distrust from religious fundamentalists, politicians, and other skeptics, and the list continues. These examples show how authority needs to be understood within ongoing struggles to achieve and maintain legitimacy.

The contested nature of authoritative status has been most fully developed in the "boundary-work" concept advanced by sociologist Thomas Gieryn.[40] Like Starr, Gieryn directs attention to the relational workings of authority in his study of science. He labels this "epistemic authority," defined as "the legitimate power to define, describe, and explain bounded domains of reality."[41] This view positions authority as both restricted and dynamic. To Gieryn, science has no natural boundaries, only the contingent, malleable, and inconsistent ones humans create in their bid to protect or dispute the allotment of cultural authority. These struggles play out in public through competition over epistemic authority and the privileges conferred by this position regarding knowledge, prestige, and resources.

In looking across these five premises, an idea of authority as a stable, trait-based object to be possessed by certain speakers is replaced by a conceptualization of being an authority as the right to be listened to occurring within a context-bound asymmetrical relationship through the performance of discourse that includes control over particular knowledge and that is subject to contestation and change regarding its modes of legitimacy. These elements provide the building blocks for a theory of journalistic authority.

THE RELATIONAL THEORY OF JOURNALISTIC AUTHORITY

Moving from these five premises that define authority generally to the specific case of journalistic authority begins with a definition of journalistic authority sensitive to its various components and their interrelations: journalistic authority is a contingent relationship in which certain actors come to possess a right to create legitimate discursive knowledge about events in the world for others.

Although the succinctness of this definition permits ambiguity, this statement provides the core of the relational theory of journalistic authority developed in this book. It emphasizes authority's principal components, including journalistic authority's fundamentally social character, its reliance on context, and the continual remaking of these relations through interactions among a fluctuating set of diverse actors. Starting from this theoretical center, the sections below further develop the relational theory of journalistic authority through careful attention to four aspects specific to journalistic authority: the journalist-audience relationship, discursive patterns, control over knowledge, and the balance between durability and malleability.

Journalism's Asymmetrical Relationship with Its Audiences

"You give us 22 minutes, we'll give you the world." The slogan of the New York–based news radio station WINS doubles as a general statement about journalism. It captures a particular exchange between journalists and news audiences—we give the news our attention to gain knowledge about events taking place outside our experience. This exchange forms the basis of journalism's "authority relation"[42] between a journalistic actor who has knowledge and the audience that lacks it. In this exchange, journalists' asymmetry with their audiences arises through the condition of "awayness," to use Jay Rosen's term, in which news happening outside audiences' immediate observations is presented.[43] This inequality of access is most powerfully encompassed in the act of bearing witness. Journalists are present where audiences are not. This may be in places off-limits to most, such as armed conflicts; it may be standing in for us when we simply lack the time or inclination to attend, such as city council meetings; or where we want to be present vicariously, such as the sidelines of the big game. Journalists enjoy unequal access to events of the world. In turn, the audience's dependence on information gathered from this access shapes its relationship with journalism.[44]

Distant presence itself is not enough to ensure authority. Journalists mark themselves off as a distinct group largely through claims to professionalism (a topic more fully explored in chapter 1). The linkage between professionalism and cultural authority has a historical trajectory. The adoption of objectivity and neutrality norms during the twentieth century marked a considerable shift from earlier forms of partisan and popular news. In many respects, professionalism was a conscious effort to mimic other professions to enhance authority.[45] This movement was borne out through such developments as the founding of journalism schools and the establishment of the Society of Professional Journalists in the early 1900s. The preamble of the latter's code of ethics— "Professional integrity is the cornerstone of a journalist's credibility"[46]— succinctly demonstrates the degree to which professionalism has come to reside at the heart of arguments journalists make for why they deserve to be trusted as society's chroniclers.

Even as journalistic professionalism lacks the boundary-making qualities exercised by the classic professions,[47] the benefits of professional status as a means of seeking authority are clear. Professionalism provides a normative prescription for how journalists should behave, a shared understanding of acceptable practices, and an institutional guide for organizing journalistic practices—usually within hierarchical structures. The combination of professional norms and professional practice gives rise to what Seth Lewis calls a "professional logic" that legitimizes journalists' work and helps establish boundaries between journalists and nonjournalists.[48] Work matters as journalists tout their skills and expertise as the basis for exclusive control over news.[49]

Journalism's professional logic reaches beyond the actions of journalists to include understandings of how other social actors ought to behave. News production and consumption are intertwined so that the norms and practices that underlie news production contain within them embedded notions of appropriate knowledge forms and citizenship practices. This duality is especially visible with audiences as the ways in which a news text is created shapes how it should be read.[50] The assumptions contained in journalism's professional logic also extend to its relationships with other social actors outside the newsroom, including news sources, corporate management, and advertisers.

Journalistic Authority as Discursive

A relational perspective of journalistic authority should be sensitive to how different actors position themselves—and others—through the creation of an authority relation. But through what means does this positioning occur? The authority relation is not a static social arrangement but one arising through continual discursive production. This view aligns with James Boyd White's understanding of authority as "a certain kind of thinking and talking" that entails "a way of using language, a way of creating an identity for oneself and making a relation to others."[51] But because journalists and their audiences rarely interact in direct, one-on-one spaces, the communicative authority of journalism is mediated through news texts. Recognizing this invites a closer examination of how the shape of news texts—their formal conventions, visual style, and so on—act to both communicate meanings about events being covered while also signaling the legitimacy of the news account.

Positioning a news text as an "authoritative utterance"[52] helps connect the particularity of news discourse with the establishment of legitimacy. Teun van Dijk considers the news to be a "speech act of assertion"[53]—journalists present their stories as factual. Epistemologically, this sense of factuality is achieved largely through sourcing practices favoring direct quotations or sound bites (see chapter 5). Rather than argumentation, news stories adopt a declarative narrative style premised on journalists' ability to adhere to set conventions.[54] Outside of editorial and opinion spaces, news content rarely utilizes persuasion as its chief mode of address. An obituary does not persuade the reader that someone has died—it states it as fact.[55] However, the news is not merely a recitation of disconnected facts but a narrative form following particular patterns and conventions.[56] Understanding journalistic authority requires careful attention to how stories are crafted and to the assumptions these story forms contain regarding the audience.

Clearly, journalistic authority cannot be separated from news forms. Yet two initial cautions are needed. First, an overemphasis on textual properties risks ignoring the actors behind the texts. To avoid depopulating journalistic authority, the conceptual lens of performativity helps bridge the space between news texts and the creators and consumers of news.[57] Marcel Broersma argues that the translation from the specificity of an event to its rendering as news through repetitive story forms and styles contains an excess of meaning. Instrumentally, these templates make news work possible but symbolically they provide "a shared social code between journalists and their public" that establishes meaning around the individual story while reiterating the authority of journalists to create a legitimate account.[58] As performance becomes conventionalized, naturalized narrative forms escape scrutiny. Broersma goes further to connect the repetition of story forms to journalistic authority: "Journalistic texts then should not primarily be understood as attempts to mimetically describe events, but as strategic interpretations of them, that offer journalists the possibility of asserting moral authority and, as a result, obtain power."[59] The news is not neutral description but the product of a host of institutional practices and necessities—not least of which is the need to be authoritative.

A second caution is to avoid examining news discourse from within the normative vocabulary of journalism. Narrative aspects often go unarticulated in journalism's normative language of factuality and objectivity.[60] At heart, news stories are stories, and examining journalists as storytellers brings to light extraprofessional attributes that shape journalistic authority. For example, television news forms create a level of intimacy through their visual conventions that needs to be understood on its own terms. The authoritative air of former CBS News anchor Walter Cronkite derived not merely from his reporting skills but largely from an on-air demeanor summed up in the familial nickname "Uncle Walter."[61] Acknowledging the news as story and journalist as storyteller complicates normative or informational understandings of how journalists produce authoritative utterances to instead suggest a broader picture of the relationship between journalists and their audiences.

Journalistic Authority as Control Over Knowledge

To many, equating the flood of daily news, from Montenegro to Miley Cyrus, to knowledge stretches the concept too far. Rather than an insult to journalism, this disconnect exposes the deep-seated bias of associating knowledge with the high standards of rigorous, rational inquiry enshrined in the scientific method. As philosopher Michael Williams argues, "'Know' is an honorific term." To accept knowledge from someone signals a "double endorsement" of the knowledge itself and the legitimacy of the one espousing knowledge.[62] Within journalism, reporters know by following procedures of observation and information collection that they then use to construct news accounts intended to inform audiences of happenings in the world.[63] This claim is not new. Three-quarters of a century ago, Robert Park recognized both the importance of considering news as knowledge and the challenges in differentiating journalism from the knowledge-producing activities of history, philosophy, and science. Borrowing from William James, Park placed news within a continuum bookended by the more fleeting *acquaintance with* and the more involved *knowledge about*. The crowded environment in which journalists operate necessitates this differentiation. Rejecting images of news audiences studiously contemplating the knowledge journalists produce, Park admits: "Public attention . . . under normal conditions is wavering, unsteady, and easily distracted." Given this constraint, Park recognizes news to be a form of mediated perception: "It does not so much inform as orient the public, giving each and all notice as to what is going on."[64] This view may limit the depth of knowledge contained in any single journalistic account, but it extends its reach across the public. The ability of the news to reach a wide audience is central to journalism's claim to facilitate political action and to circulate collectively shared stories.

Treating journalism as a knowledge-producing activity invites questions regarding its epistemological basis, or what Mats Ekström calls the "*rules, routines* and *institutionalized procedures* that operate within a social setting and decide the form of the knowledge produced and the *knowledge claims* expressed (or implied)."[65] Operationally, established procedures make possible the consistent production of knowledge claims—the news—within bureaucratic organizations. Journalists are inculcated with rules and routines institutionalized within journalism. These procedures are more than just functional; they simultaneously justify why *these* practices support knowledge claims. Such justification is necessary once news is recognized not as a mirror of events but as a particular mode of storytelling predicated on the claim of providing an accurate account. The legitimacy of journalism as a way of producing truthful accounts of events in the world is bound up in its procedures as well as the display of these procedures within news texts—for example, a quoted source or a video of an event. Particular patterns of news discourse yield "recognition by journalists and audiences of the authority of news language,"[66] in Donald Matheson's view. For journalists to produce knowledge, the audience must recognize their underlying procedures as legitimate. Journalists cannot force audiences to accept their accounts but must instead rely on the public acceptance of journalistic knowledge.[67]

Even if journalists create knowledge, their dissimilarities with such knowledge-based professions such as medicine or science raise questions about whether they can act as an authority in the above conceptual model.[68] In these other fields, being an authority requires the command of particular literacies to comprehend specialized knowledge not understood by outsiders without translation. But journalistic authority is not predicated on the demonstration or command of esoteric knowledge. Aside from a few trade-based publications, news discourse must be constructed so as to be easily accessible and understood within a society marked by stratified educational levels. Both political and commercial imperatives impel this need to appeal to a wide audience. If a journalist is an authority in the way R. B. Friedman describes it above, this particular way of being an authority differs from other knowledge producers. Journalists lacking expertise over a subject area can lay claim to expertise in interacting with the sources, documents, and audiences that makes news possible.[69] This is a fraught position, as journalists remain precariously perched between the often-diverging interests of sources and audiences.

As a final word, efforts to understand the control of journalistic knowledge must take care not to amalgamate all of journalistic practice. Journalism encompasses a wide variety of news forms across different media, which gives rise to a diversity of epistemological approaches.[70] For example, Matheson views blogs as adopting "a journalism of connections" in which a blog post does not speak as an isolated text but relies on links to other sources.[71] Moving from the declarative voice of a traditional news item to a partial and collaborative voice of a blog post alters how knowledge is produced as well as how claims to authority are made.[72]

These developments complicate the core question concerning journalism's control over knowledge: how do journalists produce authoritative knowledge that is accepted by news audiences? This question brings us to the topic of journalistic authority as malleable and open to contestation.

The Malleability of Journalistic Authority

Much of this chapter has focused on the meaning of authority, but the noun *journalism* also requires attention.[73] Trying to condense a wide range of news-generating practices into the same noun creates problems, as do efforts to make black-and-white distinctions separating what counts as journalism from what does not. Adding temporality into the mix further complicates efforts to arrive at stable definitions. Even a cursory historical tour of journalism reveals many divergent strands of news.[74] The continual introduction of new media technologies has transformed the terrain of news time and time again, often with accompanying struggle between old and new (see chapter 6).[75] In any age, answers to Jay Rosen's question "what are journalists for?" will vary.[76] Outside of technological change, journalists' move toward professionalization has altered both news practices and normative understandings underlying these practices, even if such exertions are hampered by journalism's often difficult fit as a profession.[77]

The definitional ambiguity of journalism as a collective entity has become increasingly fraught in the twenty-first century. Media convergence has blurred boundaries separating once discrete news platforms; the spread of networked technology has altered the nature of participation; algorithms have automated some news tasks; mobile devices allow fluid news gathering and dissemination; and so on. One demarcation tactic has been to append *mainstream* or *legacy* as prefixes for journalism—although these labels have also taken on pejorative connotations in some circles. It remains possible that the journalism practices being honed by emerging news forms and evolving legacy organizations will coalesce and institutionalize, crystallizing into the same isomorphism that has marked legacy media outlets in the past.[78] Even today, flipping among local television newscasts in the United States or perusing "red top" British tabloids reveals a fairly homogeneous diet of news. Perhaps developing news forms will fall into this pattern in the next decade or so, rendering much of the present trepidation about journalism quaintly misplaced. Or, as David Ryfe wonders, it may be that journalism is "unraveling" into a profusion of different news forms along with the further winnowing of the boundary separating actors within journalism from those on the outside.[79] Indeed, the emerging media environment may support a heterogeneous newscape unimaginable in the mass communication era of the twentieth century. Chris Anderson, Emily Bell, and Clay Shirky raise this issue in their exploration of what they label "post-industrial journalism." Looking to the near future, the authors envisage "the continued weakening of the very idea of what constitutes news, and thus what constitutes a news organization."[80] In this environment, it becomes less clear what is meant when pointing to journalism.

To confront the issue of authority at such a moment of ambiguity, this book considers the imprecision embedded in the referent *journalism* to be an important site of inquiry rather than a lexical weakness. The development of new forms of news takes place in conjunction with the rhetorical elaboration of innovative ideas of what journalism should be.[81] When routines and structures that had been taken for granted in moments of greater stability compete with alternative routines and structures, the conditions of journalistic authority gain attention. This can be seen in the comments made by Bill Keller at the start of this chapter: what would have seemed like a superfluous discussion of news practices in the past becomes a concrete plea for their preservation against rival ideas in the present.

From the perspective of malleability, each of the above characteristics of journalistic authority appears entangled in uncertainty. The hold of professionalism as the basis for journalism's asymmetrical relationship with its audience cannot be assumed as journalism continues to fracture and adopt new forms. The push for participatory journalism raises many questions about the journalist-audience relationship and its bearing on journalistic authority.[82] Networked digital technology has altered this dynamic through such emergent practices as "citizen witnessing," which, according to Stuart Allan, challenges "the journalist's self-proclaimed status as a professional observer"—a position that had been simply implied.[83] Increasingly, the assertion of an unequal relationship between communicators and audiences runs up against a celebration of participatory opportunities and user-generated content.[84] Social media provide important new avenues for public expression, multiplying the number of communicators. Although a dependence on journalists persists, claims that journalists' professional status grants them omnipresence or a social position above the rest of society are sure to draw criticism. These trends point to the remaking of the authority relation between journalists and the audience, although not in unilateral ways.

The rise of the productive audience also alters the connections between journalistic authority and discourse. In treating journalistic authority as performative and embedded in news discourse, we are left to question what happens when the forms of journalism multiply and proliferate. If discourse and performance are linked, it follows that different discursive styles correspond to different kinds of performances. For example, presidential debates in the United States draw heightened levels of attention and scrutiny, as journalists pore over the candidates' statements. Yet clearly this news coverage will differ widely among the factual recitation of a front-page news account, the in-depth critique of a columnist, the rapid-fire contentious interchange of a cable television news program, the partisan analysis of talk radio, the personalized interpretation of a blog, and the succinct snark of a tweet. Instead of one type of news discourse or journalistic performance, individual forms vary in how they establish authority.[85] Performance may still be at the center of journalistic authority, but a less cohesive news landscape compels careful attention to its divergences.

Finally, a wide range of communicators increasingly challenges journalists' control over knowledge. While classic knowledge professions are able to use control over knowledge to maintain jurisdictional control,[86] journalism has no inbuilt protections. It is perennially open to competition from other forms of public account. To return to an earlier example, ubiquitous camera-equipped, network-connected mobile phones offer users powerful tools for chronicling and sharing happenings in front of them, which may then eventually circulate through the news media or entirely through nonnews communication networks. This has become true of terrorist attacks; from the July 7 bombing attack in London in 2005 to the attacks on Brussels in 2016, witnesses provided images of the aftermath that quickly became widespread even before the facts of the attack were established. Certainly journalists seek control over knowledge by presenting themselves as experts over the jurisdiction of news production.[87] Many professional journalists are quick to point out their virtues while warning about the dangers of relying on the accounts of untrained observers.[88] But control of knowledge cannot be assumed.

One question is how the emerging digital media ecosystem affects the authority of news organizations. The reputation of a news outlet often supersedes individual journalists such that an affiliation with the *New York Times* or CBS News is itself a marker of authority. In some sense, this authority derives from the recognition of these news organizations as popular channels with broad audiences, but there is also a conferral of esteem from the affiliation. The proliferation of digital voices does not automatically necessitate the destruction of these news brands, but it does complicate how to understand journalistic authority in a diverse media environment.

The shift to digital news has been accompanied by numerous public conversations, experiments with news forms, novel organizational structures, and other reactions, all of which provide ample analytical opportunities for interrogating journalistic authority. As Bruce Lincoln writes, "The best way to study something like authority is not when it operates smoothly and efficiently, for its success in some measures depends on naturalizing itself and obscuring the very processes of which it is the product," but instead to "investigate select moments of crisis."[89] This statement presents an invitation to look more closely at what is happening to contemporary journalism with the understanding that to define journalism is to define its authority.[90]

JOURNALISTIC AUTHORITY AS MODEL AND ANALYTICAL TOOL

In putting forward a relational theory of journalistic authority, this book must navigate two significant challenges that plague attempts to make sense of contemporary journalism. The first challenge is to examine journalism as a distinct object of inquiry without rending it from the context that gives it meaning. A key assertion regarding journalistic authority is that journalism cannot be understood apart from its social, cultural, and technological moorings, even as its practitioners often adopt a rhetoric of detachment. As a cultural form, journalism's soft edges blend into other expressive, political, and social forms. Sensitivity is needed to assess how internal structures relate to external influences. A second difficulty can be encapsulated in what Henry Jenkins describes as the problem of vantage point. There is no place to stand above a changing media environment that continues to rapidly shift under the analyst's feet.[91] Sifting out enduring trends from passing crazes or significant rifts from superficial occurrences is difficult without the perspective of hindsight. These two challenges indicate that both "journalism" and what makes it authoritative are never settled objects, but ideas constantly constructed, promoted, and contested by an array of actors working from different social positions.

With these claims in mind, the analysis of journalistic authority presented in this book cannot provide a static explanation that contains within it the definitive answer to what authority looks like. Such an attempt would be both partial and instantly outdated. Instead, this work builds off the core premises of the relational theory of journalistic authority identified above to offer two different kinds of contributions: a conceptual intervention and an analytical tool.

In making a conceptual contribution, the relational theory of journalistic authority developed in the following chapters provides a generalized structure to explain the components of journalistic authority. This theory replaces simplistic notions of authority with a multifaceted framework resting on three core premises. First, the relationships through which the news attains authority can be understood only by accounting for an array of actors (including technological actors) both inside and outside the newsroom—reporters, owners, sources, audiences, programmers, legislators, critics, and so forth. Second, these relationships are contextual. Drawing together an array of actors, objects, and discourses into an intermeshed and variable system necessitates temporal, spatial, and cultural specificity. Third, authority cannot be explained with any single variable. How journalists align themselves as a group, the forms of news that develop, and the stories journalists tell to justify what they do all matter. A relational theory of journalistic authority is necessarily antireductionist. No single part explains the others.

The importance of establishing a general framework is that journalistic authority will appear differently depending on time and place. To analyze journalistic authority in a specific context requires a model containing several general components, including group identity, textual forms, and discourses about journalism. Doing so necessitates a schema for unearthing particular components endemic to journalistic authority. The shape of anxieties over professionalism reviewed in chapter 1, the emergence of news forms examined in chapter 2, and the narratives about journalism recalled in chapter 3 will undoubtedly change over time, but general questions of group identity, legitimated news forms, and discursive context are central to journalistic authority. Moreover, treating journalism as inseparable from its context shifts attention to the patterns of interaction between journalists and their audiences, sources, technologies, and external critics (i.e., the topics taken up in part 2). Even as the operation of journalism changes, the relationality of authority remains. Erecting a durable schema moves past the dynamism that marks much of contemporary journalism to instead provide a basic model for how journalistic accounts become legitimated.

My second goal is to offer an analytical tool for interrogating—and critiquing—the present state of journalistic authority. In doing so, the majority of the examples provided throughout the book pertain to journalism in the United States. This geographical isolationism may be limiting, but its necessity derives from the centrality of context in examining journalistic authority. The particularities of any national milieu shape the types of arguments that develop around journalistic authority. This specificity is not meant to infer that what is happening in the United States can be extrapolated and exported to the rest of the world. Far from it. Instead, scholars ought to apply the basic framework for thinking about journalistic authority to other national contexts. Comparative perspectives on journalistic authority promise to further illuminate authority's situated and contingent nature. Finally, the relational perspective advanced here suggests new ways of thinking about how to critique the news. Understanding the means by which journalists come to claim authority opens up space to assess, propose, and defend alternative relational forms. Ultimately, a relational theory of journalistic authority not only describes a set of associations to explain their workings; it also provides a critical space to challenge what authority looks like.

PLAN OF THE BOOK

This introduction has argued that journalistic authority must be understood as emerging through an interconnected array of normative articulations, relational dynamics, institutional workings, knowledge practices, technological developments, and formal patterns that coalesce and diverge across time and continue to morph as conditions inside and outside of journalism change. In foregrounding complexity, the difficulty becomes avoiding oversimplification while providing coherent explanation. The rest of the book confronts this balancing act by breaking down journalistic authority to explore its key components individually in separate chapters. However, this isolation should not be construed as an argument for their disconnection from one another. They all work in concert, and certainly overlaps emerge across chapters.

Part 1, "Foundations of Journalistic Authority," takes an internal, journalist-centric perspective to survey the legitimating practices journalists engage in to bolster their claims to authority. Chapter 1 examines how journalists draw on notions of professionalism to establish authority, construct boundaries around acceptable norms and practices, and create distance from others. It also tracks forces of deprofessionalization and how they affect understandings of the usefulness of journalism as a system of knowledge production in the digital era. Chapter 2 takes up the question of news forms as markers of authority and how the patterns that have developed over time transcend their role in communicating information to also establish a particular journalist-audience relationship. Finally, chapter 3 considers how journalists publicly position their work as an authoritative cultural practice through discourse supporting the legitimacy of their social role.

Part 2, "Journalistic Authority in Context," moves beyond the analytical vacuum of part 1 to bring journalism back into the wider realm of social practice. These four chapters build off the premise that journalistic authority is not some material object or quality possessed, but a relationship between actors pursuing an authoritative social position and the outsiders who recognize it. Chapter 4 explores the often neglected role audiences play in the establishment journalistic authority. Theories of authority always involve an authority relation between those claiming authority and those who consent to it. Chapter 5 shifts the focus to how journalists and their sources cocreate news. Journalists' reliance on entrenched sourcing patterns leads to the efficient gathering of information, but it also provides an argument for their position as legitimate knowledge actors that reaffirms a map of the authorized knowers within society. Chapter 6 spotlights the complex connections between journalism and technology that persist throughout the book. Even though technology has come to occupy a causal role in much of the discourse around journalistic change, journalism has always involved technology that shapes what news looks like, just as journalists shape technologies to their needs. Chapter 7 examines how media criticism shapes the consumption environment for news by adding layers of meaning around news discourses and the journalists that produce them.

The conclusion draws together key points from across the book to present a comprehensive model of the theory of journalistic authority. What emerges is a politics of journalistic authority in which the very basis of journalism's legitimacy becomes open to contestation. This environment strikes fear in the hearts of many journalists, but it is also a moment of opportunity to think about what we expect from the news.

PART ONE

Foundations of Journalistic Authority

CHAPTER ONE

Professionalism as Privilege and Distance

Journalistic Identity

As the press crowded into a Dubuque, Iowa, rally for presidential hopeful Donald Trump in August 2015, Univision's Jorge Ramos, one of the most well-known Latino television journalists in the United States, engaged in a heated exchange with the candidate over his consistent disparagement of Latino immigrants. The encounter ended with Trump berating Ramos, a scene repeated by news outlets and circulated on social media in the ensuing days. Later, Trump appeared on conservative talk radio host Hugh Hewitt's show to complain that Ramos's behavior at the press conference was inappropriate. Hewitt concurred with this assessment of Ramos, adding succinctly, "It was not professional."[1] This accusation could be read as a dismissal of Ramos for acting impolitely or conflicting with Hewitt's political preferences, but this would be an incomplete view. Professionalism has great currency when speaking of journalism. It connects to the arguments journalists make about how they do their work and why it matters to the public. Professionalism provides the basis for arguments that journalists ought to be respected. Given this importance, what does it mean *not* to act professionally?

The critique of Ramos was that he abandoned his objectivity when he adopted a specific political position to challenge Trump. In doing so, Ramos was making news instead of reporting it. By accusing Ramos of acting unprofessionally, critics denied him legitimacy as a journalist. He was vacating professional prestige by deviating from expected behavior. By contrast, some commentators saluted Ramos for holding Trump accountable. These supporters squarely placed him in the bounds of news professionalism (perhaps more so than journalists who failed to challenge Trump's unsubstantiated claims and inflammatory rhetoric). What this episode indicates is that professionalism is both a constraining force affecting the behaviors of journalists and a contested realm concerned, at heart, with what makes journalism authoritative.

The inherent thorniness contained within the concept of professionalism makes it a useful place to begin developing an understanding of how journalism presents itself to be authoritative—that is, as deserving of the right to be listened to in its creation of knowledge about the world. Professionalism and objectivity have long been staples of research on journalism, but how do these concepts relate to the larger topic of journalistic authority? Too often this linkage is left unarticulated. Part of the reason why has to do with how issues of journalistic professionalism are talked about. For journalists, the difficulties of objectivity and distinctions between professionals and amateurs are familiar topics, taking up much of the public discussion around journalism.[2] By contrast, journalists don't often talk explicitly about themselves as authorities. It is not part of their vocabulary. If anything, many journalists would bristle at being labeled an authority because it hits too close to the types of authorities they cover as news topics. Meanwhile, scholars who have usefully explored journalistic professionalism have not always taken the further step of examining its connection to authority. To others, the link between professionalism and authority, particularly the idea of being an authority put forward in the introduction, is assumed.[3]

The central claim of this chapter is that journalistic authority, as it has developed over the past century, is deeply interwoven with professionalism. Appeals to professionalism provide journalists with what Mark Deuze calls a path to "self-legitimize their position in society."[4] Journalistic professionalism—constructed as a particular set of beliefs, a particular collection of practices, a particular way of relating to sources and audiences, and a particular type of organizational form—affords journalists an argument for why they deserve to be considered culturally legitimate producers of knowledge. Professional legitimation is about being recognized as providing something of social value—news, in this case—but it also necessitates recognition as the exclusive provider of this activity by those on the outside—news audiences and sources.[5]

As a strategy for journalistic authority, professionalism should be understood as deeply relational. Arguments for professionalism carry within them understandings of how journalists should interact with their audiences (see chapter 4) and their sources (see chapter 5). In short, professionalism contains a totalizing system of relations. The tenets of professionalism have become so entrenched as to obscure its choice as one way of legitimating journalism among others. The professional stance is a particular one that stakes out a manner for journalists to think and to act. In this chapter, I analyze journalistic professionalism and how it relates to authority, as well as how it shapes the struggle for control over news in the face of uncertainty regarding the future direction of journalism.

PLACING JOURNALISM AMONG THE PROFESSIONS

Examining journalistic professionalism begins with acknowledging a contradiction: ascribing to journalism the status of profession is notoriously problematic, yet journalists often understand their work to be of a professional sort. This is not quite the paradox it may seem when so plainly expressed, but this disconnect raises some of the semantic calisthenics necessary to properly explain journalistic professionalism and explore its relation to the larger idea of journalistic authority. Journalism famously lacks many of the boundary-making mechanisms available to other professions—licensing, educational requirements, testing, professional organization membership, etc. Scholars grappling with journalistic professionalism have also qualified the professional label in various ways. Jeremy Tunstall, in his groundbreaking surveys of journalists in the United Kingdom, denied professional status to journalists on the grounds that journalism could never emulate more established professions like medicine and law.[6] Likewise, in the United States, David Weaver and colleagues found it problematic to assign professional status to journalism.[7] Clearly, from a trait-based perspective, journalism lacks many of the prominent characteristics associated with other professions. The confusion regarding professionalism is compounded by its use as an analytical term applied by scholars and a label used popularly, even by practitioners (e.g., the Society of *Professional* Journalists). This usage should not be assumed to be the same, unless practitioners are expected to adopt the language of journalism studies. Nonetheless, how journalists define their relationship with professionalism remains important. Many journalists even reject the label, favoring instead such nomenclature as occupation, craft, or vocation.[8] The point is not to judge such denials but to explore the ambiguities (and even reluctance) surrounding journalistic professionalism. In sum, journalistic professionalism appears messy at best.

Rescuing the value of professionalism for thinking about journalistic authority requires first looking at how the study of professions has moved past the enumeration of traits as a means of identifying and distinguishing professions to instead follow Everett Hughes in focusing on professionalism as a source of meaning.[9] The shift from profession to professionalism—from an entity to how its members define their control over a particular domain of work—spawned new historical and constructivist approaches examining the means by which a group positions itself as a profession.[10] Viewing professions as culturally negotiated constructs of group identity has produced sophisticated questions about professionalism and its social impact.[11] The replacement of profession-as-entity with professionalism-as-process relocates attention to what Magali Sarfatti Larson calls "the professional project" through which groups struggle for social recognition—and the spoils that accompany such status.[12] Thus, professions adopt a rhetoric of altruism to support their social position, but they do so in a way that also bolsters their self-interest.[13] And because these struggles persist, professions remain embedded in complex webs of social relations that are themselves not stable.

These perspectives move past whether journalism is a profession to instead question how the narratives and practices of professionalism support journalistic authority. The markers of journalistic professionalism connect to a constellation of familiar ideals: autonomy from the market, independence from the state, pursuit of quality and accuracy, shared norms and practices, work freedom, legal rights, and control over news content. These attributes all rest on the position of journalism as a distinct practice with a distinct social purpose that can be expressed in the proposition that journalists ought to be left alone to do their work. Silvio Waisbord indicates the complex nature of the concept when he describes professionalism as "a conceptual category, a normative ideal, a narrative that reveals how journalism intersects with economic, political, social, and cultural forces that shape media systems."[14] In keeping with this line of inquiry, Michael Schudson and Chris Anderson wed journalism studies with the sociology of the professions when they direct analytical attention to "the circumstances in which journalists attempt to turn themselves into professional people."[15] Again, this is not a claim that all journalists identify themselves as part of a profession but rather the assumption that professionalism best captures the declarations journalists make about the social value and specificity of their work. It provides a perspective situating journalism as a form of knowledge production aimed at producing truthful accounts of the world. Focusing on how and why these ideas get articulated bypasses the problems of journalists' failure to attain professional status or to wholly adopt a coherent professional self-understanding. Even if journalists avoid the label of profession, they lay claim to its chief components: autonomy-as-independence is built into the fabric of claims supporting journalistic authority, as is a belief in public service and a collective sense of acceptable practices. Given these conditions, one way forward is to adopt Meryl Aldridge and Julia Evetts's proposition that journalistic professionalism is, at its core, "polyvalent."[16] Its many meanings complicate efforts to discuss professionalism without first clarifying how the concept is being used.

The following sections break down the larger issue of journalistic professionalism into three components suggested by Henrik Örnebring: organization, autonomy, and knowledge.[17] In his book chapter, Örnebring uses *organization* to refer narrowly to professional organizations, but it is invoked here in the broader sense of professionalism as providing an institutionalized collective identity. Next, the component of autonomy moves outward to consider how professional norms and practices regulate the relationship between journalism and external actors. Finally, the section on knowledge links journalistic professionalism to the epistemic assumptions bound up in news forms. The discussion of knowledge also takes up the topics of objectivity and expertise. Each section explores these notions while also considering ongoing challenges to journalistic professionalism.

Örnebring notes that unlike other professional groups, journalists tend to have little or no relationship with professional organizations. In the United States, membership in the Society of Professional Journalists has never been high nor has the group been an advocate on par with the American Medical Association or the American Bar Association.[18] News outlets provide a level of institutional support to the journalists they employ but not in a way that unites the field. Faced with this lack of organizational membership, a broader view is necessary to capture less formal shared understandings of journalistic professionalism. Aldridge and Evetts do so by emphasizing discursivity: "Journalism's standing as a profession in North America is . . . not a matter of legal protections and institutional forms. It is a *discourse* shared and nourished by practitioners, employers and [the] public."[19] This discourse creates shared commitments giving rise to a sense of a journalistic community while providing a public argument for those outside of journalism.[20] It shapes the authority relation between journalists and audiences.

The force of professionalism in creating a collective sensibility among journalists is central to Deuze's argument that journalism's shared "occupational ideology" provides a better approach to defining what unites journalists than other collective identifiers. Ideology joins understanding and action as "a collection of values, strategies and formal codes characterizing professional journalism and shared most widely by its members."[21] This conceptualization draws its strength from highlighting what John Soloski calls "the cognitive base of news professionalism."[22] Professionalism provides a way of thinking about news by creating a "professional culture" that generates both meanings and actions related to those meanings.[23]

Deuze's foregrounding of ideology shifts attention to questions of shared meanings and therefore how journalists choose to accept certain norms, practices, and actors as journalistically appropriate while ostracizing others as deviant. One example is the uneasy pairing of the *New York Times* with WikiLeaks, a site not shy about its activist inclinations, to publish stories about a trove of leaked documents that the latter had acquired in 2010. The newspaper worked with WikiLeaks to acquire and publish the documents but carefully distanced itself from the site by avoiding the language of being partners.[24] This tightrope walk by the *Times* over its relationship with WikiLeaks stemmed from its desire to protect an occupational ideology that it so closely connected to its legitimacy.

Journalists expressing themselves as a community through the discourse of professionalism also craft a sense of their work as supporting the common good. Jenny Wiik points to the altruistic tendencies in the discourse journalists produce about their work.[25] Journalistic professionalism supplies journalists with a robust set of rhetorical arguments for why they are worthy, enabling them to connect professional news with providing an essential public service to their audiences. Most forcefully, journalists define their role as the fourth estate, making democratic governance possible through the mass circulation of information and holding public institutions accountable. There is a long history of this argument. Even before the establishment of the US Constitution, Thomas Jefferson famously wrote, "Were it left to me to decide whether we should have a government without newspapers or newspapers without a government, I should not hesitate a moment to prefer the latter."[26] Of course, the late eighteenth-century press did not resemble contemporary news, but this sentiment has become an argument for the professional press as an independent press and therefore a worthy arbiter among a sea of self-interested public actors. Conversely, journalists lamenting the decline of traditional—or perhaps professional—journalism emphasize the social harm of diminished news coverage rather than the individual fate of unemployed reporters.[27]

The fourth-estate argument linking journalistic professionalism to authority is woven into the fabric of journalism. It draws authority from outside itself by conflating journalism with democratic institutions. At the same time, the proclivity to connect professionalism to the public-trustee model in conceptions of journalism results in a narrow vision.[28] This will become apparent in later chapters, but two core weaknesses merit attention here. First, the focus on fourth-estate functions obscures the broader universe of what journalism does. It should be recognized as a partial discourse that sharpens the focus on the subset of so-called hard news associated with politics and governance while ignoring other topics—sports, entertainment, and so on—that are nonetheless part of news. The news is not all city council meetings; care should be taken not to reinforce rationalist models of news consumption. Second, arguments for journalistic authority predicated on the fourth-estate model command high expectations of news content and its consumers.[29] As a result, journalism falls prey to the inevitable gulf between journalistic rhetoric and actual practice.[30] Journalism becomes an easy target for its many critics.

If not all journalism is made authoritative through democratic normative commitments, then more basic questions of how a news account comes to communicate an event need to be asked. Professionalism—and its concomitant value of objectivity—lends support to the truth claims underlying journalistic work. The news, in essence, is presented as fact, not fiction. Or, with the dogma of objectivity somewhat weakened, the news attempts to provide as close an approximation of factuality as possible. Wolfgang Donsbach gets to this basic role when he asserts that the purpose of professionalism is to provide a "validation of assertions about reality with a high degree of responsibility."[31] The professional press is considered to be a responsible one. This matters because news discourse does not present information in argument form. News stories rarely build a case to win over an audience; instead, news is declarative. It tells us what happened. What is persuasive is not the content of a news story but the apparatus of authority invoked through claims to professionalism and appeals to the objectivity norm—an argument further explored in the next chapter.

While professionalism provides journalists with a source of collective identity and shared meaning, other scholars point to professionalism as a source of discipline, or what Soloski terms a "trans-organizational control mechanism."[32] Although different newsrooms have their idiosyncrasies, journalistic values and norms persist across individual news organizations. Journalists socialized into collective ways of thinking about journalism internalize ideas of acceptable practices and norms while learning what is unacceptable or deviant.[33] To return to Deuze's claim, the shared ideology underlying journalistic professionalism disciplines actors so that management does not have to.[34] The new reporter arriving in the newsroom already knows the expectations regarding how to write news stories. In this way, professional identities make possible autonomous work practices while maintaining control. This is especially important for journalism, as deadline-driven reporters produce an unceasing output of news stories covering various domains of public life.[35] In short, professionalism provides meaning for actors while simultaneously governing conduct.

In an increasingly heterogeneous media environment, the notion of professionalism as an overarching identity—or ideology—for journalists runs up against competing forms of journalism predicated on a more diverse set of normative grounds. Given the weakening hegemonic power of traditional modes of professional journalism and the momentum of "post-industrial journalism,"[36] it becomes more difficult for "a single model of journalism to firmly control the jurisdiction of news."[37] What this means for journalistic authority will be taken up below.

CLAIMS TO AUTONOMY AND EXCLUSIVITY

A hallmark of professionalization is autonomy. Professional actors laying claim to a particular jurisdiction of work assert their ability to control this area independently. This core insistence on autonomy is that of self-rule without interference. In this sense, autonomy is itself normative in that it provides a way of thinking about how professionals ought to operate. Yet stark declarations equating autonomy with professional self-control must be tempered by context. No social group exists independently. As the sociology of the professions has made clear, professions are imbricated with society in complex ways with many crosscurrents of influence. Professions define themselves through their relationships to those outside their borders. Just as the doctor must relate to patients, administrators, insurance companies, and policymakers, so too do journalists operate within a complicated social environment in which they interact with audiences, sources, lawyers, management, and others.

Autonomy works on a collective level to create a normative bulwark against interference from external influences.[38] This sense of autonomy closely aligns with Andrew Abbott's concept of jurisdictional control. Looking across what he calls the "system of professions," Abbott locates professional power in being able to stake out a domain of work. This entails exclusivity, or the ability to set boundaries and exclude other actors from entering into or externally influencing the community. But from the other direction, a professional community can legitimately occupy a specific domain of work only through cultural assent. Waisbord makes this point clear: "The notion of professionalism presupposes that certain people by virtue of their training and acceptance by peers are uniquely qualified to perform certain services that are particularly appreciated by society. Professions are about social distinction, not democracy."[39] Exclusivity pertains to the erection of boundaries recognized from the inside and the outside. It becomes a right attained through ongoing boundary work by the community to achieve recognition.[40] To reiterate the basics of authority outlined in the introduction, authority should be understood as relational and therefore requiring a measure of assent. Following this argument, the conferral of professional status is steeped in offering value to those outside the profession, including the news audience.

Normatively, autonomy is central to journalists' claims to authority. Stephen Ward uncovers pledges of press independence and impartiality dating back hundreds of years in the efforts of British publishers to convince readers of the veritableness of their accounts.[41] Yet, in practice, the limitations of journalistic autonomy should be made clear.[42] Notions of journalistic independence have evolved over time. In the United States, the political party–sponsored newspapers of the nineteenth century competed against populist papers with strong editor-publisher figures. Even as party control diminished, the specter of powerful owners—from William Randolph Hearst to Lord Beaverbrook to Rupert Murdoch—dictating editorial decisions has remained. Commercial media are faulted for being beholden to the market, while state-owned media face accusations of toeing the government line. These examples complicate claims to autonomy.

Critics of the commercialization of news, particularly in the political economy vein, raise objections to simplistic images of an independent press.[43] As J. Herbert Altschull argues: "The content of the news media inevitably reflects the interests of those who pay the bill."[44] These critics point to market pressures placed on nearly all news organizations to generate profits for owners; they are not immune from the economy. Another threat to journalistic autonomy as a professional norm arises through the persistent reliance on sources to create news accounts.[45] What comes to be news is the product of interaction through sources, both in person and through documents. This reliance is the main topic of chapter 5, but at this point what should be made clear is that journalists seeking to retain their autonomous status must do so while depending on others for the core information of their accounts.[46]

Even as autonomy continues to serve as a normative guidepost, journalism can never be assured exclusivity because of its reliance on external actors for news, ties to the market economy, the spread of digital communication technology, and a lack of strict boundaries demarcating insiders from outsiders. Journalism remains more pervious when compared to other professions' ability to retreat cognitively to abstract knowledge or structurally to credentialism.[47] Schudson underscores the importance of journalism's normative commitments in the face of a lack of constraining mechanisms:

> Journalists live in the public eye. They are uninsulated from public scrutiny—they have no recondite language, little fancy technology, no mirrors and mysteries to shield them from the public. There are strong reasons for journalists to seek publicly-appealing moral norms to protect them from criticism, embarrassment, or lawsuits, and to give them guidance in their work to prevent practices that would provoke criticism or even lawsuits, and to endow their occupation with an identity they can count as worthy.[48]

Journalists are caught in the position of promising much to society in exchange for authority, particularly in their twinning of journalism and democracy. Resorting to professionalism to bolster authority acts as a stabilizing force through appeals to continuity across actors and organizations. But it is also a fraught strategy in that it provides both an argument for journalistic authority and a normative means through which to attack journalism.

More recent developments alter the shape of journalistic autonomy both in theory and in practice. With journalistic professionalism during the mass communication era, exclusivity had been largely enforced through economic and technological barriers. The costs involved in generating and exhibiting news have long been quite high. As a result, much of the boundary work surrounding the exclusivity of professional journalism involved distinctions between journalistically appropriate hard news and journalistically suspect soft news.[49] Yet understanding the present state of journalistic professionalism necessitates foregrounding how technological changes weaken journalists' near monopoly on knowledge production involving current events. With the expansion of access to mediated communication, the dichotomy between professional journalists and grassroots amateur production has become a focal point for researchers and practitioners.[50] Nonjournalists can easily become citizen witnesses capable of relaying information quickly through social networks thanks to camera-equipped smartphones and platforms for the quick distribution of content.[51] But this extension is not the only change occurring with the circulation of public knowledge. Perhaps even more significant are new opportunities for disintermediation. Digital communication technologies have given institutions and public figures new ways to reach audiences directly. For example, politicians have long been able to reach the public directly through advertising or direct mail, albeit with a significant price tag. But social media alter this dynamic in ways that are still evolving.

PROFESSIONAL KNOWLEDGE PRODUCERS

A simple view may hold the news to be an informational account of happenings in the world. But this stress on information threatens to obscure what makes the news a particular type of discourse that differs from casual conversation, gossip, literature, or history. To understand better what the news entails and how it relates to journalistic professionalism—and ultimately authority—a useful perspective is to consider news as a form of *knowledge* about the world. Following Robert Park, journalists produce knowledge that is geared toward collective orientation rather than specialized study, but it is also one beholden to set conventions.[52] This section focuses on *professional* journalistic knowledge by examining two elements central to this position: objectivity and expertise.

No other norm or ideal of journalism has received as much attention as objectivity.[53] Practically its own subfield within journalism studies, objectivity has been studied through historical inquiry, ethical considerations, and newsroom ethnography. It is also a term marked by misunderstandings—like professionalism, objectivity too is polyvalent. Is the journalist being objective? Or are her methods of news gathering objective? Or is objectivity the quality of a text? Or the absence of an overt political orientation? This lack of precision contributes to easy arguments for why objectivity, in journalism or elsewhere, is impossible. The lessons of postmodernism and poststructualism have inspired suspicion of value-free knowledge or claims of neutral language. Within journalism, the rejection of mirror theories and emphasis on the necessity of framing in the construction of cohesive stories have erased a belief that journalists merely capture an event.[54] Criticisms of objectivity's consequences abound: Instead of removing journalists from bias, objectivity is its own source of bias.[55] Instead of weakening the power of elite sources, it supports the status quo.[56] Instead of connecting journalists to what they cover, it provides a "view from nowhere."[57] In all these ways, the notion of a naive journalistic objectivity has been discarded.

Yet journalists, who are not so naive about objectivity's problems as the literature seems to suggest, still cling to some idea of objectivity as part of their professional identities. Looked at in conjunction with professionalism, objectivity provides a guiding principle for how to gather and report news. It is often defined negatively—objectivity is *not* giving over to conjecture, gossip, or hidden prejudice. In doing so, journalists place themselves apart from other communicators, including the realm of public relations. On the level of practice, Steven Maras points out that journalists need not believe wholeheartedly in journalistic objectivity to follow practices grounded in the objectivity norm.[58] Others have suggested objectivity-related normative commitments, such as balance.[59]

Understanding the enduring relationship between professionalism and objectivity requires taking a long view of journalism history. From its origins, purveyors of journalism—or protojournalism—have insisted on giving evenhanded accounts of the world.[60] However, close state control, especially in the British context, shaped news coverage, as did the partisan press in the United States. Dan Schiller dates the rise of objectivity as a journalistic value to the birth of the penny press in the 1830s.[61] Self-supported through sales and advertising, the populist penny press grew up alongside the spread of positivism as a way of knowing the world. Objectivity also accompanied professionalizing maneuvers by journalists, including the birth of the Society of Professional Journalists in 1909 and the founding of journalism schools at the University of Missouri in 1908 and Columbia University in 1912.

Michael Schudson presents the clearest linkage between objectivity and professionalism in his classic history, *Discovering the News*.[62] For Schudson, objectivity slowly developed from the penny press era through the rise of the informational ideal articulated by Adolph Ochs in his re-branding of the *New York Times* in 1897. The momentum accelerated in response to widespread dismay following the experiences of World War I and the success of the Committee on Public Information's propaganda efforts, which, consequentially, was a marquee moment for public relations. In this same moment, Walter Lippmann decried the dearth of facts in newspapers and called for more disciplined news practices.[63] It is in this context that, for journalism, objectivity becomes a "fully formulated occupational ideal, part of a professional project or mission. Far more than a set of craft rules to fend off libel suits or a set of constraints to help editors keep tabs on their underlings, objectivity was finally a moral code."[64] Objectivity gave journalists a way to understand their work and an argument for controlling the domain of news based on the social good. It allowed journalists to establish fealty to a supraorganizational code rather than to an owner or a party.[65] This is not to assert that journalists completely accepted objectivity as even possible. Just as objectivity attained its dominance as a news norm, it was also cast as suspect.[66]

Even with its shortcomings, the objectivity norm has provided journalists with a portable stance from which to stake out their claims for professionalism. While equating journalistic and scientific objectivity conjures core differences, their shared faith in objectivity can be summarized by a belief that the world is observable from a distance. From this viewpoint, professionalism provides not only a practical system for making observations and translating them into news but a means of legitimizing these practices. Less attention has been given to the related question of how journalistic work—the work of observing—relates to expertise.

Broadly speaking, expertise denotes the possession of specific knowledge. However, the control of knowledge is not socially isolated but a contextual practice, often with sharp lines between those who know and those who do not. For professions, the importance of expertise is clearly visible in the arguments they make for their right to control a particular social domain.[67] In this capacity, expertise serves as boundary-making device separating out those in possession of abstract knowledge from the rest of society. Expert status becomes something to be attained. In addition, even as expertise may be seen as serving society, only other experts are in a position to judge one's expertise.[68] For many professions, an elaborate system of accreditation and licensing provides the mark of expertise, evidenced by the diplomas and other certifications that adorn the walls of many professionals. For the rest of us outside of the profession, we lack the knowledge to assess expertise and are left to trust that these procedures properly establish expertise and that self-policing mechanisms work. Being unable to judge expert knowledge, expertise instead becomes a heuristic device to legitimate the professional work of the expert—or an authority. Hannah Arendt understood the power of expertise not to be a form of force or persuasion but a position that "commands confidence" from the lay public.[69] We are persuaded not by the force of argument or coercion but by who is speaking.[70] But how do journalists accomplish this?

A major roadblock to accepting journalism as a profession is the lack of expertise comparable to other professions.[71] Howard Tumber and Marina Prentoulis point out the vulnerability of journalism as a professional practice because of "the absence of a theoretical and scientific framework that supports the claims to 'truth' and guards against deviations from the duties of social responsibility."[72] Expertise provides a mechanism for control within a professional community as actors invoke seemingly inviolable tenets of the profession to demarcate appropriate action and therefore specify who is deserving of recognition.

The problem of journalistic expertise is most clearly understood when considering how knowledge is expressed—or made knowable—through discourse.[73] Communities use the discourse of expertise to share knowledge and patrol boundaries.[74] Journalists are, in essence, producers of discourse—news. But journalistic discourse, unlike scientific, legal, or medical discourse, is rarely abstract. Conversely, abstraction makes for bad journalism. Clarity, especially in the explanation of complex topics, makes for good journalism. Often, the public relies on journalism to translate complex discourses into understandable ones. For example, after Peter Higgs won the 2013 Nobel Prize in Physics for his predictions of the Higgs boson particle, the *New York Times* created an animated video on its website to explain this enormously complex principle of quantum mechanics to its audience of nonphysicists.[75] News tends to be easy to digest, even to the point of being displayed on a ticker along the side of buildings or the bottom of television screens.[76] This is not to denigrate the value of long-form or explanatory journalism. Some of the most vaunted news reports, like John Hersey's reporting on the aftermath of the Hiroshima atomic bomb for the *New Yorker*, are meticulous accomplishments. But, again, this type of reporting is aimed at a general audience, not a specialized one. In the end, journalistic expertise does not stem from the creation of abstract knowledge.

What, then, do journalists have an expertise in? Or, what does the "odd form of specifically journalistic expertise" entail?[77] One answer is a set of "technical competencies,"[78] or skills more closely resembling a craft.[79] Journalists learn how to interact with sometimes hard-to-get sources—either human or documental—and to construct stories from this material. Journalism education, after all, has a curriculum. And in an era marked by the rise of media convergence and a decline in newsgathering resources, the expectation that individual journalists be proficient at a wide array of skills and technologies grows. Journalism is also not monolithic, but comprises different specializations, particularly through the beat system.[80] For example, covering the Supreme Court requires an extraordinary command of legal procedures and case histories to be effective. Expertise also relates to experience. Journalists openly draw on the past to interpret news events in the present.

Zvi Reich captures these ideas of expertise in conceiving of journalists as "interactional" experts adept at working with and among other experts. Journalistic work requires constant interaction with a wide array of sources—many of which may be considered experts in their own fields. Journalists rely on expert sources while portraying themselves as independent.[81] To be successful, journalists develop an expertise in managing these relationships and a proficiency in translating material from sources into accessible news discourse. Reich further argues that journalists are "actually *bipolar* interactional experts" because they must also manage interactions with their untrained news audiences.[82] This ability of journalists to mediate, in both senses of the word, between sources and audiences is a form of expertise. Nonetheless, while journalists hone their craft, the skills-based view of journalistic expertise fails to provide the insulation of professionalism found in other domains.

Expertise goes beyond news-gathering practices and the assembling of news texts to entail the cognitive patterns Waisbord calls "thinking journalistically."[83] Instead of worrying about the possession—or lack thereof—of abstract knowledge, this perspective examines how journalists act as an epistemic community.[84] This accent on journalistic epistemology, including its "rules, routines and institutionalized procedures," foregrounds knowledge production—news—as resulting from a learned sensibility of how to construct accounts of events.[85] This claim calls to mind Deuze's argument above that a common *ideology* is the basic shared trait of journalistic professionalism. Waisbord borrows from Bourdieu to make a similar point: "Journalistic logic or *doxa* refers to the specific rationality of journalism articulated in the observance of news values—the criteria commonly used to define and report news. This knowledge is a unique way of apprehending the world that characterizes journalism by sifting massive amounts of information to churn out a tangible, manageable, recognizable product—news."[86] News emerges out of the shared logic of journalistic professionalism.

Another difficulty for journalistic knowledge production is that journalists have to respond reactively to events in the world. While the scientist conducts controlled experiments in the lab, the journalist responds to a mix of the predictable and the unpredictable that they rarely control.[87] Journalists must agilely sift through far more happenings than could ever be covered to identify what is newsworthy. Professional judgment is among the distinguishing features of what it means to be an authority. It invites respect while ordering the world symbolically. To do this, journalists engage in the selective spatial deployment of resources to produce what Gaye Tuchman calls the "news net"—the institutionalized patterns of attention to only certain topics and actors.[88]

Recognizing journalists as professional knowledge producers requires us to account for both rampant criticisms questioning the viability of objectivity and the special conditions of journalistic expertise. Objectivity is inherently tricky. Even as it may be dismissed as impossible or even undesirable, it remains an important touchstone for journalists advocating continued control over the jurisdiction of news. Likewise, because journalists lack the epistemic shelter afforded by the control of esoteric knowledge, they require an alternative path to expertise through the collection, sorting, and production of news discourses for large, unspecialized audiences. These peculiarities confine and shape the role of professionalism in supporting journalistic authority.

JOURNALISTIC PROFESSIONALISM IN QUESTION

Much scholarly attention has been directed at professionalization—including Larson's professional project—as a social process of attaining prestige and laying claim to particular domains of work. Yet the reverse trend of *deprofessionalization* has also attracted attention since the 1970s. At the time, sociologist Marie Haug surveyed an array of deprofessionalizing forces on the horizon, including a prescient suggestion that the ease of accessing information via computer technology would have an adverse effect on the possession of professional knowledge: "No longer need knowledge be packed only in the professional's head or in a specialized library, where it is relatively inaccessible. It can be available not just to those who know, but also to those who know how to get it."[89] To Haug, control over information stood at the precipice of transformation. Four decades later, the extent of deprofessionalization may be a bit overstated, but clearly the revolution in networked digital computing has altered control over knowledge. When we want to know something, we go to Google.[90]

The deprofessionalization of journalism inevitably invites questions about its coherence as a practice and as a concept. Looking across a variety of changes taking place within journalism, including changes in technology, the encroachment of commercialism on editorial decisions, and the rise of nontraditional journalists, Tamara Witschge and Gunnar Nygren question the viability of journalism as "a homogeneous profession."[91] In the face of these challenges, the conservatism inherent in professionalism becomes evident as journalists react to external changes by falling back on their normative base "to protect the boundaries and values of their profession."[92] These findings should not be too surprising, as belief in the normative commitments of journalistic professionalism makes shifting to new ways of thinking difficult. David Ryfe conceives of the attachment to professional ideas through a tripartite model of habits, investments, and definitions.[93] Journalists develop habits that make regular news work possible, which grow into investments in certain ways of doing things. But the final level of definitions is where the hold of professionalism is the strongest. In line with the view of journalists as knowledge producers advanced above, they develop cognitive attachments that are difficult to break. As a result, deviations from past practices are met with reactions ranging from confusion to resistance.[94]

Outside the walls of traditional newsrooms, deprofessionalization helps us understand the expansion of mediated voices. The decline of journalism's monopoly on the creation, provision, and circulation of information has coincided with what Sue Robinson and Cathy DeShano call a "feeling of entitlement" for new actors wanting to participate.[95] This is not to assume that professional journalism will cease to exist but only that it increasingly operates alongside a bevy of new forms promulgated by new actors.[96] Blogs and social media have become important platforms for public expression that supplement journalistic output with a mix of opinions, challenges, extensions, and fact-checking. Yet in the face of the rise of "citizen expertise," journalists continue to cling to notions of "asymmetric expertise" to define and defend their social role.[97] Even as journalists welcome many attributes of news in the digital era, they consistently express apprehension at the prospect of giving up entrenched professional values.[98]

In considering the state of journalistic professionalism, Örnebring makes the important point that professions are not static or isolated from the external world. Viewing professionalism as either moving forward or receding would be a fallacy. Rather, professionalization is a process that can move in different directions.[99] While the forces of professionalism are resilient, they are also subject to shifting external conditions.[100] This tension between forces of conservatism and dynamism shapes the path of journalistic professionalization, as well as how journalists position themselves to be authoritative. Old arguments based on information monopoly or a more homogenous view of what constitutes appropriate journalistic norms and practices require renewed attention, as part 2 of this book demonstrates.

THE PERSISTENCE OF JOURNALISTIC PROFESSIONALISM

Scholars have paid copious attention to journalism as an occupation, even as it remains, at best, "an anomalous profession."[101] Despite these anomalies, professionalism persists because, in a basic sense, journalists argue that what they do is special. They highlight their skills, promote their commitment to ethics, laud their institutional legacies, point to an instinctual notion of newsworthiness, and, most importantly, fall back on a core argument that their work is socially important, if not entirely central to the functioning of democracy.[102] Each of these characteristics is a bid for distinction, and together they comprise what Seth Lewis refers to as "the collectively shared and taken-for-granted assumptions underlying the belief that journalists, acting in their normative roles, ought to wield gatekeeping control over news content on behalf of society."[103] The notion of control here is central. Authority over the domain of news would mean nothing if it was not restricted through the complex workings of professionalism within the larger society. A commitment to professionalism, and its close association with news organizations, works to control what journalism is. This occurs against the backdrop of actors developing new forms of news that may be only partially beholden, if at all, to this understanding of journalistic professionalism.

The connections bonding professionalism, authority, and exclusivity point to the need to consider boundary work taking place around notions of appropriate journalistic actions, attitudes, and actors.[104] Journalists seek to capture and recapture their jurisdiction over news. But it is not just journalists who should be considered in defining and demarcating journalism. A broader view illustrates the degree to which journalism occurs in a complex social space with many actors on the inside and the outside having an effect on its workings and understandings.[105] Professionalism is, at some level, an argument about why one's judgment is valid—an argument that requires both an actor to make it and an actor to accept it.

Treating professionalism as dynamic, contested, and embedded rather than stable and self-contained exposes the interplay between emerging cultural and technological dynamics and the self-understandings employed by journalists seeking to legitimate their work. In describing the myriad attacks on the cornerstone idea of journalistic objectivity, Maras connects external assent and internal norms: "If the assumptions upon which journalists carry out their work are suspect, then this can impact negatively on public confidence."[106] This is putting it mildly. But the statement points to a greater need to understand the calibration between the understandings developing within the profession and the expectations of those on the outside—and whose judgment should be included in any conceptualization of journalistic authority.

Conceiving of a basis for journalistic authority that does not include professionalism is difficult. In modern Western societies, professionalization remains a key path toward establishing legitimacy, attaining a measure of self-control, and defending the provision of value to society. But, like authority, professionalism should not be mistaken for an immobile force. Instead, the shape of journalistic professionalism is dynamic and reactive within the larger context in which journalism operates. Whether or not the legitimating force of professionalism will weaken in the future, it is imperative to attend to the shape of the transformation taking place within journalism, particularly among competing definitions of journalism.

This is not to say authority can be explained wholly through professionalism. Professionalism provides a powerful lens for viewing authority, but like all lenses, it affords an incomplete view. Other elements of journalistic authority must be simultaneously considered, namely, extra-professional journalistic attributes, the role of news forms, and the narratives that journalists tell about their work. It is only through looking across these elements that an understanding of how journalism comes to possess the right to be listened to can be established.

CHAPTER TWO

Texts and Textual Authority

Forms of Journalism

Like many politicians, Rep. John Fleming, a Republican congressman from the state of Louisiana, uses social media to connect directly with constituents. Fleming often shares updates and links to news stories, and in February 2012 he tagged a story about a new abortion services facility in Kansas and added the comment "More on Planned Parenthood, abortion by the wholesale."[1] Only this story, headlined "Planned Parenthood Opens $8 Billion Abortionplex," was not from the Associated Press or the *New York Times*, but the satirical online news site the *Onion*.[2] Needless to say, no abortionplexes were in the works, and word of the embarrassing gaffe circulated widely. Congressman Fleming's slipup, while quite public, is apparently not rare. Confusion over the veracity of *The Onion* has resulted in a website consisting solely of social media users mistaking *Onion* stories for real news.[3]

Confusing *The Onion* with *real* journalism is certainly absurd, but it is also telling. As an experiment, quickly scan the front page of *The Onion* website and then switch to the *New York Times*. The experience is jarring not because of the difference in content—one hopes—but because of the similarity of form. Consider these two ledes, published a day apart:

WASHINGTON—A flurry of last-minute moves by the House, Senate and White House late Monday failed to break a bitter budget standoff over President Obama's health care law, setting in motion the first government shutdown in nearly two decades.[4]

WASHINGTON—With legislators unable to reach an agreement on health care and other issues before the start of the new budget year, Washington insiders confirmed Monday that the United States is rapidly approaching a full-scale government hoedown.[5]

The second one, of course, is from *The Onion*, while the first one appeared in the *New York Times*. But the difference is palpable only in the final word of *The Onion*'s story, which goes on to describe the antics of a government hoedown (with pictures!). The rest is recognizable boilerplate news lede, including the Washington dateline and the basic summary description. The mimicry of *The Onion*—both in its layout and its narrative structures—contributes to its comedic impact. But it also brings to light the standardization of news form. *The Onion* succeeds partially through political satire but more directly through parodying journalistic forms with ridiculous tweaks. Beyond understanding how *The Onion* uses news conventions to generate humor lies a broader question of what the repetitious familiarity of news forms tells us about the workings of journalistic authority.

News forms are too often taken for granted when they should instead be interrogated for how they shape and constrain the production of journalistic knowledge. Like any cultural form, news texts have conventions that reveal much about the purposes of their creators. From narrative conventions to the sequencing of items in news content to image use, the material choices speak volumes about how journalism understands itself and its relationship to its audiences. This point has been summed up by Robert Manoff and Michael Schudson: "Journalism, like any other storytelling activity, is a form of fiction operating out of its own conventions and understandings and with its own set of sociological, ideological, and literary constraints."[6] The label of fiction might seem demeaning to journalism, but it is not so much a value judgment as an acknowledgement that all news texts are *not* the events being reporting but a constructed account beholden to long-standing rules for what such an account can and should look like.

News forms should also be recognized as dynamic and medium-specific. Over time, print news developed conventions, but the arrival of new media—newsreels, radio, television—required their own conventions suitable to their capabilities. Other technologies, like the Associated Press's wirephoto and satellite video transmission, further altered news forms. The arrival of digital media and the growth of mobile technology in particular upend expectations of what news form should be by ushering in a diversity of forms and experiments with respect to both news content and its delivery. This media environment further complicates the connections between news form and journalistic authority.

It is in this context that this chapter examines how the conventions that govern news forms come to legitimate news texts as authoritative. On one level, news forms are the expression of journalistic professionalism. Over time, news conventions develop in sync with journalists' efforts to imbue understandings of their work with the logic of professionalism.[7] Yet, as will be seen, professionalism cannot fully explain journalistic authority. Comprehending the connection between journalistic authority and news forms requires a wider frame that is sensitive to what may be termed the extraprofessional qualities of news content.

THE AUTHORITATIVE EXPRESSIONS OF JOURNALISM

In his study of medical professionalism, Paul Starr argues that doctors gained power not through some outside mandate but rather through accruing cultural authority, which he defines as "the construction of reality through definitions of facts and values."[8] In gaining this authority, the doctor-patient relationship is one in which the doctor controls the knowledge of the maladies and the subsequent courses of action for the patient. Journalists too seek to define reality through their reporting but must do so by communicating from afar with largely unseen audiences. Journalists rely on the impersonal influence of their news texts rather than the interpersonal interactions that dominate other professions.[9] Journalists work to establish what we may call "mediated authority" through ingrained news conventions that convey information through repetitive story structures. In turn, audiences encounter journalism impersonally through interactions with news texts. This distance reinforces the asymmetry bound up in storytelling between producer and consumers—even as these lines continue to blur.

How journalists cultivate authority at a distance can best be conceptualized by examining journalism as a form of cultural production. This nomenclature places journalism alongside other expressive occupations—writers, poets, painters, sculptors, academics, and the like—by stressing the *output* of journalism as what the public encounters. The focus on output—on the materiality of news and its media—allows us to draw connections between form and journalists' self-understanding of their work expressed in the previous chapter. Each news item presented to the public is simultaneously an argument for the legitimacy of journalism, encompassed in the forms of news journalists use to tell their stories. The shift from actors to texts also allows for a better view of how audiences connect to news and reveals elements of journalism's discursive authority that go beyond what can be found in the discourse of journalistic professionalism.

But how do recurring visual and narrative news forms legitimate news texts?[10] And what exactly is meant by *form*? A useful starting point is Kevin Barnhurst and John Nerone's definition of form as "the persisting visible structures of the newspaper." In examining three centuries of changes in the enduring elements of newspaper design—layout, typography, and visual images—they demonstrate the close connections between form and ideas of authority. Design elements do not arise from neutral decisions. Although aesthetics do matter, news forms are deeply social in their patterns: "Form embodies the imagined relationship of a medium to its society and polity."[11] Changes in form indicate shifts in journalism's understanding of itself and its relationship to its readers. Yet Barnhurst and Nerone are careful to judge newspaper form not as an exact expression of journalistic self-understanding but as a reciprocal force that also acts on how journalists understand their role. In this dual relationship, meanings shape form while "form constrains meaning making."[12] Form is not reducible to professionalism but exists as a separate entity deserving of study on its own terms.

Extending the language of Barnhurst and Nerone, I define journalistic form as *the persisting visible and narrative structures of news*. This broadened definition encompasses design elements, narrative conventions, and image use across different media. Moreover, examining journalism through the lens of cultural production emphasizes the relationship between journalism's material expressions and the construction and circulation of meaning. The accent on news as a discourse of meaning sits awkwardly next to the claims of distance embedded in journalistic objectivity.[13] Normatively, journalists speak of their work in such value-neutral tones as providing facts or information for their readers to interpret as they will.[14] Despite such pronouncements, if mirror theories assuming journalistic accounts to be exact reproductions of the events being covered are to be rejected, then what journalists really produce are *meanings* about the world. All news stories involve an interpretation of an event rendered into a meaningful account through an adherence to set forms.[15] The story gives meaning to the event being covered in explicit and tacit ways.

John Hartley recognized the determinant effect of news forms on the shape of a news report decades ago: "It is not the *event* which is reported that determines the form, content, meaning or 'truth' of the news, but rather the *news* that determines what it is that the event means: its meaning results from the features of the sign-system and the context in which it is uttered and received."[16] Journalism does not begin anew with each event but instead works through established formal conventions and structural constraints to make events meaningful through existing news structures. On the one hand, this slavish devotion to reporting conventions makes the unending tide of news work a practical endeavor, as ethnographic studies have shown.[17] News would not be possible without adherence to preexisting forms.[18] But what also must be acknowledged is that news conventions are not neutral. The structures they impose on news accounts attach layers of meaning to the events being communicated. Through formal conventions, news stories communicate to audiences such basic meanings about the world as what is important or serious and what is unimportant and dismissible, what is right or desirable and what is wrong and deviant, and what is worth public attention and what falls off the social map.

Of course, repetition and the familiarity of conventions are not enough to make the news authoritative. Instead, connecting form with authority begins with returning to the premise that authority is not a thing possessed but a relational dynamic arising through interactions between an authority and those dependent on this authority. This authority relation takes place through mediated interaction with news content. Journalists produce familiar news texts at regular intervals consumed by audiences. News forms structure the production of journalistic knowledge, but they are themselves meaningful, as will be explained below. Putting aside normative claims underlying journalists' arguments for why their work benefits the public, the authority relation occurs through audiences' encounters with news texts—and the forms that govern these texts. For the audience, to enter into a news story is to enter into this particular authority relation. Newspapers, for example, deliberately order the news, deciding what goes in what section and what gets left out and highlighting certain stories while burying others in a sea of text. Readers see this ordering and understand its conventions, even if they flip to the back to read the comics.

The remainder of the chapter examines how news forms structure the authority relation by dividing form into three subparts—story forms, positioning, and images. Story forms pertain to the narrative and verbal conventions that make news accounts intelligible and meaningful. By contrast, the focus on positioning moves beyond the linguistic realm to highlight the importance of news design and layout to generate meaning. The section on images delves into the particular representational issues that pertain to the use of visuals in news presentation. On some level, this is an artificial distinction, as the textual is embedded in the visual—and vice versa. However, treating textual and visual modes as analytically discrete underscores the particularities of news forms and their relationship to journalistic authority.

STORY FORMS: NEWS AS AUTHORITATIVE NARRATIVE

Walter Fisher famously christened us *homo narrans*—the human as essentially a storyteller.[19] Stories are central to social life, but what type of stories do journalists produce? One succinct answer comes from a basic newswriting course the author took as an undergraduate. In differentiating news writing from other forms of storytelling, the instructor offered the example that if a generic mystery novel was to be refashioned as a news story, the first line would be "The butler did it." This, of course, would not be a very satisfying book to curl up on the couch with, but it illustrates well the narrative biases embedded within the inverted pyramid structure. This format provides a template for structuring information into a coherent narrative, but it also contains a particular tacit argument supporting the journalistic values of immediacy and factualness over other modes of expression. Conversely, a reporter accused of burying the lede—presenting important details further down in the story—is castigated for poor newswriting.[20]

The story has always been the basic unit of news, even as what constitutes an appropriate news story varies across time, across media, and even within a news outlet. The news story is not a constant but an evolving form, dependent on the context of its production and reception.[21] Recognizing this variability prompts questions about how news stories come to be cast as authoritative utterances, secured by journalism's epistemological practices for generating knowledge about the world. As an *expression* of journalism's professionalist ideals, a news story concretizes abstract normative commitments to objectivity, impartiality, and distance that undergird much of the argument journalists make about why they deserve to be considered authoritative. To reimagine Bruno Latour's aphorism that "technology is society made durable,"[22] we can claim that news forms are journalistic ideology made durable. They freeze into place a set of particular authority relations between journalists and others. For example, the rise of such taken-for-granted narrative conventions as the summary lede and the inverted pyramid accompanied the professionalizing efforts of journalists at the start of the twentieth century.[23] These elements are expressions of journalism's professional hopes as well as a means of structuring news production and news consumption. With regard to the latter, news stories are always written for an audience, and the conventions they employ contain an understanding of this audience and how it should know about the world through news.

It would be a mistake to read news forms as *only* the material expression of professionalism. As a form of cultural production, journalism is beholden to the demands of narrative, and narratives involve the selection and sequencing of textual aspects into a meaningful whole. Or, put more simply, journalists produce stories. The news story must be recognized as a negotiation between journalism's epistemic practices and the necessities of narrative building incumbent in all forms of storytelling. Journalists are bound by "two impossible ideas—the demands of 'reality,' which they see as reachable through objective strategies, and the demands of narrativity."[24] Weaving information into a coherent narrative necessitates interpreting how disparate parts interrelate as well as developing a coherent storyline. Thus journalists respond to the seemingly discrepant demands of information conveyance and a commitment to narrative through the standardization of news formats.

One way the tension between narrative and information is managed is through familiarity. Stuart Allan identifies a number of formal elements—headlines, ledes, narrative order, vocabulary, and forms of address—that persist across newspaper stories.[25] Similar patterns exist for broadcast news as well. On the level of utility, this standardization helps tame the continuous demands of news production by allowing journalists to quickly write stories and editors to edit them. The news story, while isolatable in the finished news product, must be recognized as emanating from what Allan Bell calls the "news assembly line."[26] But unlike the Fordist production techniques of incremental additions, the news text evolves through multiple layers of editing that shape the story. This is only possible through standardization. On the reception end, news audiences internalize routinized patterns of news writing and can quickly comprehend news texts. For audiences, conventionalized news forms make news graspable while masking its conventions.[27] The news report is a genre with limited variations, and its authoritativeness is a product of convention as much as it is an epistemological feat. The familiarity accompanying unending repetition should not be overlooked.

The notion that news forms structure knowledge is central to Robert Darnton's account of being socialized into the newspaper crime beat. Learning to be a reporter meant, in part, learning to internalize formulas for telling stories. Faced with new information, "we simply drew on the traditional repertory of genres. It was like making cookies from an antique cookie cutter."[28] The dependence on repetition was more than merely a time-saving strategy. Instead, Darnton argues, story forms are so ingrained in the minds of reporters that they can conjure a new story only by relying on preexisting archetypes: "Without pre-established categories of what constitutes 'news,' it is impossible to sort out experience."[29] The story mattered more than the content, an imbalance that resulted often in the fabrication of quotes to complete a story—not out of duplicity but out of narrative expectancy. The fidelity to formal conventions topped the fidelity to accurate facts. The point is not to cast journalists as fabricators but to accentuate the degree to which journalists think *through* news conventions that are always already laden with inbuilt meaning.

While news forms may be functional, they are hardly neutral—a point made above. This claim must be recognized, even if it clashes with journalists' claims that events drive stories. The formal conventions of news writing constrain how any news story can be told. Journalists may view this sameness "as a vindication of objective reporting, rather than the triumph of formulaic narrative construction."[30] But shifting the focus to the latter brings to light the relationship between news forms and the range of meanings that arise within the news. News stories tend toward the proclamation of certainties while masking uncertainties.[31] The reliance on direct quotations tends to privilege institutional sources while making it harder for alternative voices to be heard.[32] Meanwhile, in the absence of the author's voice, and particularly the lack of first-person address, impersonal news accounts seem absolute or unimpeachable. These characteristics support news accounts as authoritative utterances assembled by professional journalists. To borrow from Stuart Hall, news stories aim to convert what may be controversial understandings of the world into common sense declared so by journalists.[33] This process is further masked by journalists' claims of impartiality.

The conventions of news discourse are important not only for what they indicate about how journalists imagine their role, but also for how journalists imagine their audiences. All news forms carry within them assumptions about the social world. As Peter Dahlgren notes: "Texts foster specific ways of seeing the world, hinder other ways and even structure specific ways of relating to the text itself."[34] The inverted pyramid structure and use of quotations and attribution are bound up in an image of the news conveyed to rational audiences drawing on this information to make choices about their governance. This vision finds expression in Jürgen Habermas's conception of the rise of the public sphere in early modern Europe, with newspapers bolstering deliberative interaction.[35] From this view, news becomes information put together by professional journalists to be made use of in specific ways by the audience. While this is, of course, an ideal, it persists within professional arguments for journalistic authority. But the stress on information also leads to questions about what this view of news fails to enunciate.

In sum, the narrative conventions of news texts do more than provide information; they adopt a particular mode of seeing and representing the world for news audiences. News discourse is dominated by the ideal of the objectively written, inverted pyramid–style account with few adjectives and frequent attribution to sources. As an archetype, this form expresses the professionalist ideology of journalists. It is the goal for what journalistic knowledge looks like. This stress on factuality, detachment, and the assuredness of the journalistic voice produces knowledge in a particular way that shapes the range of responses for audiences. For this reason, conventional news narrative forms have long engendered critiques. Daniel Hallin levies such an attack:

> The style of modern American journalism, with its attribution, passive voice constructions, and its substitution of technical for moral or political judgments, is largely designed to conceal the voice of the journalist. But as journalism has become increasingly interpretive, it seems to me this form has become increasingly problematic—both alienating in the wall it throws between the journalist and the reader, and fundamentally dishonest.[36]

Even as social construction in its many guises demonstrates the situatedness of all knowledge, journalists continue to operate within narrative limits designed to stress detachment and unobtrusiveness.[37] Critics have argued for decades that this style hides ideological commitments behind seemingly objective news discourse.[38] Taken together, these criticisms result in what may be called formal wariness about the constraints and abuse of this form.

Some critics have pushed back at the constraints of newswriting they view as simply tiresome. British documentary maker Adam Curtis speculates "the reason we don't read newspapers these days is because the journalism is so boring."[39] Curtis goes on to argue that by refusing to adopt the narrative conventions associated with story forms such as documentaries or fiction, journalists fail their audiences by not making important information interesting. Such arguments have spurred decades of narrative experiments breaking from this model. Aesthetic and political wariness of the constraints embedded in news forms has led to such innovations as literary journalism,[40] alternative and advocacy journalism,[41] public journalism,[42] and more personal writing in new media forms.[43] They all arise out of a shared belief in alternative narrative forms, which gives rise to alternative strategies of legitimation and different ways of structuring the authority relation between journalists and audiences.

POSITIONING: CREATING MEANING THROUGH SPACE AND TIME

News stories are not experienced in isolation—at least not traditionally. Instead, the meaning of any news story derives in no small part from where it is situated among other news stories. All stories are subject to positioning—the purposive sequencing of news stories to signal the relative weight and meaning of individual stories and the larger social map created by the news product. Layout and design are central to how journalists produce knowledge about the world. Journalistic authority is not merely about conveying knowledge through a story; it is about selecting stories for inclusion in the news (while ignoring most happenings) and arranging them in an intentionally meaningful way.

Michael Schudson captures the interpretive work of journalists in including and emphasizing certain stories:

> A news story is an announcement of special interest and importance. . . . It suggests that what is published has a call on public attention. Placement on the page or in the broadcast indicates how noteworthy; readers understand the hierarchy of importance this creates. It is a hierarchy of moral salience. It is no wonder that the sacred center of the working day on a metropolitan newspaper is the editorial conference to decide what stories will make page one, and where on the page they will go.[44]

The invocation of morality underscores the importance of story placement in determining the meaning of news items. Even if journalists might avoid the language of morality, they emphasize their role in generating a hierarchy of news as an expression of their authority.

The centrality of story positioning as a journalistic activity emerged over time, beginning with print news. Barnhurst and Nerone's historical study of newspaper design connects changing patterns in front-page layouts to ideas of how journalism has understood itself during different eras. The dense and disorganized hodgepodge of the nineteenth-century newspaper reflected the dizziness of urban life, climbing literacy rates, and the rise of the mass newspaper audience. In the 1900s, newspapers progressed to more orderly designs with fewer stories sporting larger, interpretive headlines, and eventually the accompaniment of photographs. This shift occurred alongside a shift in journalistic understanding from providing one account of an event among others to giving "*the* news" of the day, arranged hierarchically.[45] In the 1920s, these design shifts "amounted to the visual analog of professionalism."[46] For Barnhurst and Nerone, the newspaper became "the social map"—a cartography of the day's important events.[47] Just as mapmakers seek to index real spaces, journalists sought to portray the social map with neat divisions. Placement in the newspaper, along with associated elements like headline size and illustrations, came to connote importance. The visual arrangement signaled to readers how to interpret a story even before reading the first word. Altogether absence conversely indicates a lack of importance. As remarked upon in the introduction, the *New York Times*'s motto of "All the news that's fit to print" serves as an ideology of news selection—the journalists as arbiter of what matters to readers, with readers standing in for all of society.

Visual forms communicate more than relative importance. As journalists turned increasingly to the discourse of professionalism to build their arguments for cultural authority, they adopted a normative stance as objective purveyors of information to rational audiences able to transform such information into political viewpoints. This logic required newspapers to embrace a position that Barnhurst and Nerone identify as "monovocality"—the stance that each news story is an accurate, objective account arranged in a meaningful way by professional adherents.[48] The newspaper gives the day's news, neatly packaged, without equivocation. This may be the fullest expression of journalistic professionalism—the eradication of divergent subjectivity in favor of an encompassing singular voice.[49]

Ironically, just as monovocality becomes the prevailing journalistic stance, bylines begin to appear within news stories.[50] In previous eras of what would look to modern eyes as a more colorful age of journalism, the byline was mostly absent. This omission supported a perspective that authority did not derive from any individual, but from the full force of the newspaper. Meanwhile, bylines arose first for opinion writers, where individual voices were touted and marketed. However, just as professional practices were becoming standardized so that, in theory anyway, the identity of the individual journalist should not matter in how a story was covered, bylines began to proliferate for common news stories.[51]

Broadcast news also imposes meaning through positioning. In place of the spatiality of print journalism, broadcast journalism operates through tight control over temporality in guiding audiences through a linear account of the news.[52] Metaphorically, television journalists invoke a top story, which is often top both in its place in the sequence of news stories and in the assertion of its importance. Like print formats, so-called soft news—sports, entertainment, lifestyle news—is normally cordoned off for later in a broadcast, along with humorous anecdotes. In the compressed space of a radio or television news broadcast, news selection is closely connected to journalistic authority, with importance signaled through both inclusion and sequencing.

Efforts by broadcast news organizations to maintain monovocality faced challenges first from the intimacy of human voices on radio and later human faces on television. For example, the BBC has long stressed monovocality through appealing to the authority of the corporation—and not its individual journalists—to vouch for its news accounts. In the earliest days of radio news, this meant not identifying individual newsreaders on air. This practice continued until 1940, when the BBC introduced identification out of fear that the Germans would imitate British newscasters. Television proved to be more vexing for the BBC. As Stuart Allan notes: "The danger of 'personalizing' the news as the voice of an individual, as opposed to that of the corporation, was considered to be serious enough to warrant the preservation of anonymity."[53] In its early television broadcasts, the BBC attempted to solve the danger of personalization by simply displaying a clock face on the screen while the news was read. Only over time did newsreaders gain full identification, a move that was popular with audiences. Monovocality gave way to the familiarity of individual presenters as undergirding journalistic authority. This has been true in the United States with news anchors ranking among the most well-known celebrities. Their authority then becomes a matter of presence as much as any professional acumen.[54] Television news succeeds with its direct address to viewers watching at home. The personal and professional intermesh as evening news becomes part of household rituals.[55]

DIGITAL NEWS FORMS: BLURRING AND DETACHING

The act of positioning a news story is as much a part of establishing authority as is the content of the story itself. Barnhurst and Nerone equate news selection and presentation as a social map, and, like points on a map, all content is relational. However, the ability of journalists to provide a social map is increasingly at odds with digital news consumption practices. Certainly, the legacy of monovocality survives, as most online news sites continue to arrange items hierarchically, interpreting for the reader the relative importance of each item. But beneath this apparent similarity are two opposing trends that sharply deviate from previous norms governing news form—a blurring of content that undoes the neat boundaries found in legacy media and the detachment of stories from the stream of news. Through these two shifts, emerging digital media forms complicate the connection between form and journalistic authority.

The blurring of content in digital news spaces arises in part from the lack of space and time constraints for online news sites. Newspapers have a finite number of pages, while broadcasts are limited in time. Digital sites are not bound by these limitations, so that the neatly delineated news product gives way to the ever-growing databases of online news. Furthermore, the topical separations enforced through the use of sections in newspapers or in broadcasts have less hold with online news, as different topics vie for the top spots. In some cases, news site design reflects this unending abundance of items. For example, the front page of the site for UK newspaper the *Daily Mail*, one of the leading English-language news sites in the world, features a continuously updated mix of topics. Stories about politics sit side by side with celebrity gossip. In this sense, the sheer quantity of stories confronting online news audiences calls to mind the jumble of the nineteenth-century newspaper.[56] However, unlike the unchanging newspaper, news sites constantly update their front page because of the pressure to keep audiences reading.[57]

Online, the top story on a news site retains that spot only temporarily before being supplanted by something newer. The growth of audience metrics means that this selection process can be guided by instant feedback on reader preferences rather than the guesswork of news ordering or journalists' judgment of what matters most.[58]

Even more radical than the intermingling of news topics is the blurring of established formal boundaries between news content and advertising content. While advertisements have tended to fall to the margins of newspaper front pages and are clearly delineated in broadcast news, online news sites integrate digital ads alongside content. The *New York Times* and *Washington Post* websites both place a display advertisement running the width of the screen in the space between the nameplate and the top news stories—a practice that would not be tolerated on the print front page, one would imagine, without drawing consternation from subscriber and journalist alike. Likewise, the sites for NBC News, CBS News, and ABC News all place advertisements in prominent spots at the top of the page, creating a visual mix of news and advertising content.

The blurring between content and advertisements has become even more acute through the practice of native advertising—paid content created by or for an advertiser that appears alongside editorial content. This practice is not without controversy, as the *Atlantic* discovered when it published on its site a sponsored content item that was little more than a press release for the Church of Scientology.[59] This was an embarrassing moment for the venerated news outlet, and critics accused it of abandoning its autonomy in pursuit of increasing revenues. While this was a particularly egregious example, it brought into focus an ongoing trend toward more native advertising. News sites became eager to capitalize off the practice's success in generating income well beyond traditional online advertising. The practice continues to grow, with sites like BuzzFeed deriving all of its revenues from sponsored content. Debates continue on how to signal the difference between news and advertising, but the underlying blurring of these two content types once held to be discrete has become more prominent over time.

The blurring of formal news spaces upends the established connections between journalistic authority and news forms by introducing practices that had fallen away in other news outlets. The separation of news and advertising, which is a defining element of professional autonomy, gives way to looser barriers.[60] At best, these practices reimagine journalism for a digital age of abundance, with new tools, new expectations from audiences, and new sources of revenue necessary to sustain reporting. At worst, they undermine the legitimacy of journalism without adequately constructing new grounds to reestablish this legitimacy. In any case, they should not be dismissed as mere design choices but instead recognized for how they reflect a reimaging of the relationship between journalists and their audiences.

The detachment of news stories from their original context marks another departure from traditional modes of journalism. The trend has been toward disintermediation in which individual stories no longer remain embedded within the original context established by a news organization. Disintermediation affects existing modes of journalistic authority by altering the path from story to reader. An early instance of this disruption occurred when Google launched Google News as a standalone news search engine in 2002. Journalists responded warily at the suggestion that algorithms could replace a human editor.[61] A key aspect of professionalism is control over abstract knowledge, long considered a uniquely human trait. When algorithms automate news selection and organization, increasingly "it is code that determines our frame of reference and shapes the way we see the world."[62] In recent years, new services like Narrative Science's Quill software have gone beyond story search and curation to actually convert data into news stories without the need for reporters—a topic taken up in chapter 6.[63] The literal dehumanization of journalism raises questions about the connections between journalistic authority and embodied journalists.

While full automation may not be near, the news landscape has witnessed the rise of new intermediaries through news search engines, social media sharing, and the practice of aggregation. With regard to the latter, Chris Anderson shows that although many traditional journalists disdain aggregation as profiting off the news work of others, news aggregators have developed their own expertise in curating news.[64] Putting aside value judgments regarding intellectual property, these new intermediaries demonstrate how the fluidity of digital content alters the presentational horizon for news content. Aggregation allows for the reinterpretation of news stories by placing them in new contexts. If meaning is contextual, then this meaning is altered depending on a news story's relationship with other content on a news site. But this is not just the work of professionals. What we may call citizen intermediaries circulate news through social media, embedding stories in new contexts and assigning additional meanings.[65] This action has become normal to the point of escaping serious consideration for how it diminishes the monopoly of news outlets to hierarchically sequence the news.

Increasingly, news sites *encourage* their users to share content to drive traffic and brand recognition. When readers go to a story on the website of the *St. Louis Post-Dispatch*, they encounter three options for sharing stories—Facebook, Twitter, and e-mail—prominently sandwiched between the headline and the byline. This conspicuous placement indicates the newspaper's efforts to spur readers to share stories, which acts both as a yardstick for gauging reader interest and a method of extending its brand through readers' active sharing. Certainly, readers of print media have always been able to cut out and save or share news stories, but it has never been built into the news-reading experience to the degree to which it has become entrenched within online news design. Content sharing is unfortunately one of the least remarked-upon shifts taking place in journalism. Online, each news story normally occupies its own page with its own URL, which allows users to easily distribute individual stories through e-mail or social media. This architecture also works in the reverse way, with shared links and search engines allowing users to bypass a news site's home page and go straight to a story.[66] These patterns of news navigation have become a normal part of the online news experience, but the present focus on journalistic authority necessitates stepping back to ask how these developments profoundly alter the circulation of news.

The detachment of a news story from the total news product alters— if not destroys—the traditional role of journalists in presenting a map of what's important. Some may find this a lamentable loss of journalism's ability to concentrate attention, while others may see it as empowering audiences formerly at the mercy of what others think is important— arguments that both have merit. Nonetheless, from the standpoint of journalistic authority, disintermediation transforms journalism's role of mapping social space. Stories become atomized as they are recirculated through various media channels. This shift flattens news stories so that they may be treated equally or rearranged without consequences. Indeed, the recommendation engines of news sites turn to algorithms to reshuffle news stories according to the personal interests of individual readers. In contrast to a news story possessing a claim on the public's attention as central to journalistic authority, news stories become isolated and interchangeable texts.

NEWS IMAGES: BETWEEN FACTS AND AESTHETICS

Much attention to news texts goes to its verbal aspects, with far too little attention to news images.[67] News images have long been part of how journalists legitimate their accounts. In particular, news photographs have become a regular staple of news stories, and television relies heavily on video accounts. Viewed through the normative lens of professionalism, photographs become the ultimate expression of objectivity.[68] Visual evidence has a deep association with objective knowledge in the sciences.[69] Within journalism, the photograph has come to bear the trace of a reality easily reproducible in a superior manner to the written account; a photograph is a recording of something that *happened*. With the rise of photographs, the journalistic role of witnessing, as John Ellis argues, shifts from an emphasis on the written account to the direct account of the news photograph.[70]

Yet journalists have long wrestled with the ontology of news photographs. Photography has always invoked dueling understandings as both a tool for achieving objective realism *and* subjective expressionism.[71] The former stresses the mechanics of picture making as substituting for human partiality, while the latter situates photography as a creative form creditable to the skilled use and aesthetic sensibility of the photographer. The overlap between the realms of photojournalism and art highlight the entrenched aesthetic dimensions of news photographs. As Loup Langdon argues, "Photojournalism at its best . . . has always been intentionally subjective, emotional, and intimate."[72] News photographs are forever bound up in competing conceptions as expressions of truth picked for their newsworthiness and selective renderings chosen for their aesthetic merit. Dona Schwartz identifies this dualism when noting that photojournalists "insist on the objectivity of their pictures at the same time that they attempt to demonstrate their mastery of the craft."[73] It is no surprise then that allegations of manipulation and staging have always surrounded news photographs, even some of the most vaunted exam-ples.[74] The objective quality of news images is also mitigated by their interpretive dependence on text.[75] The journalist has already decided on how a photograph is to be understood based on how it is positioned, ed-ited, sized, and captioned. Even so, photographic meaning cannot be isolated from reception, as the assignment of meaning by the public takes place in the context of viewing.[76]

In the end, the connection between news photographs and journal-istic authority rests on an amalgamation of material and symbolic prac-tices. Images provide evidence of events and deliver information visually rather than linguistically to news audiences. But the authority of the im-age cannot be reduced to indexical fidelity. Doing so omits its emotional and communal power from conceptions of journalistic authority.

As with other modes of journalism in the digital era, the use of news images is changing. Certainly, image norms vary across media and formats, as the tabloid press demonstrates.[77] But the rise of digital pho-tography alters how images can be produced and circulated. Witnessing extends beyond the purview of the professional journalist.[78] At news-papers, photojournalism staffs have been hit hard by ongoing budget cuts. The *Chicago Sun-Times* went as far as to eliminate its photojour-nalists, choosing instead to entrust reporters with cameras and smart phones.[79] In addition, the switch to digital photography and the wide availability of photo-editing software facilitate widespread image ma-nipulation, whereas the darkroom was limited to a few esoteric tricks.[80] Contemporary society is awash in digital images, and revelations of in-appropriately manipulated or fabricated images have become a normal occurrence. One high-profile incident occurred at the start of the 2003 Iraq War, when Brian Walski, an award-winning *Los Angeles Times* photographer, submitted a harrowing photograph of a group of cower-ing Iraqi civilians with a US soldier looming over them. The dramatic photograph was then featured prominently in several US newspapers be-fore a closer inspection of the photo revealed duplicated elements. When reached by his editor, Walski admitted to fabricating the photograph by cobbling together separate images to improve its aesthetics, and he was quickly fired.[81] What was remarkable about this incident was that the manipulation took place on a laptop in the middle of a war zone thou-sands of miles from the newsroom. Given the ease with which digital photographs can be manipulated, journalists holding up news images as faithful evidence that an incident occurred as it was recorded face increased scrutiny from suspicious audiences.

Even with technological developments, shifts in use, and questions about their fidelity, images remain central to news while photojournalists cling to established norms.[82] The power of images, as unexplained as it is, retains its driving force for those wanting to bear witness. Julianne Newton acknowledges the ontological challenges besetting photography but also the sustained desire to use images: "Even as some argue the impossibility of making truthful images, photojournalists across the globe are fighting for the right to photograph things they are passionately convinced people need to see."[83] To demand this right to be listened to is to invoke the authority of journalism.

WHAT PROFESSIONALISM CANNOT EXPLAIN ABOUT AUTHORITY

Journalistic authority cannot be fully explained through the lens of professionalism or by assuming that news discourse can be reduced to merely the expression of this professionalism. News texts produce an excess of meaning that also needs to be accounted for and which is no less important to the construction of journalistic authority.[84] In short, "journalism works differently" than many of its assumptions.[85] This argument is made clearer by returning to the contention that journalism should be understood as a form of cultural production.

The shift from professionalism as the privileged explanation for journalistic authority to journalism as an embedded cultural practice calls to mind James W. Carey's dualist perspective of communication as both transmission and ritual. From a transmission perspective, what journalism produces is portable information capable of being mass-produced and extended through space to large audiences. Transmission-based understandings stress the movement of information from one place to another. As an institution, journalism produces and circulates information to distant audiences. Carey argues this incomplete view distracts from a more basic understanding of communication as central to the creation of a shared world, with journalism as a key mode of cultural production. Instead of favoring transmission, a ritual view shifts journalism from "the act of imparting information" to "the representation of shared beliefs."[86] As "a presentation of reality that gives life an overall form, order, and tone,"[87] the news is a particular symbolic system charged with generating shared meaning about the world. From this perspective, the repetition of form is meaningful in itself.

A stress on ritual and cultural continuity over the transmission of individual news stories shifts attention to the symbolic power of news. Elizabeth Bird and Robert Dardenne stress this point in showing how the constancy of news forms and story formats supersedes individual stories: "The facts, names, and details change almost daily, but the framework into which they fit—the symbolic system—is more enduring."[88] Jack Lule takes this argument further in ascribing to journalism a mythic cultural function of "telling the great stories of humankind to humankind."[89] Examining news stories as myth moves attention from specific content to how familiar archetypes structure narrative forms and add meaning to stories. Like all myths, these stories define the normative social order by iterating collective values and rejecting deviancy. Lule's work suggests the need to account for enduring symbolic structures when considering the meanings journalists create about the world through the close adherence to set story forms.[90]

In all likelihood, the preceding discussion would be anathema to journalists.[91] Page one meetings do not devote time to discussions of myth. Yet the value of this perspective lies in shifting attention from the atomizing discourse of news as information for rational actors to the cultural role of news as a collectivizing force. In a classic example, John Fiske and John Hartley identify the "bardic function" of television in producing, as a bard does, highly stylized accounts that speak to audiences as a collective, orienting them to the world and creating a sense of shared identity.[92] Shifting from news as informational to news as bardic or ritualistic sheds light on the collective meanings that arise through news consumption. This function is readily visible in studies of media events in which journalists focus society's attention in moments of celebration or grief.[93] During such media events, journalists dispense with their self-proclaimed detachment and become participants in these rituals.[94] Although they bring society together, critics have ascribed to ritual a hegemonic role of reinforcing existing social hierarchies.[95] Simon Cottle argues against the simplistic equating of media ritual as either the preservation of the dominant ideology or the consensual flattening out of society to instead point the journalism's complex relationship with the polity.[96]

Despite the research cited above, the clout accorded to journalistic professionalism too often overshadows journalism's ritual functions.[97] The continued joining of news content to rationalist ideals informed by public-sphere theory discounts journalism's contribution to what Barry Richards calls the "emotional public sphere."[98] While emotions are left out of normative models of journalistic professionalism—and by extension arguments for authority—clearly much news content does work on an emotional level. Journalism can be stimulating rather than merely informative.[99] Karin Wahl-Jorgensen challenges dominant assumptions about objective journalism by emphasizing the "strategic ritual of emotionality" in Pulitzer Prize–winning articles.[100] She finds that while journalists face constraints from engaging in emotional expression, they readily draw on their sources to provide emotion in their stories. This move calls to mind Norman Fairclough's claim that nonjournalistic voices are ventriloquized through their emplacement within news discourse.[101] Journalists go through great lengths to incorporate emotion in their stories, even if this inclusion lacks a conventional normative justification.

The role of emotions can be clearly seen in the specific role of journalism as healer. Carolyn Kitch and Janice Hume reveal the myriad ways that journalists confront grief and death in news coverage. In the face of disaster, journalists retreat to a pattern that "conveys cultural stories employing familiar elements arranged in recognizable order, stories that recur across media and over time to create a broader understanding of the meaning of death."[102] In the marathon coverage following such tragedies as the Kennedy assassination or the September 11, 2001, attacks, journalists do more than deliver information about these events. They also mediate tragedy, collectivize attention during moments of intense grief, and stabilize order in the face of apparent instability. Grief may not be on the curriculum in journalism school, but it remains necessary to account for such ritualistic functions of journalism as confronting death and tragedy when conceptualizing journalistic authority. In those moments when journalists mediate exceptional events, they collectivize attention and create shared experiences.[103]

The power of news to convey emotion is perhaps most apparent with photographs. The discussion of images above acknowledged their complex interconnected roles in indexing reality, bearing witness, and invoking emotional responses. Clearly, photographs are often understood within the dominant modes of journalistic professionalism and the emphasis placed on creating objective accounts.[104] But journalistic authority cannot be explained by this mode alone. If journalism is to possess a right to be listened to as a way of knowing the world, its role in generating meaning beyond what can be accounted for through the lens of professionalism should be recognized. To return to news coverage of the September 11 attacks on New York, television news constantly replayed the video of the plane striking the World Trade Center and the collapse of the towers, newspapers devoted room to pictures of the attack and its aftermath (including pictures of the victims), and online news further circulated visuals. This was not merely informational—no one had missed what happened. Instead it was part of the reaction to the trauma of the attack and the attendant grief.[105] Recognizing this role via the use of news images invites an engagement with the cultural authority of journalism that includes its role in creating shared meanings about the events being covered and abetting the public in confronting difficult moments collectively.

Images from the September 11 attacks quickly became iconic news images firmly pressed into cultural memory as a part of how the past is understood.[106] News reporting and the events being reported become stuck together as specific images are indelibly printed into collective memory. Moreover, the traits of their iconicity are telling. For example, Michael Griffin shows how images of war persist across decades not through the specificity of an account but through generalizing conflict.[107] These images have little news value in terms of conveying information about an event, but they have cultural value in being made to capture the feeling of conflict, as in the cathartic Iwo Jima flag raising or the blank stares of war-weary US soldiers in Korea. Images work on an emotional level in ways that rarely fit with journalism's self-proclaimed norms.[108] Nor do they always fit with broader notions of citizenship.[109] Nonetheless, the durability of images in collective memory further underscores the cultural working of journalistic authority in conveying emotion, establishing collective meanings, and providing continuity to social life.[110] These values may not always find expression in how journalism talks about itself, but they deserve attention nonetheless.

IMAGINING JOURNALISM THROUGH ITS FORMS

Journalistic authority cannot be properly understood without a close examination of news forms. The conventions that govern narrative styles, layout and design, and images are not haphazard or impartial elements but the material basis for the authority relation between journalists and audiences. News forms are laden with epistemological premises that shape the type of knowledge they communicate and, by extension, contain an argument for their legitimation. News forms are also complex in how they are at once a manifestation of journalists' understandings of their work—the realization of journalistic professionalism—while also beholden to the dictates of such extraprofessional qualities as narrativity, emotion, and aesthetics. Finally, news forms are not static but instead evolve in response to changing technologies, changing self-understandings, and changing social conditions.

These attributes are all vital for examining news forms, but so too is an acknowledgement of the increasingly fractured state of journalism. The discussion of news forms in this chapter has more or less assumed the news to be homogeneous. Much of what has been discussed above pertains to the standard news form and its hold on collective understandings of journalism. While this reduction allows connections to be drawn between form and journalistic authority, it also omits emergent news forms popping up across the larger mediascape. Analytically, trying to draw broad conclusions inductively leads to privileging some forms while omitting others.

Journalism has many faces, and digital technology continues to facilitate novel forms that do not conform to traditional journalistic standards. As a result, new entrants operating through online sites, social media, and mobile apps have brought news forms that differ from those specified above.[111] For example, news blogs, many of which have grown into thriving organizations over the past decade, often depart from the isolated and impersonal tone of conventional news to instead stress the personality of the writer and signal connections to others through copious linking and quoting.[112] But these emergent forms are not only about changing formal presentations. More crucially, new conventions contain new ways of imagining the relationship between news producers and consumers, sometimes explicitly blurring the line. The proliferation of novel news forms continues to make journalism much more heterogeneous than what existed through its twentieth-century mass communication models.

This transformation is not merely about different styles but also about new authority relations that arise from these styles. These shifts in form also shift the basic premises of journalistic authority in directions that are unfamiliar or even publicly contested for their deviation from traditional norms and practices. What needs to be examined is how departures from traditionally taken for granted news forms suggest new grounds for legitimation, and what this authority relation looks like. The medium-specific constraints of print and broadcast news give way to a different news experience with digital media. New digital tools alter what journalism can look like. Digital media bring new potentialities to how journalists connect to news audiences as well as create new challenges in managing the flood of available content. Expecting news presentation to stay the same prohibits scrutiny of new modes of news. Instead, attention must be paid to how formal news innovation gets articulated in ways that shape how journalists present arguments for their legitimacy.

CHAPTER THREE

Telling Stories About Themselves

Journalism's Narratives

No award in American journalism matches the prestige of a Pulitzer Prize. For nearly a century, the annual awards have conferred their recipients with public recognition as the pinnacle of the journalistic profession. Each year brings rampant speculation and clandestine leaks leading up to the official announcement. Once revealed, newspaper editors stand among the desks of the winning newsrooms to deliver good news—for a change—to the assembled staff. The Pulitzer Prizes provide an annual occasion, and a very public one at that, to spotlight journalistic achievement and tout examples of journalism fulfilling its normative commitment to public service. Their symbolic power extends beyond the winners to act as a beacon of what journalism can and should do. In crucial ways, their meaning is shaped by the larger context in which they are bestowed. This was made abundantly clear with the announcement of the 2013 crop of winners. The *New York Times* asserted the awards "were especially valued" that year since "so many news organizations were battling their own financial troubles."[1]

The somber theme continued through the luncheon to fete the 2013 prize recipients. In his address to the gathered honorees, Pulitzer Prize board chairman Paul Tash celebrated their collective accomplishment while also observing the difficult conditions besetting traditional print journalism: "What makes this year's crop of Pulitzer finalists even more remarkable is the punishing economic pressure on most of the news organizations that have sponsored the work." Tash continued, diagnosing the cause as "the combination of economic crisis and competition from digital alternatives [that] has sent advertising revenues plummeting by more than half." Yet even in these challenging work conditions, Tash vouched for the quality of the prize recipients, adding, "Journalistic ambition burns both in organizations and individuals, despite the financial challenges."[2] It was a rallying cry amid continuing gloom surrounding the news industry.

The Pulitzer Prizes and accompanying speech by Tash provide a prime example of the final dimension of journalistic authority described in part 1 of this book—the public narratives journalists create about their work. Journalism's right to be listened to—that is, its ability to establish its authority relation with the public—depends on the arguments journalists craft to position their practices as legitimate means for generating knowledge about the world and their organizations as the legitimate venues for this to occur. They do so in an increasingly complex media landscape that facilitates all manner of voices, including journalism's critics. Whole conversations take place around what the news is and what it ought to be.

The Pulitzer Prizes provides one such example for the public arguments journalists make. Recipients, both individual journalists and news organizations, earn bragging rights in perpetuity. Winning entries become models—both specifically to others coveting a future Pulitzer and broadly to the public—of what quality journalism looks like. But something else is also going on here. The conferral of the prizes provides meaning about the state of contemporary journalism. In 2013, this narrative involved the financial health of print journalism. Tash took the prize luncheon as an opportunity to publicly engage the adverse conditions of the news industry. His interpretation accentuated external elements, namely, the industry's financial woes due to the decimation of advertising revenues and technological changes expanding the terrain of news. In defining the problems the industry faces this way, Tash omitted culpability on the editorial side of newspapers or larger cultural shifts in media consumption and creation. The prizes, by contrast, demonstrate the continued relevance of traditional print journalism.[3]

The Pulitzer Prizes can be understood as just one example of what Peter Dahlgren calls the contest over "definitional control" of journalism.[4] The journalistic community, as fractured as it is, works to define its own problems and solutions. This occurs through narratives about journalism produced by a multitude of speakers within a multitude of sites—including awards luncheons. This chapter looks inward at how the journalistic community engages in narrative construction about itself and how such talk about journalism fits into a fully formed conception of journalistic authority.[5] It begins by theorizing as to what narratives about journalism do and then proceeds to investigate the many sites in which such efforts occur and the many actors involved.

WHAT NARRATIVES ABOUT JOURNALISM DO

The argument at the core of this chapter—and perhaps more accurately at the core of this book—is the need to recognize journalism as a contingent cultural practice involving both the materiality of news and ways of imagining journalism. In moving from narratives *of* journalism—the news account—to narratives *about* journalism, attention switches from the implicit relations embedded in news forms to the explicit articulations of journalistic norms and practices occurring alongside the news. Journalism, as the fusion of practice and belief, is both malleable and durable, prone to contingencies and contradictions, and undeniably woven deeply into cultural, political, economic, and social life. Accepting this set of premises requires probing the mechanisms through which journalism, as a mode of cultural production, comes to have the requisite meaning to provide a legitimate discourse of the real—as well as how this meaning is upheld, transformed, and contested. In short, where do ideas of what journalism is and what it should be come from?

To answer this basic question, we can first divide news narratives from narratives about journalism. The latter can be condensed under the somewhat clunky name "metajournalistic discourse."[6] This type of talk is conceived as a *meta*discourse, or a secondary discourse that intrinsically and reflexively relates back to a primary discourse—news, in this case. Discussions of what news ought to do, critiques of a particular story as inaccurate, portrayals of reporters in popular culture all fall in this category of discourse. So too can we add Pulitzer Prize luncheons. To accommodate this variety, metajournalistic discourse is a purposely broad discursive field defined by the topic of journalism rather than speaker, venue, or mode of address.[7] Given this breadth, we can begin to trace metajournalistic discourse across an array of topics including debates over the appropriateness of particular news-gathering procedures, skirmishes involving the legal rights accorded to journalists, the lauding of journalists through awards or reminiscences of storied careers, and the identification and denunciation of journalists for deviant practices. Any one of these examples pertains to some concrete aspect of journalistic practice while also providing interpretive space to engage larger questions of journalism surrounding morality, legality, quality, and normalcy. In one sense, metajournalistic discourse can clearly be identified as a discourse, full of recurring textual patterns that seem to follow conventions (an awards speech, for example). But the sense of discourse employed here signals something deeper: talk about journalism shapes and constrains how we think about journalism.

Journalistic authority cannot be fully conceptualized without a theoretical link to metajournalistic discourse. We have to consider journalism as an idea, as something imagined, as much as we consider its material and organizational forms. The ability of journalists to position themselves as an authority over a particular domain of public knowledge—news—requires continual maintenance to support claims for journalists' right to be listened to. In lieu of chicken-and-egg arguments about whether practices or discourse supporting practice come first, they should be seen as developing together. Proponents of any new journalistic practice, normative commitment, or formal convention espouse the value gained from the innovation.[8] These developments are also unevenly distributed so that some actors may argue on behalf of a particular change while others oppose it. For example, familiar news elements like the inverted pyramid or the interview were not always central to journalism but practices that developed to occupy a central place in how journalism is imagined as a legitimate social practice. We can see how these practices progressed through the benefit of historical perspective, but it becomes difficult in the present moment of digital upheaval to discern isolated trends that only ever occupy a corner of journalistic thinking from emergent forms that possess the same transformative potential as the inverted pyramid. This lack of clarity is all the more reason to recognize how practice and discourse develop in tandem to compete for legitimacy.

Metajournalistic discourse cannot be removed from its context. Its power to delineate the meaning of journalism requires careful attention to its production and circulation. Statements about journalism are not free-floating aphorisms of some general nature but statements *from* somewhere. The need to wed discourse with context leads to a necessary distinction between metajournalistic discourse originating within journalism and emanating externally or from its rough edges. Changing media have altered the means through which this discourse can be produced and circulated, which vastly increased the mediated sites through which metajournalistic discourse moves. Within this terrain, Meryl Aldridge and Julia Evetts observe journalism to be "an intensely reflexive occupation which constantly talks to and about itself."[9] Much of this owes to journalists' structural position as cultural producers. In controlling the means of discursive dissemination, journalists are able to directly convey inward-looking talk about journalism to their audiences. Surveying this output, Tanni Haas argues for three types of journalistic metacoverage, which include "news media reporting" on organizational and economic happenings, "news media criticism" evaluating developments across journalism, and finally "news media self-criticism" in which the critical eye is turned inward.[10] Haas argues that the latter is the most rare and chalks up the lack of sustained reflexivity to fears that truly critical self-evaluation threatens to scare away audiences and advertisers. Nevertheless, this lack of self-reflexivity should not detract from an interest in just what all this talk about journalism does. Instead, following Barbie Zelizer and Peter Dahlgren, I argue that journalists rely on narratives about their work to support their claims to cultural authority and to retain "definitional control" over its conduct and reception.[11]

FACING CRISIS THROUGH DISCOURSES OF CONSOLIDATION AND DIFFERENTIATION

The discussion of metajournalistic discourse thus far has tended toward the abstract. To make this more concrete, we can turn to efforts by journalists—including Paul Tash above—to confront the struggles of the newspaper industry in recent years in what many label a time of crisis. This is not all rhetoric, as the following case makes plain. In 2009, amid a combination of long-term industry trends—e.g., declining audiences for print and the decline of markets with multiple newspapers—and short term circumstances—e.g., the global recession and drastic decrease of advertising revenues—caused the demise of two major US newspapers. In the span of a few weeks, the *Rocky Mountain News* closed for good while the *Seattle Post-Intelligencer* ended its print edition and laid off most of its staff in a bid to survive as a scaled-down, online-only news site.[12] Both newspapers had operated in their respective cities for over a century, and their circulations placed them among the top hundred newspapers in the United States. Notably, the two failed newspapers existed in competitive newspaper markets in which they faced off against larger rival newspapers—the *Denver Post* and *Seattle Times*—for circulation and advertising revenue. While once common, intracity newspaper competition had fallen away by the 1980s. The changing economics of news and rise of broadcast media made newspaper competition a rarity outside of New York and Chicago. For smaller cities, even in good economic times, competition was barely sustainable.

When the *Rocky Mountain News* and the *Seattle Post-Intelligencer* announced their back-to-back fates in early 2009, journalists largely ignored the peculiarity of their competitive newspaper environments to instead cast them as representing the fragility of newspapers everywhere. They became symbols of what was widely considered to be a crisis of traditional news, canaries in the coal mine presaging the possible failure of the entire industry. Through metajournalistic discourse, journalists sought definitional control over how the problems of newspapers should be understood, which, in turn, suggested potential remedies.[13] With the newspaper industry seemingly in peril, journalists mounted a defense of norms and practices to be preserved even if printed newspapers disappeared. For example, an editor writing in the final edition of the *Rocky Mountain News* warned of the dire consequences that would follow: "Corruption at all levels of government will grow some. Politicians will escape embarrassment. Businesses will hoodwink their employees and shareholders. More taxpayer money will be wasted. And far fewer people will be looking out for you. I'm talking about trained, dedicated, experienced journalists who know what to look for and know how to get it in front of you to read in digestible form."[14] This quote suggests the inadequacy of nonprofessional journalists compared to the professionalism epitomized by newspapers. But it was also an effort to define what may appropriately be considered journalism irrespective of medium. Journalists also demonstrated their open disdain toward emergent news forms. One columnist wrote: "You can go online and read no end of fiction and smear about public figures. But when you read content in a newspaper, you consistently can rely on it."[15]

However much the journalistic community rallied around these newspapers, the public response to these claims was next to nothing. No meaningful efforts to save the two newspapers occurred, and newspaper circulation continued to drop even as news appetites remained strong. We may then ask who was served by the construction of the newspaper crisis. Journalists shaped the narrative around the newspapers largely by pointing to the failures of the business side of newspaper companies to be inventive while eschewing cultural changes leading to the decreased consumption of print news or newspapers' poor record of online innovation.[16] This context indicates how journalists' reactions are not neutral interpretations of the newspaper industry but a particular way of narrativizing the complex set of factors involved in the decline of newspapers. Controlling this narrative is a way of controlling both the naming of symptoms and the corresponding means of suggesting a cure.[17] Of course, any industry engages in discourses of self-protection amid fear of intrusion from others or outright demise. But journalists occupy a unique cultural space in that they control direct channels of communication with their audiences that they can use to report on the news industry.

Another way to examine the discussions surrounding the *Rocky Mountain News* and the *Seattle Post-Intelligencer* is how journalists used the twin rhetorics of consolidation and differentiation to create boundaries. In consolidation mode, talk about journalism represents journalism as a coherent practice applicable across a large and diverse swath of news-related activities. The rhetoric of consolidation flattens difference while constructing the elements of a common journalistic ideology—often one beginning from the newspaper as journalism's center.[18] As the rhetoric of consolidation imagines a coherent corpus for journalism, the rhetoric of differentiation institutes a stark division between what may be considered appropriately journalistic and what should be discounted as inadequate. Journalism has always comprised difference, whether by medium, geography, audience, or normative orientation, but contemporary trends portend greater variety, making consolidation appear more fraught.[19] Differentiation then acts as a way to build walls within journalism. Defenders of newspapers, in the above example, situated new digital forms as insufficient or even dangerous.[20]

Rhetorics of differentiation and consolidation demonstrate how metajournalistic discourse categorizes certain norms, practices, or actors as acceptable or improper, included or excluded, the same or different. The drawing of contrasts certainly gets attention, but consolidation in particular highlights the community-making aspects of metajournalistic discourse. Treating them as separate helps bring to light how they each connect to journalistic authority, but it is also important to explore how these two forces interrelate. Making this clear necessitates an example of how journalists publicly confront deviance.

ESTABLISHING COMMUNITY THROUGH DEVIANCE

In 2014, the venerable liberal political magazine *New Republic*, cofounded by Walter Lippmann, celebrated its centennial with a special issue. Typical of anniversary issues,[21] the lineup contained a mix of features commemorating the magazine's century of political commentary and extolling the *New Republic*'s place in American intellectual life. But the issue was not all laurels. Editor Franklin Foer's lead story, "The Story of How the *New Republic* Invented Modern Liberalism," was followed by Hanna Rosin's article: "Hello, My Name Is Stephen Glass, and I'm Sorry."[22] Glass may have disappeared from the magazine sixteen years earlier, but his story is well known within journalism. He was fired in 1998, after being exposed for fabricating scores of magazine articles. His offenses were not minor peccadilloes, but rather elaborate ploys involving fake business cards, fictitious notes, and even a forged website for a nonexistent technology company. Buzz Bissinger chronicled his story in *Vanity Fair*,[23] which became the basis for the movie *Shattered Glass*. Given both the lengths Glass went to hide his lies and the attention his transgressions received, Rosin's label of Glass as "the perpetrator of probably the most elaborate fraud in journalistic history" may not be an overstatement. Rosin's 7,000-word article combines a recapitulation of Glass's actions, Rosin's own self-reflection as his one-time friend and advocate, and Glass's postscandal life, including the State Bar of California's recent refusal to allow him to practice law.

The decision for the *New Republic* to so prominently feature a story on Glass indicates just how deeply intertwined the legacy of journalistic success and failure are. Charles Lane, Glass's editor when he was exposed, told Rosin: "Steve did something so spectacular and so dishonest on such a world scale that it's going to stay with him forever, and not unfairly." But the episode is also forever tied to the *New Republic*. Glass may have left the magazine and journalism altogether, but his tenure left such a lasting mark on the magazine that years later the editors felt they had to confront this legacy in an in-depth manner amid its celebratory self-examinations—even as it dredged up such adverse memories.

Episodes of journalistic deviance lead to particularly pronounced efforts by the journalistic community to explicitly denounce deviant actors. Studies of reactions to such incidents often use the framework of "paradigm repair" in which journalists seek to avert larger threats to journalism by isolating and ostracizing individuals.[24] This concept derives from Thomas Kuhn's seminal work on the role of paradigms in dictating scientific practice and shaping epistemological assumptions.[25] Journalism, as a cultural practice, contains its own paradigms that direct how the world can be made known through news discourse. Incidents of deviance requiring paradigm repair reveal the fragility of this paradigm by exposing the contingency of journalistic legitimacy and the contradictions that lay below the surface. When an incident threatens to expose shortcomings and instill doubt, journalists engage in interpretive labor to remove the threat through isolation. In an act of differentiation, journalistic violators are cast out of the community as deviant. Simultaneously, in an act of consolidation, members of the journalistic community reaffirm core commitments and the solidity of news practices. Such moves transform the story from the deviant action of an individual to the restorative action of a community. Yet this approach is reactive rather that constructive; it does not confront structural issues but smooths over them.

To return to the *New Republic* case, Glass's much-publicized dismissal symbolically demonstrates the removal of the fabricator as an act of rooting out deviance, even if larger questions of the nature of journalistic factuality go unasked. What's more, the larger narrative of Glass extends beyond his extraordinary actions to also include the work of then editor Charles Lane to expose Glass's lies (this is also the crux of the drama in the movie *Shattered Glass*). In her article, Rosin comments on how Lane's successful career has become inextricably tied to, if not overshadowed by, his exposure of Glass. As Lane admitted to Rosin, "It was a great feather in my cap," but it also "tends to distract from everything else I've done in my career." In this story, if Glass is the villain, Lane is the hero. This juxtaposition acts to reinforce the self-regulatory potential of journalists to monitor their own kind. The problem of Glass found its solution in the dogged work of Lane to expose and correct the fabrications. It may not be a happy ending, but it reinforces a narrative of journalists striving to protect their reputation and practices. Journalists advocate for the virtue of their self-policing against the need for outside investigations. This argument is often made salient in discussions of press freedom. For example, the British newspaper industry responded to the *News of the World* scandal by arguing for its ability to monitor itself in an effort to forestall a government-sponsored regulatory body.[26]

Even as individual journalists accused of wrongdoing by the community find themselves exiled, the resulting stories of deviance become part of the narrative through which journalism defines itself. The individuals may be gone, but their legacy becomes an interpretive tool employed in the face of new allegations of journalistic misconduct.[27] In this complicated way, these stories contribute to arguments for journalistic authority made by journalists by turning attention from deviance to repair. After isolating deviance, journalists can then use these stories to argue for their own self-regulatory prowess as means of supporting autonomy. In addition, the attention to deviance reinforces communal notions of correct journalism through discursive consolidation. While journalists may not wholly control the narratives of their scandals, they nonetheless engage in metajournalistic discourse to repair and preserve the arguments that they make to support their authority.

What's not known is how successful the *New Republic* was in exorcising Glass from the rest of the magazine. Perhaps stirring up his memory had the opposite effect of suggesting the tenuousness dwelling in any news account that attempts to provide an accurate depiction of events in the world. This ambiguity reminds us that metajournalistic discourse comprises narratives that can be interpreted in different ways. Nonetheless, this episode provides an example of how journalists publicly confront their work in ways that establish boundaries and establish community.

METAJOURNALISTIC DISCOURSE AS
BOUNDARY MAKING

The expulsion of Glass is just one example of how the journalistic community seeks to establish boundaries. The study of boundaries has a long history within sociology.[28] Societies are marked by difference, leading to the need for careful analysis of how various demarcations develop and disappear, how they are enforced or altered, and the consequences of these forces of consolidation and differentiation in generating social hierarchies. The introduction touted the work of Thomas Gieryn in the sociology of science,[29] which provides a promising conceptual lens for thinking about journalism.[30] To return to this argument, Gieryn moves away from the laboratory to instead foreground public struggle over definitions of science through rhetorical "boundary-work." His approach is stridently antiessentialist, vacating all preconceptions to privilege how actors undertake efforts to erect, police, or demolish boundaries in pursuit of "epistemic authority" over the creation of knowledge about specific parts of the natural and social world while placing competitors outside the bounds of such authority.[31] In the absence of enduring essential qualities, science emerges as the result of an ongoing making and remaking of allegiances contingent on time and place—which Gieryn calls "credibility contests." Knowledge creation, despite the normative claims to autonomy bound up in professionalism, is deeply rooted in and reactive to context. For an example of boundary work, scientists intent on maintaining autonomy stand up to the state to try and expunge the influence of politics from its domain.[32]

Although the concept of boundary work may seem deeply resonant with journalism, adapting Gieryn's view of science is more fraught than it appears on the surface.[33] Certainly, both scientists and journalists follow procedures to record and relay knowledge and, therefore, both require epistemic authority to portray domains of reality to the wider public. But it would be a mistake to consider them overly analogous. Efforts to transpose Gieryn's work on science to journalism encounter three barriers.[34] First, journalism can never have the sharp boundaries found in other professions, and the ambiguousness of what may be called journalism continues to increase in the digital media environment. Second, the type of knowledge output journalists produce differs from scientific knowledge. Unlike the esoteric technical discourse of science, journalists seek to produce lucid stories accessible to a wide audience stratified by education level. Unclear language makes for bad journalism. Finally, journalistic expertise is more accurately understood as interactional, in contrast to the substantive, abstract expertise governing science.[35] Taken together, any effort to import boundary work into journalism must account for the porousness of the news profession and the lack of abstract knowledge and expertise as supplying a means of delineation. This is not meant to detract from the usefulness of Gieryn's concept, but rather to recognize the ways in which the peculiarities of journalism shape how boundary work can be used to understand it.

Boundary work sheds light on how journalists define appropriate practices, values, and actors while excluding others. These discourses of differentiation demarcate the bounds of legitimate journalism as a mode of cultural production tasked with relaying society's stories to itself. They are not merely rhetorical exercises but deliberate efforts to shape the structural conditions in which news is created and the epistemological grounds on which it is legitimated. In the Glass case, journalists railing against his actions went beyond disassociating the news industry with this single individual to signal a defense of the credibility of their work and their ability to represent reality. Glass's fabrications, as extreme as they were, invoked the overall fragility of journalism as a cultural system capable of depicting reality through news texts. This is, of course, a perpetual challenge since the account will always be separate from what is being recounted. There is always a gap between representation and object, and Glass's offenses—as they were constructed—expose this gap to the public. Journalists reacted through boundary work to expel Glass in order to protect the system.

Another conceptual asset of the boundary work perspective is that it permits an interpretation of metajournalistic discourse that is at once self-interested and earnest. Certainly, a wide range of actors—newspaper reporters, amateur bloggers, politicians, media owners, and so on— seeking to install or erase boundaries stand to gain—or lose—depending on the outcome. But journalists seeking definitional control through metajournalistic discourse should not be reduced to only self-serving motivations. On the contrary, journalists' pledges of acting as watchdogs or their expressed desire to inform the public are often heartfelt. Journalists may be accused of being self-important, but journalism remains a system of knowledge creation and distribution accruing cultural authority through its anticipated benefit to society. Journalists attacking Glass did so because they felt that their profession had been impugned. The anger over his actions was genuine, even if it was also in journalists' interest to create a distinction out of self-protection. Perhaps the best evidence for motives beyond self-interest is the interminable supply of journalistic aspirants despite the profession's generally low wages and precarious working conditions.[36]

Boundary work provides metajournalistic discourse with a sense of why attending to talk about journalism matters when examining how the contemporary conditions of news affect journalistic authority. The examples of the *Rocky Mountain News* and *Seattle Post-Intelligencer* above suggests the economic difficulties many news organizations find themselves in as they adjust to the loss of legacy advertising and circulation revenue. Digital media have further expanded the possibilities of what news can look like and who can create it. Connected to this, conventional news forms and normative commitments are increasingly challenged by alternative perspectives, such as a call to abandon neutral reporting in favor of an advocacy or partisan stance. In this, or any, context, journalists' right to be listened to—the basis of being an authority—rests on perpetual rhetorical work that both supports the basis for this right while also seeking to make clear who exactly should possess it. Boundaries divide insiders and outsiders and define their relation through this opposition. With journalistic authority, the boundaries define the authority relation by providing a dividing line between those with authority and those that lack it *but* who assent to it. Yet this authority relation is not permanent or stable but a bond that is continually fashioned through the interaction between journalists and their audiences. From this perspective, the explicit definitional labor of boundary work can be understood as an adaptive response to journalism's ever-changing conditions. Its lack of systemic professional barriers makes this discourse all the more important.

METAJOURNALISTIC DISCOURSE AS COMMUNITY MAKING

The banishment of Stephen Glass illustrates how journalists use metajournalistic discourse to differentiate between insiders and outsiders. Certain people, practices, and sites are argued to be journalistic—and therefore eligible for journalistic authority—while others are excluded. Equally important to boundary work is how metajournalistic discourse also defines the territory within these boundaries. The rhetoric of consolidation operates in the opposite direction from differentiation; instead of erecting boundaries between things, consolidation erases boundaries to assert commonality. Speakers collapse a diverse news sphere into a generalized amalgam (albeit while still suggesting that the journalistic field has boundaries). This interpretive action implies coherence and asserts the transferability of journalistic authority across the domain of journalists.[37] But it also imposes on journalism a singular vision—or a limited set of visions. In short, metajournalistic discourse should be examined not just for how interpretive differentiation is created, but also for how a shared identity among journalists is constituted, by whom, and for what purpose.

In seeking to reconcile metajournalistic discourse as both boundary making and community making, Dan Berkowitz provides the concept of discursive "double duty."[38] The term developed from a study of efforts by journalists to publicly distance themselves from their paparazzi counterparts after the latter were implicated in the automobile crash that killed Princess Diana in 1997. Following public outcry, journalists eagerly contrasted their work practices from reckless celebrity chasers. But beyond wishing to avoid seeing their reputations dragged down by paparazzi, journalists also sought to establish a collective sense of ethics to dictate what newsgathering tactics should be considered off-limits. In addition to exiling paparazzi as deviant to restore public trust, this discourse also performed the double duty of instilling a collective sense of acceptable journalism among practitioners. Extending Berkowitz's notion of double duty to metajournalistic discourse generally provides a way to appreciate this type of talk as both definitional control aimed at outsiders and community-making efforts directed inwardly. This can be seen in how treatment of Stephen Glass as deviant reinforces community norms and commitments. Glass's deviancy provides a contrasting other from which the journalistic community can distance itself. The collective pillorying of Glass doubles as an implicit—or even explicit—argument that the community can be trusted.

Of course, not all controversies are as pat as Glass. Disagreements within news threaten discursive efforts to unify journalism. For example, most mainstream news outlets prohibit paying sources for their information, out of the belief that such monetary interactions taint the information received. ABC News and NBC News also don't pay their sources, but they do license media materials from sources, in effect equaling a payment. This practice draws criticism from some as corrupting news, while others see it as minor.[39] This discussion occurs in public, argued through competing claims about what is journalistically appropriate and what lies outside that boundary. These episodes bring to light the myriad variations within the larger field of journalism—if even such a field can meaningfully exist.

The need for metajournalistic discourse to be community making stems from the same peculiarities of journalism outlined above. Hampered by a lack of rigid borders common in traditional means of establishing group identity, journalists nonetheless tend to coalesce around a common ideology and understanding of practice.[40] This insight regarding communal norms arises in Barbie Zelizer's efforts to move beyond the privileging of professionalism in explaining journalism.[41] She appropriates the concept of "interpretive community" from literary studies,[42] which she then applies to journalism as "a group that authenticates itself through its narratives and collective memories" with the "aim of collective legitimation."[43] Journalists establish a collective identity and legitimate their authority through shared narratives and symbols.[44] This argument forms the backbone of Zelizer's *Covering the Body*, which traces the development of the Kennedy assassination coverage as a symbol to be wielded by journalists—and particularly nascent television news—in arguing for their authority.

Zelizer's study of the Kennedy assassination as a symbol of journalistic authority also reveals the importance of examining collective memory.[45] Through strategies of remembering and forgetting, narratives about the past provide journalists with a discursive means to legitimate their work in the present.[46] Shared stories of the past provide the journalistic community with a common stock of symbols around which to make sense of and promote its work, particularly in changing times.[47] As journalists endeavor to understand the present media environment, they draw on a long history to defend entrenched practices and norms. Such narratives do not only dictate journalistic practice; they situate news audiences within a particular social formation by invoking historical moments that carry particular valences for the wider culture. For example, Bob Woodward and Carl Bernstein's reporting on the Watergate scandal for the *Washington Post* has become enshrined in journalistic lore, transforming the complex events and intermeshing of actors into a tale of two intrepid reporters bringing down the president of the United States.[48] More recently, the critical success of the movie *Spotlight*, winner of the 2016 Academy Award for Best Picture, further props up a heralded vision of investigative journalism as a model of what news can be. Nonetheless, the stories journalists tell about themselves are always open to challenge, both from internal factions and external critics.

Treating journalists as an interpretive community locates communal coherence around the circulation of shared meanings rather than other organizational, professional, or educational traits. Yet stressing the creation of common understandings also requires mindfulness regarding the disparate body of actors laying claim to the title of journalist. Given variations across time, space, medium, and so on, no one can speak for all of journalism. This lack of fundamental coherence may persist, but it should not disqualify the usefulness of the interpretive communities approach and the role of narrative in defining journalism. Instead of dismissing totalizing claims, journalism studies should critique the discursive means by which certain speakers attempt to homogenize journalism through the rhetoric of consolidation. Especially in periods of upheaval, examining who speaks about journalism and how their claims consolidate and differentiate perceptions of journalism reveals patterns of symbolic power. To return to the opening example, the awarding of Pulitzer Prizes creates a hierarchy entitling its winners—as well as those who judge and administer the awards—to special status within journalism. They gain a perch from which to speak, supported by the reputation of the award. Other voices, particularly those outside elite news organizations, find it difficult to speak for more than themselves. New entrants into the news industry have even more trouble gaining a voice.

Ultimately, what is at stake with metajournalistic discourse is the ability to make pronouncements about journalism: what forms it should take, what its practitioners should do, and what underlying arguments for authority it should pursue. Such a position also entails proscribing certain forms, practices, and norms as outside of journalism. Metajournalistic discourse provides the conceptual lens to carefully scrutinize who shapes journalism's public arguments for authority, engages in boundary work, and speaks on behalf of the larger community—and who does not. If interpretive communities exist through narratives, it should be asked where these narratives come from, how they are challenged, and how they change over time.

AUTHORITY AND THE MYTH OF THE MEDIATED CENTER

All statements about journalism, from a book-length disquisition on the problems of contemporary journalism to a 140-character tweet complaining about a vapid news story, exhibit assumptions as to what journalism is and what it ought to be. Journalism studies scholars have long fixated on what news looks like and how it is made, with far less attention going to how the news is talked about—even if this is, by definition, what journalism studies does. The vast terrain of talk about journalism—metajournalistic discourse—accompanying news discourse needs to be included in understandings of journalistic authority. Journalistic authority cannot be fully accounted for through the discourse of professionalism or the formal patterns of news texts. Both the practices of news production and consumption are deeply shaped by the conditions in which they occur. A news story is not an isolated text but one understood within a larger cultural context that includes expectations of what journalism ought to do to be authoritative. The production and consumption of news need to be recognized as embedded within complex sets of publicly articulated beliefs about journalism. Ultimately, the ability of journalists to engage in the creation of legitimate knowledge about the world rests on this larger realm of discourse articulating and defending this role.

To end this chapter, an important question needs to be asked about the consequences of metajournalistic discourse for authority. How effective are journalists in building their case? When journalists define the authority relation that joins them with those outside of journalism—audiences, sources, advertisers, etc.—they conjure a broader social arrangement dictating how journalism ought to be embedded into the functioning of society. Arguments for journalism's social role, from spirited defenses of the need for healthy journalism to quotidian assumptions about what the news does, often situate journalism as vital to democratic functioning and the maintenance of community. In making these arguments, journalists defend their function of relaying what Nick Couldry calls "the myth of the mediated centre"—the idea that an existing social center is not only discoverable, but is what journalists reference in everyday reporting.[49] Couldry applies the term to media generally, but it is particularly useful to understanding journalists' arguments as being socially central yet distant from what they report. A belief in a preexisting center allows journalists to create news accounts of social, political, and economic normalcy and deviancy while obscuring journalism's role in creating this center through their news-making strategies.[50] This position bestows legitimacy upon journalists charged with communicating this social center to their audiences.

The counterpart to imagining society's center is the reinforcement of "the myth of the media's social centrality."[51] This mythic positioning, Couldry argues, is the means by which journalists situate themselves as *legitimate*—a term we could easily slide into being authoritative. Journalists deserve authority, the argument goes, because they mediate society to society. Returning to the above question, how effective are journalists at accomplishing this positioning? After all, the claim to represent society's center is steeped in power. The center is always a construction derived from a particular vantage point through particular practices of knowledge creation and circulation. Journalists make topical decisions about what is important, epistemological decisions about how a topic can be known, and interpretive decisions about what these topics mean. Journalists locate themselves within their authority relation with audiences so that the former speaks on behalf of the latter: "Every media claim to speak 'for us all' naturalises the fact that generally we do not speak for ourselves."[52] In the sense that this happens, journalists effectively support their social position within society. But this statement also identifies the representational power of the news media resting on journalism's public arguments of being at the center, and speaking on behalf of the center. Attending to metajournalistic discourse should not be merely about particular utterances on a particular topic but understood within the totality of the social context in which this discourse occurs. The myth of media's social centrality provides a lens for examining metajournalistic discourse as seeking to establish—and protect—a particular vision of journalistic authority within a larger social space of competing forces.

In the end, Couldry's argument reminds us that all social visions of journalism matter because they simultaneously present an image of society. Like any group seeking authority, journalists are self-interested in protecting control over their jurisdiction, to use Andrew Abbott's term.[53] This view does not render such attempts as conniving or negate their claims to serving the public interest, but it does underscore that arguments made on behalf of journalism are always only one option out of many alternative possibilities. Chapter 7 demonstrates how the entry of new voices into metajournalistic discourse portends a wider variety of viewpoints that challenge journalists' claims to mediate the center. Metajournalistic discourse is an act of imagining journalism with the goal of having these ideas accepted as natural and legitimate. It is the means by which journalists—and others—articulate the idealized authority relation between journalism and its audiences.

PART TWO

Journalistic Authority in Context

CHAPTER FOUR

Recognizing Journalistic Authority

The Public's Opinion

When the *New York Times* launched a new internal project dubbed The Upshot in April 2014 run by former Washington bureau chief David Leonhardt, the site-within-the-site promised news stories driven by the voguish deciphering of big data[1] and explanatory pieces providing primers on developing issues, all with a stronger voice than run-of-the-mill news stories. On the day of this writing, new stories focused on such hotly debated issues as the gender pay gap and the Affordable Care Act. Given the ample attention it already devotes to these topics, why would the *Times* feel the need to carve out a unique project? The answer lies in the defection of onetime *Times* blogger Nate Silver with his *FiveThirtyEight* blog to ESPN and the departure of Ezra Klein from the *Washington Post* to start the similarly themed news site *Vox*. The common approach adopted by these three sites—and the copious attention their launches received—indicate the search for new ways of telling the news: the emphasis on data suggests distance from anecdotal or source-quote derived stories, the stress on deeper explanation contrasts with the incremental updates of continuous news coverage, and the more personal narrative style diverges from the standardized formal conventions governing much news output. In short, these sites react to existing news forms by trying something new to lure audiences.[2]

The quest to develop novel news forms matters beyond stylistic elements, epistemological innovations, or even the search for new market niches. Each attempt to reinvent news simultaneously reimagines the journalist-audience relationship. The enunciation of a new journalistic form requires a corresponding set of claims clarifying how it provides the audience with content it both wants and needs (two separate issues, to be sure).[3] Put differently, these claims are central to defining the relationship with audiences on which journalistic authority rests.

The debut of The Upshot provides a noteworthy example of how new journalistic forms contain within them ways of imagining the audience. In a note introducing the aims of the initiative, Leonhardt explicitly took up the position of his readers: "We believe many people don't understand the news as well as they would like. They want to grasp big, complicated stories . . . so well that they can explain the whys and hows of those stories to their friends, relatives and colleagues."[4] This particular motivation imagines audiences feel deficient in their understanding of current events, perhaps even fearing social stigmatization over their lack of knowledge. The note further defended both The Upshot's unique voice and its emphasis on judgment: "We will not hesitate to make analytical judgments about why something has happened and what is likely to happen in the future. We'll tell you how we came to those judgments—*and invite you to come to your own conclusions.*" Emphasis has been added to the end of this sentence to highlight how Leonhardt constructs the journalist-audience relation in his note. On the surface, even with a move away from impartiality, this statement reaffirms the conviction underlying information-based theories of journalism: audiences should draw on news for information but decide for themselves on the issues. Yet this was not the typical traditional interpretation of the journalist-audience relationship as a one-way flow of neutral information provided to rational audiences. Instead, Leonhardt situated cooperation with the audience as a guiding principle for The Upshot:

> Perhaps most important, we want The Upshot to feel like a collaboration between journalists and readers. We will often publish the details behind our reporting . . . and we hope that readers will find angles we did not. We also want to get story assignments from you:

Tell us what data you think deserves exploration. Tell us which parts of the news you do not understand as well as you'd like.

The second-person voice underscores the relational aspects of this message by encouraging interaction as a positive for all. It is interpersonal and direct in tone, despite the audience for the *Times* website exceeding 31 million monthly unique visitors.[5] But beyond the practicality of achieving meaningful interaction with a mass audience, the sentiment expressed encourages some level of cocreation, even if only openness to suggestions or, at most, readers' own analyses of the data. Time will tell. But the point worth emphasizing is how ideas about journalism, such as the ones expressed by Leonhardt, are also ideas about audiences. Although not his explicit aim, Leonhardt is rethinking the basis of journalistic authority by reimagining the relationship between the production of news texts and their audiences. It provides an entry point for thinking through the role of the news audience in a relational perspective of journalistic authority.

From the starting point of accepting news audiences' role in journalistic authority to be both necessary and psychologically and culturally complex, this chapter probes the authority relation between journalists and the news audience.[6] Much of the focus is on public opinion surveys about news performance, which are arguably the most visible measure of how audiences understand journalism. Even if they are by no means perfect, surveys occupy such an outsized place in the discourse about journalism that they cannot be ignored. The patterns they reveal about public opinion of news are important, but so is their place in creating particular cultural narratives about journalism. The chapter then switches from opinion to actions to examine how digital technologies transform how journalists and audiences conceptualize their relationship with each other and with the mediated public sphere. The fracturing the "unitary public"[7] and an expansion of mediated voices complicates the authority relation between journalists and audiences—in some ways even erasing meaningful distinctions.

RECOGNIZING JOURNALISTIC AUTHORITY

What does it look like for journalistic authority to be recognized by society? This question may appear straightforward, but it is deceptive in its simplicity. Answering the question requires an explanation of the meaning of recognition when speaking about authority. In its weakest sense, recognition is a matter of simple identification, as in how one learns to recognize the outlines of one's country on a map. In this case, recognition is a form of knowledge. But when speaking of authority, recognition becomes a matter of granting legitimacy to whatever thing is being recognized. The map example is not just about geographical contours. It also indicates the complex cultural and political factors that envelop the individual doing the recognizing. Finding one's—or another's—country on a map shapes ideas of identity and difference. It is an act of power in how it organizes social space in a way that includes the recognizer. A similar relationship among authority, recognition, and identity holds for journalism. To recognize journalism as a distinct activity charged with certain normative and functional duties is to place one in relation to what is identified. Or, more concretely, to identify a news story as an account of something that happened somewhere relies on a relationship between reporter and reader.

This emphasis on recognition connects to the assertion that journalistic authority always involves an authority relation between those claiming authority and those who consent to authority. In a sense, authority *is* this relationship, as no one can claim to be an authority without recognition from others who are not making such claims. To be clear, recognition is not synonymous with deference but a complex idea more in tune with ideas of hegemony as the consolidation of symbolic forms.[8] The power of journalism to represent reality to society relies on the consent of audiences who, at least historically, are unable to dictate the conditions of their consumption beyond the indirect means of granting or withholding collective attention—that is, buying or not buying a newspaper; watching or not watching a news broadcast. But beyond these market-based reactions, audiences are enveloped in discourses about the centrality of journalism that have a powerful hold over how they imagine themselves within an authority relation with journalists.[9] In short, the power of journalists should be understood both as representational through the crafting of truthful stories and as epistemological in the legitimation of these texts.

The power relations inherent in relational perspectives of authority have received ample attention in social psychology, where a key analytical problem has been determining why people voluntarily defer to authority. Outside of reward power and coercive power, how do authorities attain and hold on to legitimate power?[10] Psychologists Tom Tyler and Allan Lind find that issues like procedural fairness matter quite a bit, but in arguing authority to be relational they suggest that people voluntarily comply with authority out of a desire to protect their own self-image.[11] In conforming to authority, people identify traits that they wish to be true of their own selves and of the larger society. This perspective extends a relational perspective beyond authorities' arguments for legitimacy to include how those acted upon recognize their own identity as bound up with shared systems of authority.

In making the leap from social psychology to journalism, a relational theory of authority must recognize two factors. First, the type of authority journalists possess is much more nonbinding than that which Tyler and Lind study. And second, journalistic authority develops not through interpersonal interaction but through mediated texts produced by recognized news organizations. Although news permeates much of modern life, from Twitter feeds to televisions installed at gas pumps, most people rarely encounter journalists. This peculiarity is often overlooked. Nonetheless, Taylor and Lind's research suggests a deep-seated psychological relationship with authority. Authority relations organize the world and our place within it; they orient us to others and define our roles, news audiences included.

VIEWING THE AUTHORITY RELATION FROM THE AUDIENCE'S SIDE

If journalistic authority is truly relational, we need to address how audiences understand the news. The crassest way to attack this issue is through simple metrics of consumption. News organizations studiously measure their audiences, touting their success and ruing their losses. The logistical need for such measures is, of course, the setting of advertising prices, in which case audiences become a commodity whose attention is sold off to advertisers.[12] Over time, methods for measuring news media have spawned new techniques, from print circulation measures to broadcast news listenership and viewership to the increasingly sophisticated metrics for measuring online audiences.[13] Much scholarly attention has been paid to the commodification of media audiences, with the shift over time from the massing of aggregate attention to the personalization of individualized pitches.[14] But this chapter engages the question of *authority*, and for this the value of audience measures grows murky. News consumption tells us next to nothing about how journalistic authority is understood. At most, audience gains or losses can be surmised to indicate the gain or loss of authority, but only in a surface way. News consumption patterns—i.e., the decline of print news and the rise of attention to certain online news sites—are useful for directing scholarly inquiry, but getting to authority requires deeper prying.

Another way forward is to ask people what they think about journalism. One of the most famous examples of this tactic comes from Bernard Berelson's seminal paper "What the Missing Newspaper Means."[15] The study took place in 1945 during a seventeen-day strike by newspaper delivery drivers in New York. Other polling organizations sought to measure public opinion about the absent dailies, but Berelson dismissed these efforts as only attaining surface facts rather than the meaning of the newspaper in the fabric of readers' daily lives. Taking a different tack, his researchers fanned out across Manhattan, ultimately engaging a diverse set of sixty news readers for interviews. When queried about the missing papers, respondents almost all answered by drawing on normative tropes of journalism. In these initial responses, missing the newspaper meant missing vital information about current events. Berelson was suspicious of these pat answers, noting that even though "nearly everybody *pays tribute* to the value of the newspaper as a source of 'serious' information,"[16] on follow-up, most readers could not name what serious stories they had been following before the strike. To Berelson, something else was evidently happening. Further pressing by the interviewers to get beyond the automatic espousal of tropes turned up such nonnormative uses of newspapers as respite from the toils of daily life, social prestige as means of conversation (similar to Leonhardt's suggestion above that audiences want to be conversant about current events), and even social contact. Finally, people just enjoyed reading.

Looking back through this study reveals some interesting findings for considering the authority relationship between journalists and audiences from the audience perspective. Bereslon's study has been invoked to show the noninformation uses of the news, but the "stereotyped responses," in Berelson's words, may be the least remarked-upon aspect of the study despite what they indicate about readers' relationship with journalism. Respondents' automatic appeal to serious news as what they most missed reflects what psychologists call social desirability bias: telling interviewers what they think they should be saying, even if it is not the most honest answer.[17] In a more specific sense, the easy accessibility of democratically oriented answers to queries about news habits demonstrates what I call normative absorption—the internalization of authorities' legitimating arguments by nonauthorities.

Learned cultural narratives about journalism are part of the wider process of socialization. For example, the use of newspapers—or perhaps digital news these days—to acquaint children with current events is a common educational experience. Teaching students to be citizens also teaches them to be news consumers—a connection that reproduces journalists' own narratives about the source of their authority. The 1945 pedagogical text "Newspapers in the Classroom" made this argument clear: "A free press is one of America's most cherished institutions, and every child should be taught how to make use of it. Future policies of the nation depend largely upon the public opinion formed through the medium of newspapers. The schools should see that every child develops a newspaper habit."[18] This quote is notable for its assumptions about the place of the press in US society and its frankness in advocating for teaching an appreciation for journalism. Keeping up with the news becomes the responsibility of the citizen. John Pauly traces the history of the news-reading movement to reveal how its promotional underpinnings instill the value of news without challenging underlying journalistic structures.[19] A largely neutral, for-profit news system becomes naturalized as the only way for journalism to operate. Nonetheless, this example shows the extent to which journalistic norms are deeply embedded in public life.

Applying these ideas to the Berelson study shows the difficulty of drawing conclusions about respondents' motivations from their answers to survey questions. It cannot really be known if they internalized these norms or if they only wanted to say the correct thing to an interviewer from Columbia University. However, the common recitation of democratic norms points to some level of internalization of metajournalistic discourse propping up the social importance of journalism. Newspaper readers had a cognitively accessible schema for thinking about journalism, one that they understood to be both widespread and socially desirable. More recent evidence that survey respondents often overstate their use of hard news provides further evidence of the absorption of this way of thinking.[20] News audiences publicly avow normative arguments not of their making.[21]

Berelson's study also reveals complex social practices surrounding news consumption. Newspaper readers openly expressed sentiments of separation to describe what missing the newspaper meant. As one respondent put it: "You feel put out and isolated from the rest of the world. It practically means isolation. We're at a loss without our paper."[22] Berelson attributes such feelings to the interruption of the newspaper reading habit. But it more powerfully underscores James W. Carey's arguments that communication should be understood not only as transmission but also as ritual. He invokes the newspaper as an example of a collective ritual more notable for fostering a shared culture than for any particular bit of information it contains. In one of his more well-known passages, Carey compares news reading to religious services in that meaning stems from inherent repetition: "News changes little and yet is intrinsically satisfying; it performs few functions yet is habitually consumed." Rather than bits of information, news "is a presentation of reality that gives life an overall form, order, and tone."[23] Berelson's findings support these claims by moving beyond the rational meanings of the absent newspaper—i.e., the loss of a conduit for important information—to nonrational meanings arising from the cultural impact of commonly shared news texts.

Seven decades later, the Berelson study continues to yield fruit. Labeled here as "normative absorption," the phenomenon he uncovered suggests that audiences internalize arguments defending journalistic authority and are easily able to access the accompanying normative language when asked. But further digging revealed that the audience's engagement with journalism echoes the diversity of journalists' authority-seeking strategies. Just as no single aspect of journalistic authority—professionalism, formal conventions, and narrative—can single-handedly explain the concept, news audiences too maintain a complex relationship with the news they consume. Finally, the lasting lesson of the Berelson study is to be critical of what surveys gauging public opinion about journalism really measure—an important reminder before turning to what surveys indicate about public attitudes toward contemporary journalism.

PUBLIC OPINION AND JOURNALISTIC AUTHORITY

The public opinion survey has attained an indelible spot in the functioning of democracies, for good or for ill.[24] If in a democracy the opinion of the people—and not just elected officials—matters, surveys supply a mode of tapping into opinions about the conduct of public institutions to provide a representative tally of what people think. In large-scale democracies—basically any modern nation-state—this can occur only through quantification, both in terms of sampling and survey design. Quantification requires sacrificing nuance, the value of which the Berelson study showed for thinking about journalism, but it makes knowable a reliable estimate of what people think at a given time. This argument is not without its problems, as the discussion below will make clear, but the persistence and pervasiveness of public opinion surveys should be recognized as a staple of democratic political culture.

As one of the core public institutions of democracy, journalism is regularly subjected to survey research. This position itself demonstrates how journalism is imbricated with other governing institutions.[25] But before reviewing the public opinion of journalism, it should be made clear that the term *journalistic authority* does not appear in surveys—nor should it. As a conceptual construct imposed on journalism, it is not part of the everyday vocabulary of journalists or their audiences. The lack of direct engagement with journalistic authority requires a circuitous route working backward to connect existing measures to what they indicate about the authority relation between journalists and their audiences.

Just how bleak the public view of journalism is, as revealed by survey research, should come as no surprise to anyone who follows journalism. Measures of journalistic performance indicate worrying trends for contemporary news. Gallup has found a steady decline in confidence in newspapers, dropping from 51 percent in 1979 to 22 percent in 2014. Television news has seen a similar drop, from 46 percent in 1993 to 18 percent twenty-one years later in 2014.[26] Online news fared no better, with only 19 percent expressing a "great deal" or "quite a lot" of confidence in it. With the wording switched from "confidence" to "trust," the numbers improve, with 44 percent admitting to either somewhat or mostly trusting the news, and a majority of the population—55 percent—having either little or no trust.[27] In the same poll, 46 percent of respondents labeled news as "too liberal." Meanwhile, a 2013 Pew Research Project report finds broad support for the watchdog function of the press, with 68 percent of respondents replying that journalists keep a check on public officials while also finding a lack of accuracy, neutrality, and independence. Only 48 percent of respondents judge the press to "protect democracy" rather than "hurt democracy"—an improvement from an even split of 42 percent to 42 percent in its 2011 survey. Other surveys show widespread opinion of journalists as being "out of touch" (70 percent), up from 47 percent a decade earlier.[28] Among US network and cable television news outlets, only PBS had more people rating it as trustworthy than untrustworthy.[29]

What do all these negative trends show? Perhaps foremost they indicate that news audiences feel comfortable expressing their growing distrust of journalists through broadly negative evaluations of their performance. The evidence here is unequivocal in recording what respondents tell their interrogators: the majority of the population does not think journalists are doing a good job. These survey results in turn drive attention to this seemingly downward trajectory of journalistic performance. And even if these questions do not ask about authority explicitly, the assessments that we do have would seem to bode poorly for journalistic authority. If, in the relational view, authority depends on recognition from those lacking authority, then a simple reading would be that journalistic authority is fragile or even broken.

While these surveys do indicate concrete patterns, we must resist facile readings that conclude journalistic authority is disintegrating before our eyes. The semiregular pronouncement of the latest survey results often attract public attention and elicit a mixture of reactions, from the anxious hand-wringing of journalists to the smug delight of critics wishing to upend conventional news forms and practices. But, as an index of journalistic authority, or any meaningful conclusion about journalism, they have their deficiencies. These public opinion surveys require a deeper look to reveal what these trends indicate about the cultural role of journalism.

While these measures of journalism display negative trajectories, how they pertain to journalistic authority is still unclear. A significant part of the problem in connecting survey data to authority is that much of the polling on journalism centers on questions of credibility. To argue that credibility and authority are synonymous is to claim that being an authority requires one's pronouncements over the social world—or one's epistemic authority—to be believed. This is a practical view of authority as necessitating trust in order to exist. A lack of credibility, conversely, signals a lack of authority.[30] In contrast, I argue that authority and credibility are separate concepts whose correspondence is much more foggy. The Pew Research Center's finding above that a vast majority of the population still believes in the power of the press to hold officials accountable—even as respondents harshly censure the actual practices of journalists—provides a normative basis for journalistic authority even if measures of credibility in practice are weak. This discrepancy between norms and practices is crucial to understanding journalistic authority. One may champion journalism and its attendant aspirational norms while roundly condemning what its practitioners do. To take an analogy, baseball fans may boo an umpire as a sign of questioning his credibility—like journalists, umpires deal with accusations of bias and poor performance—but this does not equate to challenging the concept of the umpire, or even more practically his right to manage that particular game. From this perspective, charges of a lack of credibility for a particular actor may *reinforce* the larger, abstract authority relation in which this actor is a part.

When it comes to interpreting surveys about journalism, credibility should be understood as a measure of performance. Consistently low ratings from the public reveal a level of dissatisfaction with what the news looks like. Although the grounds on which this dissatisfaction is based are diverse rather than monolithic, part of this low opinion can be traced back to the idealized demands of journalism's self-defined normative roles of providing objective, politically useful information. This is made more acute considering the unending critique of news practices accompanying news. The Fox News Channel, to take one prominent example, positions itself as an antidote to what it asserts to be rampant left-wing political bias in mainstream journalism.[31] It draws on an established critique of the so-called liberal media in a way that is meant to undermine the work of journalists at other outlets. In this sense, all news operates within discourses about news, and these need to be accounted for to understand survey responses. Questioning credibility is not the same as questioning an institution—the correspondence between these two aspects is more complicated. Nonetheless, the ominous trend lines for journalistic credibility raise questions about how well journalists can operate without being recognized as credible actors. At what point does lack of credibility tip over to being deauthorizing?

To return to the problem of reading authority into survey results, one answer is to move away from the numbers themselves and what they measure to instead examine how the results are placed into narratives about the state of journalism. The results of a single survey question do not matter on their own until they are made meaningful by being marshaled as evidence within narratives signifying trends in public opinion and, by extension, press performance. This interpretive labor occurs immediately within the reports accompanying polling results. For example, Gallup's June 2014 press release offering its latest confidence numbers concluded with a sobering section headed "Bottom Line" that read:

> The field of news media has changed dramatically since Gallup first began measuring the confidence the public held in newspapers or TV news decades ago. . . . Amid this rapid change, Americans hold all news media platforms in low confidence. How these platforms can restore confidence with the American public is not clear, especially as editorial standards change and most outlets lack the broad reach once available to major newspapers and broadcasters.[32]

This statement narrativizes survey data into a broader tale of the structural changes facing the journalism industry. This is a particular interpretation based on a reading of the data that becomes a powerful story about what is happening to journalism. But there is a recursive quality to such statements—the survey reports announce publicly what the results mean, fueling larger cultural discourses about the diminished credibility of news, and then the public is surveyed again with these same measures. It is not that these surveys are incorrect, but reading the questions and looking at the results raises questions about what their measures actually indicate.

SKEPTICISM TOWARD THE SKEPTICS

"A situation of widespread basic discontent and political alienation exists in the U.S. today."[33] This frank assessment sums up political scientist Arthur H. Miller's reading of survey trends, leading him to claim that decline in trust is something lasting and entrenched and not momentary displeasure with ruling incumbents. While this judgment sounds familiar, it was made nearly fifty years ago in an analysis of surveys conducted in the 1960s. Its relevance to the current political climate should ward off searches for a golden era of political trust in the United States from which to draw sharp contrasts with today. But at the same time, what subsequent survey research reveals should not be ignored. Social scientists continue to voice concern that waning trust bodes poorly for democratic functioning and collective life.

By contrast, widespread fears over the decline of trust may mask a not-so-negative enlargement of political skepticism. Timothy Cook and Paul Gronke make this argument by shifting from measures of trust to gauge expressions of distrust in surveys. Their study reveals a public that does not think political leaders are trying to get away with wrongdoing but instead often fail in their attempts to do right. Read this way, declining trust in government as recorded in surveys may well reveal "the rise of a public that is—and perhaps as they should be—skeptical of many forms of power."[34] Attributing public skepticism of public institutions to matters of competency gives rise to an authority relation in which the necessity of close monitoring and criticism override the assumption that these institutions will get it right in the end on their own. That this is not a radical statement further indicates its fit with the current political culture. In his extensive history of authority, sociologist Frank Furedi traces the development of skepticism toward authority as normative in and of itself: "Obedience enjoys little cultural valuation and . . . questioning authority is interpreted as a duty of a responsible citizen."[35]

In theory, growing distrust of public institutions would seem to bolster journalism as an agent of accountability. Normatively, journalists are expected to be skeptical of public institutions—otherwise, an accountability function for news wouldn't be necessary. But what about skepticism toward the skeptics? As seen above, public opinion of journalism has declined steadily in lockstep with governing institutions. In the Gallup study measuring confidence in public institutions, the percentages declaring confidence in the news media—newspapers (22 percent), online news (19 percent), and television news (18 percent)—fare about as poorly as the three federal branches—the Supreme Court (30 percent), the presidency (29 percent), and Congress (7 percent).[36] Clearly, as a public institution, journalism does not stand outside the orbit of declining trust and rising skepticism. It falls prey to the same cultural forces as part of an interlocking system of powerful institutions.

Yet conflating trust in government with trust in journalism should be avoided given the distinction between governing authorities and journalistic authority. Whereas political actors possess instrumental power to affect policy, journalistic power occurs in the realm of symbolic production. Assessments of governance boil down to questions of action or inaction, while assessments of journalism emerge from the qualities of the news texts consumed by audiences. This is not to assume that symbols lack power but is instead an argument that journalism requires a particular conception of institutional trust sensitive to its output. Journalists do not produce laws or policies; they produce news, often about laws and policies. This distinction treats skepticism toward journalism as skepticism toward its knowledge-producing practices. In the end, declining trust in news is both part of the larger cultural decline of trust in public institutions—where journalism is part of the system of ruling elites—and a distinct distrust centered on news outputs.

Acknowledging both the general decline of institutional trust and the rise of skepticism helps us to better understand changing public attitudes toward journalism. When Berelson quizzed his newspaper-starved respondents in the 1940s, the socially acceptable answer was to laud journalism. This does not mean that newspapers were universally loved. The specters of partisanship in an era when newspaper competition was still quite common certainly colored evaluations of newspapers—including loyalty to one's own paper.[37] What has changed is the expectation that survey respondents demonstrate skepticism toward public institutions, including journalism. Criticizing journalism and displaying distrust becomes not only socially acceptable but perhaps necessary for presenting oneself as an appropriately skeptical citizen. To admit to believing everything makes one a dupe; to cop to a critical eye makes one savvy. The question then becomes what this performative skepticism means for journalism as a knowledge-producing activity. Is it true that nearly no one believes what he or she reads or sees in the news? Or is it that journalism's truth claims are out of step with contemporary postmodern sensibilities?[38] Perhaps news audiences only want to appear independent to their surveyors? Existing surveys cannot shed light on these questions.

To get beyond trust, Berelson once again provides a helpful path forward, this time in the array of motivations his newspaper readers revealed when prodded for why they missed the news. As Yariv Tsfati and Joseph Cappella find, news consumption cannot be reduced to a single motivating factor. Although increased media skepticism leads to decreased news exposure, by working from the question "How can people watch news they do not trust?" they zero in on the "need for cognition"— a measure of the desire to comprehend and order the world—as a factor that mitigates skepticism.[39] While skepticism may be rampant, it coexists with a whole set of motivating psychological and cultural factors. Ultimately, the authority relation at the heart of journalistic authority is marked by skepticism toward journalism as a powerful public institution providing ongoing factual accounts of the world. But this skepticism also does not equate to wholesale abandonment of the news or the vacating of its authority. Instead, what should be understood is how journalism operates within a complicated cultural environment.

HOW SURVEYS STRUCTURE JOURNALISTIC AUTHORITY

Certainly, journalism's poor performance in public opinion polls continues to be its own news story. How we examine the journalist-audience authority relation must account for long-term declines of trust in news that have become familiar and seemingly irreversible. But what has escaped scrutiny is the degree to which survey instruments both reflect and structure understandings of journalistic authority. Developing this argument requires that we first step back to look at how public opinion surveys work. The goal of making comparisons across demographics and across time restricts the type of questions that can be asked and the responses that can be received. A representative sample capable of being aggregated requires the collection of quantifiable answers. To realize this goal, survey authors work backward using the tools they have, such as the Likert scale, to take a preeminent example, which allows respondents only the options of strongly agree, agree, neutral, disagree, or strongly disagree. Employing such scales requires properly crafting questions that translate complicated, interconnected phenomena into uncomplicated, discrete queries. Nuance and contradiction are sacrificed for simplicity and one-dimensionality.[40] This orientation allows pollsters to aggregate data and make summary statements, such as when the Pew Research Center concluded, "Public evaluations of news organizations' performance on key measures such as accuracy, fairness and independence remain mired near all-time lows."[41] This is a temporal comparison gleaned from common questions reasked over many years.

The assumptions embedded in surveys rarely receive the attention they deserve. Justin Lewis argues that because the authorship underlying survey data is "deeply suppressed,"[42] public opinion is treated as if it "simply [existed] as an independent entity."[43] This blind spot is deeply problematic. Every survey is a carefully assembled text, one whose questions are shaped by the needs of the survey organization; its funders and/or clients; the constraints on length to retain respondents and control costs; the variation in educational and communicative skills among respondents; and the need to perpetuate questions across time for the sake of continual comparison. But no less important are the cultural assumptions embedded within survey questions or how these assumptions condition the responses they generate.

There are no neutral questions to gauge the public opinion of journalism; understandings of journalism are already built into the questions. Surveys are not disconnected queries but the product of a web of ideas and cultural assumptions about what journalism is and what it should do. In this way, surveys provide an idealized understanding of the authority relation between journalists and their audiences in line with the issue of normative absorption raised above in the discussion of Berelson. Entrenched cultural discourses about journalism challenge any idea that survey authors or survey respondents are somehow outside these preexisting webs of meaning. Instead, assumptions about journalism—and its authority relation—are already structured into questions that activate respondents' preexisting ideas of journalism.

The questions also structure how audiences can answer, even providing the very language for their opinions. What is needed then is critical attention to how survey questions about journalism are asked. For the sake of dissection, a good source is the biennial media attitudes survey conducted by the Pew Research Center every other year since 1985. The Pew Research Center is a Washington, DC–based, nonpartisan public opinion organization funded by the Pew Charitable Trusts.[44] The Pew Research Center conducts an extensive slate of polling tackling a variety of issues well beyond journalism. Even its biennial survey is integrated into a larger survey on governance that includes questions about the performance of political actors and general questions about the direction of the country. But before digging into how it asks about journalism, the first question should be why the Pew Research Center asks about journalism in the first place. As a nonprofit, Pew does not view surveys as a promotional act intended to strengthen its brand and stir up new clients, as might be expected of for-profit polling firms. Instead, the very existence of the Pew Research Center is predicated on the belief that public opinion data ought to be expertly collected and widely disseminated through the news media. The Pew Research Center is not driven by the need for revenues or by a particular partisan slant but by a broader ideology of gathering public opinion to provide, as its mission says, "a foundation of facts that can enrich the public dialogue and support sound decision-making."[45] This mission reflects a bias toward a belief in the rationalist public-sphere model of democratic society. Pew is quite effective at gaining exposure, as its survey results regularly circulate through news stories. For news organizations, Pew survey data provide cheap-to-produce stories based on a trusted source, which precludes the expense of having to do their own polling.[46] To the extent that Pew's surveys receive plenty of public notice, they contribute to the wider conversation about journalism.

The 2013 biennial media attitudes survey was conducted in July 2013 and includes answers from 1,480 respondents with a margin of error of 3 percent.[47] The survey results were compiled into a public report titled "Amid Criticism, Support for Media's 'Watchdog' Role Stands Out."[48] The opening paragraph reads:

Public evaluations of news organizations' performance on key measures such as accuracy, fairness and independence remain mired near all-time lows. But there is a bright spot among these otherwise gloomy ratings: broad majorities continue to say the press acts as a watchdog by preventing political leaders from doing things that should not be done, a view that is as widely held today as at any point over the past three decades.

From the outset, the report presents a contradiction. Evaluations of press performance continue a familiar decades-long slump, echoing other survey results. But the second sentence reveals a robust assessment of journalism's success as a watchdog, with 68 percent of respondents agreeing that the press "keeps leaders from doing things that shouldn't be done." How should these findings be reconciled? Unfortunately, the Pew survey, with its preformed answers, can only expose this apparent incongruity; it cannot explain it. The survey precludes deep explanation to instead narrow the range of responses to ensure quantifiability, leaving nagging questions about the contradiction.

Moving past the answers to the questions themselves demonstrates how the questions structure understandings of journalism through the assumptions embedded within them. For example, the watchdog question touted above is asked this way: "Some people think that by criticizing leaders, news organizations keep political leaders from doing their job. Others think that such criticism is worth it because it keeps political leaders from doing things that should not be done. Which position is closer to your opinion?" Respondents are given a dichotomized choice, with the options presented not as standalone statements but as opinions possessed by unnamed groups of "some people" and "others." The question also equates watchdog journalism with criticizing leaders—a specific interpretation that accounts for only a portion of the practice. Does an in-depth investigation count as criticism? Another way to read the question is that it is not about watchdog reporting but about criticism as partisan critique aimed at political leaders. In another sense, the question really asks about the trustworthiness of leaders rather than the ability of journalists to hold elites to account. The question is also vague about what is indicated by "things that should not be done." Is this a reference to corruption and illegality or a statement about political preference? Despite these ambiguities, the question is used by Pew to reflect the accountability role of journalists in monitoring the acts of those charged with governing.

The next three questions on the Pew survey switch from opinions of accountability to aspects of journalists' performance:

- "In general, do you think news organizations get the facts straight, or do you think that their stories and reports are often inaccurate?"
- "In presenting the news dealing with political and social issues, do you think that news organizations deal fairly with all sides, or do they tend to favor one side?"
- "In general, do you think news organizations are pretty independent, or are they often influenced by powerful people and organizations?"

These questions are clearly evaluative and contain embedded normative expectations about what journalism *should* be. Combining the wording from these questions produces a statement regarding accuracy, balance, and independence as key journalistic norms: Journalists should (1) get the facts straight, (2) deal fairly with all sides, and (3) be pretty independent. Bad journalism, by contrast, is (1) often inaccurate, (2) tends to favor one side, and (3) is often influenced by powerful people and organizations. Through this formulation, Pew internalizes journalism's own normative language about itself. In doing so, the survey limits accuracy to its factual depictions, balance to giving equal voice to differing sides, and independence to defying pressure from those in power.

This vision of journalism also contains within it a vision of what the audience should expect from journalism and, therefore, how it should act as a news audience. Even as journalists rated dismally on these questions, the normative framework visible within the questions supports a particular understanding of the authority relation between journalists and audiences. What's more, other survey questions reinforce the presumption of neutrality and the simplification of bias as pertaining only to political slant. The survey asks its respondents to decide whether journalists are "politically biased in their reporting" (58 percent) or "careful that their reporting is NOT politically biased" (30 percent) and then asks if journalists are liberal (46 percent), conservative (26 percent), or neither (19 percent). Beyond the answers here, the survey assumes neutrality to be normatively preferable and violations of neutrality to be chiefly partisan in nature. Again, this is a *particular* preshaped view of journalism within questions attempting to assess public opinion.

Survey questions about journalism cannot be detached from their built-in assumptions about the social role of news, even as these surveys are meant to represent journalism to society. As part of the overall landscape of metajournalistic discourse, these surveys reveal the extent to which assumptions about journalism are culturally embedded—and not just present in how journalists talk about what they do. Without even seeing the results, the survey questions alone reveal an idealized authority relation between journalists and their audiences. This salience is a testament to the strength of a social vision of journalism as primarily providing neutral, balanced information to a mass of rational actors. In many ways, this vision oversimplifies how journalism works by leaving out many of the more nuanced ways in which news audiences enter into a relationship with news texts. It ignores what Berelson found in his vigorous prying into what people did with newspapers. Nonetheless, it is a powerful cultural image that serves the discourses that undergird journalistic authority.

THE PRODUCTIVE NEWS AUDIENCE:
A NEW AUTHORITY RELATION?

When the survey instrument that would become the Pew biennial journalism survey first asked about journalism in 1985, the news media landscape looked very different. Peter Jennings, Tom Brokaw, and Dan Rather spoke to millions of television viewers each evening, newspaper deliveries still tended to occur in the evening, and the Internet was not widely known beyond Matthew Broderick's portrayal of a computer hacker in *WarGames*. The changing information environment will be covered more extensively in the next three chapters, but this section asks about how new media have altered the authority relation between journalists and audiences at a time when any meaningful distinction between these two sets of stakeholders is challenged.

Stepping back, one of the more radical changes to emerge out of the development and dissemination of digital communication technologies has been access to mediation, or the ability to speak at a distance to other people. To do so has always required access to both the technology of reproducibility—printing presses, cameras, microphones, etc.—and to networks of distribution—bookstores, delivery trucks, antennae, satellites, etc. Reaching wide swaths of the public often meant incurring enormous expense, but this visibility could be leveraged to collect advertising subsidies.[49] The mass communication model has not disappeared, but it does coexist with a vast terrain of online actors whose voices circulate through a variety of easily accessible digital platforms. The popularization of the term *Web 2.0* offers both a description of a media environment in which users provide the mass of content—blog posts, status updates, links, photos, tweets, etc.—and an ideology of participation celebrating the democratization of mediated forms. The cultural and political effects of these developments are uncertain at best,[50] but they have produced new ways of imagining the types of relations that inform mediated authority.

For journalism, the technological barriers limiting the creation and circulation of mass-produced news have long doubled as cultural boundaries separating who may be considered a journalist from who is not. As these technological barriers become diminished, cultural barriers also become far less stable. Audiences formerly prevented from participating in the news gain new modes of public expression, which results in the hybrid of textual consumers and producers that Axel Bruns identifies with the portmanteau *produser*.[51] Dan Gillmor provides perhaps the clearest ideological expression of what this means for news in his book *We the Media*: "We could all write, not just read, in ways never before possible. For the first time in history, at least in the developed world, anyone with a computer and Internet connection could own a press. Just about anyone could make the news."[52] The possibilities of democratized news production have been celebrated by prominent public intellectuals, including Clay Shirky, Jay Rosen, Jeff Jarvis, and Yochai Benkler,[53] for creating new possibilities for media participation. Optimistically, the combination of a greatly expanded number of voices operating in the mediated public sphere and the loss of journalists' exclusive hold on news results in a more pluralistic range of speakers able to provide information, experience, and judgment on a wider set of topics from a variety of angles.

What this extension of mediated voices means for journalism has preoccupied much recent scholarly attention. Seth Lewis characterizes this environment as a clash between the "professional logic" of journalism built around an exclusionary perspective emphasizing specialized skills and the "participatory logic" of open engagement realized through digital media channels.[54] The rise of the latter shifts understandings of journalism from an institutionalized form to a "process," to use Sue Robinson's term.[55] The convergence of these fundamentally differing views of how journalism should work has created both opportunity and tension.[56] Professional journalists have tended to downplay the inclusion of user-generated content by accentuating the content rather than their relationship with nonjournalists or by dismissing nontraditional voices.[57] A pressing question has been what the collaboration with audiences in the cocreation of news should look like.

Clearly, advocates of a participatory logic for news creation challenge entrenched understandings of how journalism works. From the perspective of this book, the democratization of public expression is notable for altering the authority relation between journalists and audiences. In its most extreme iteration, the increased permeability of production and consumption roles upends journalistic authority by destabilizing the signifiers *journalist* and *audience*. Of course, all audience members do not wish to double as reporters; Jay Rosen invokes what he calls the "one percent rule" to estimate that only 1 percent of a site's users wish to be active contributors.[58] In place of grand examples of citizen journalism, audiences have gained communicative power through much more quotidian means. For example, Facebook and Twitter offer audiences the ability to share news content along with their own commentary and experiences. Nonetheless, by altering how the boundaries of journalism can be imagined, the availability of various means of participation prompt wider rethinking of what the role of the audience should be.

While the contribution to news gathering made by the audience is hazy,[59] the developing participatory ethic suggests different ways of imagining the journalist-audience authority relation built on collaboration rather than inequality. How this will affect the other elements above—and especially understandings of journalistic norms—remains to be seen. As the news audience asserts itself in a myriad of ways, applying Richard Sennett's definition of authority as "a bond between people who are unequal" to journalism begins to sound too inflexible, if not altogether antiquated.[60] More centrally, the cultural power of journalism to interpret the importance of events for society faces increased competition. As the participatory logic takes hold, what is needed is a more fluid conception of the authority relation between journalists and audiences. The complete dissolution of reportorial authority is hard to conceive of if one thinks of, for example, war reporting. But equally important is acknowledging developing trends and examining the formation of networks between journalists and audiences. The basis of this authority relation will have to become more dynamic and responsive to an environment in which the boundaries between journalists and the audience are shifting.

THE PRECARIOUS RECOGNITION OF
JOURNALISTIC AUTHORITY

This chapter began by promoting recognition as the core basis for any authority relation. The emphasis on recognition shifts the dynamic from a coercive view of authority to one mutually established between those laying claim to authority and those who accept it. Journalists and their audiences coproduce authority in a relationship that marks them as journalist and audience, respectively, and gives meaning and expectations to these social roles. But as we move from abstract relational dynamics to the persistent negative assessments of the press revealed in opinion polls, the underlying question becomes the precariousness of recognition. More pointedly, how do we explain a continuing faith in journalism as an essential watchdog while faith in journalists' abilities to act like one continues to corrode? Part of this answer is that the surveys we have available to us lack sufficient nuance to really get to how people feel about news—respondents can respond only with the answers they are provided. Even as surveys showing journalism to be in decline are plentiful, more serious attention to how these surveys structure understandings of the news has been nonexistent. After all, the lesson of the Berelson study is that people maintain a complex orientation to the news that cannot be explained solely through rationalist modes of democratic functioning. The authority relation extends beyond the information-exchange view of journalism that is so often privileged in discourse about news. Audiences possess a great number of motives that drive how they consume and interpret news, from entertainment to community making to the desire to be informed among one's peers. The insufficiency of available polls distorts our understandings of news audiences, leading to conclusions that leave out much of what news does. We need to develop better ways to assess how audiences understand and consume news as a way of improving how we conceptualize the journalist-audience authority relation.

On another level, surveys reveal the degree to which distrust has become the default stance toward public institutions, including journalism. From this starting point, if authority and credibility are considered synonyms, then the state of the journalist-audience authority relation appears fraught at best. One could reasonably stand back and look at survey data and pronounce that journalistic authority is clearly on the wane. But this would be an oversimplification. This book has strenuously resisted thinking of authority in terms of quantifiable or even comparable units. Instead, the focus has been on explicating the conditions and qualities that persist in the authority relations through which journalists attain authority from the larger social sphere. Collapsing authority with credibility becomes a fallacy because it omits broader normative and structural issues of legitimacy. In other words, journalistic authority is not merely about press performance but more broadly about cultural expectations of journalism. Journalism is a practice that both shapes cultural expectations and is contingent on such expectations. Instead of assuming the journalist-audience relationship to be static, careful analysis reveals how contending forces shape what we, as audiences, expect of journalism as well as what we expect of ourselves in our relationship with news. The rise of skepticism as the dominant audience position signals the need to interrogate how skepticism provides a set of interpretive tools audiences use to examine news.

The ongoing precariousness of the authority relation remains an inherent part of journalistic authority as a discursive process rather than a fixed thing. Cultural forces shaping the journalist-audience relationship are variable and prone to change, affecting both what the news looks like and how audiences interact with it. Different social actors with contrasting views compete to rearrange what this relation looks like, reshaping what news should be. Optimistically, this can be a healthy debate confronting deficiencies that eventually yields a stronger journalism. Pessimistically, the clash of voices pushes skepticism into cynicism or rejection, causing a crisis of confidence well beyond where public opinion is today or a splintering of norms and practices to the degree that journalism no longer functions as a meaningful descriptor or a recognizable entity. Ultimately, either outcome—or a combination thereof—is an iterative one, forged through a clash of voices that goes well beyond what journalists say about what they do.

CHAPTER FIVE

Legitimating Knowledge Through Knowers

News Sources

On the morning of June 28, 2012, both supporters and opponents of the Affordable Care Act—also known as Obamacare—waited breathlessly for the Supreme Court to rule on the legality of the law's core feature: the individual mandate requiring all Americans to have health insurance or pay a fine. Without this requirement, the law would likely unravel. Journalists hoping to be first to report the judgment—or at least not to be left behind by their equally eager competitors—were ready to pounce. Moments after the ruling became public, Fox News Channel's Shannon Bream announced to the viewing audience, "The mandate is gone." Over at CNN, the on-screen text flashed: "BREAKING NEWS: INDIVIDUAL MANDATE STRUCK DOWN."[1] The health care law was doomed, and pundits stood by to interpret what this defeat would mean for President Obama's reelection chances in the fall. Except, as it turned out, both news networks got it wrong. The mandate had survived judicial scrutiny but only through a complicated legal argument that treated the mandate as a tax and therefore within the authority of the federal government. It took CNN six minutes to correct its mistake, while Fox much more swiftly revised its reporting simply by going online to consult the experts at *SCOTUSblog*.

Husband and wife Tom Goldstein and Amy Howe started *SCOTUSblog* in 2002 as a side project to augment Goldstein's legal practice, whose services included arguing cases before the Supreme Court. The blog quickly became a staple resource, providing more detail on the high court than any news outlet. A decade on, the blog had firmly established its reputation as the go-to site for both news and analysis. Predictably, its popularity soars with landmark rulings, including the Affordable Care Act. Shortly after the ruling became public, *SCOTUSblog* had at one point 866,000 visitors simultaneously reading its coverage.[2] The site logged millions of visitors before the day was done, solidifying its role as a key player in the news coverage of the Court's decision. As a *source* itself, *SCOTUSblog* has captured a niche by providing in-depth reporting and insight about the Supreme Court exceeding other news outlets. *SCOTUSblog* has been able to establish its authority relation with the audience both through extensive resources for the legally minded and translation of Court actions for the bulk of the not legally educated citizenry. It would seem, based on this snapshot, that *SCOTUSblog* should be considered one of the most important news sites about the Supreme Court.

Not everyone agreed. Even with its robust coverage and growing reputation, *SCOTUSblog* was stymied in its pursuit of the permanent press credentials it needed to cover the Court effectively.[3] Press credentials accord both the symbolic resource of recognition and the material resources of a guaranteed seat at hearings and workspace in the press office—both resources sought by *SCOTUSblog*. However, the blog's application was denied on the grounds that it is not, in fact, an independent news source because Goldstein's legal practice solicits cases in front of the Supreme Court. This might be decried as an episode in which an overly protective institution—the Supreme Court—is too slow or wary to adapt to a changing media environment brimming with nontraditional outlets. But it is not so simple. The Supreme Court offloads its credentialing to the U.S. Senate Press Gallery, where the designation of credentials falls not to lawmakers or bureaucrats but to a committee of journalists mostly from traditional news organizations. Despite its decadelong track record of stellar coverage of the Supreme Court, *SCOTUSblog* could not get past the credentialing committee's ruling.

SCOTUSblog's saga will be taken up below, but this episode is useful for what it indicates about source-journalist relations. The continued denial of *SCOTUSblog* demonstrates how deeply institutionalized the relations between elite news organizations and elite sources have become.

These ties do not, in a vulgar way, suggest purposive collusion among sources and journalists. Such allegations smack of conspiracy theories, and in this case the journalists rejecting *SCOTUSblog* did lay out their reasoning. Rather, this incident indicates how access to elites is closely controlled in the relationship between journalists and sources—so much so that they work in concert to establish norms of access. The *SCOTUSblog* denial reveals codified assumptions underlying how journalists and sources should interact and who should be privy to this exchange. It also illuminates divides between legacy news and new digital media forms not only over source access but, in a larger sense, what authoritative news should look like and who should make it.

This chapter explores journalistic authority from the perspective of ties between journalists and the sources they rely on to construct their accounts of the world.[4] The journalist-source relation exposes a complex network of connections that lies at the heart of the production and consumption of news knowledge. A thorough understanding of journalistic authority must account for the interactions of these actors as well as how they come to be positioned through these relational dynamics. Viewed from above, the relationship between sources and journalists may seem more a matter of exchange than of inequality, as sources provide journalists with the raw materials they assemble into stories, while journalists provide sources with exposure. Certainly, exchange is important, but it cannot adequately explain journalistic authority on its own. Making sense of the journalist-source authority relation requires digging deeper. This chapter examines the sociology of journalistic sourcing practices, focusing on which voices appear in the news as authorized knowers. It then returns to the *SCOTUSblog* example before considering how digital media upend traditional dynamics governing the journalist-source relationship.

THE SOCIOLOGY OF NEWS SOURCES

Studies examining whom journalists turn to in crafting their stories have long been a cornerstone of journalism studies research. There is a good reason for this. The journalist-source relationship marks the point at which news-making practices move outside the confines of the newsroom to the complex ties between journalists and the external world of individuals and institutions. In turn, source selection matters as a social question because particular sources will yield particular information from particular viewpoints. From this jumping-off point, the rich scholarly literature has tended to proceed in two often-related directions—an ethnographic focus on practice and a critical focus on voice.[5] Or, put a little differently, studies tend to examine the material practices of news sourcing and their symbolic consequences. Both are necessary for understanding journalistic authority.

Journalism's Sourcing Practices

Why do certain people become news sources while the vast majority do not? This question animates Herbert Gans's inquiry into journalist-source relations in his seminal ethnography, *Deciding What's News*. The answers he provides to this question vary from practical questions of proximity (geographical *and* social) to more sociological questions of the distribution of power across society. Gans demonstrates how the *authoritativeness* of the source is only one criterion of suitability, mixed in with the need for sources to be trusted, reliable, and skilled at providing useful information to journalists.[6] Position matters, but so does articulateness and consistency. The conditions in which journalists work affect the sourcing decisions they make. For example, the fast tempo of news work requires efficient practices that do not squander journalists' precious allotment of time when working under deadline. Sourcing patterns cannot be reduced to a single variable (e.g., source power), but emerge from various conditions that shape the routinized industrial creation of news. This is also reciprocal—stable news production routines continuously reproduce sourcing practices.[7] Journalists operating within constraints that mutually shape practices and the justifications for these practices turn to trusted sources both for the sake of efficiency and for epistemological reasons.

Outside of individual journalists' decisions, another key factor affecting sourcing patterns is the fundamental organization of newsrooms around specific topic areas. Any newsroom with more than just a few reporters divvies up journalistic labor by beat. In this way, journalists are largely organized around their news sources. While this is an economical choice to impose efficiency on the frenetic labor of journalism, it also routinizes attention to certain powerful actors endemic to each beat.[8] The organization of journalistic work encourages the use of certain official sources. Fishman calls this "bureaucratic affinity"—journalists hierarchically arranged in complex institutions seek out others in similar setups.[9] These institutions enjoy advantages in their communication resources, which, following Gans's criteria above, greatly facilitates interactions with journalists looking to procure information efficiently and dependably.

The normative vision of the journalist-source relation portrays the journalist as pursuing the source to actively attain information for stories. The use of the word *beat* to describe a domain of news implies a commitment to being out in the world discovering stories. But news work often originates with the source, not the journalist. Much of what public relations work does is supply journalists with story ideas, and even the basic press release form mimics conventional news writing. Oscar Gandy labels this constant input of public relations materials as "information subsidies."[10] Although the majority of press releases do not result in news,[11] journalists under intense time pressures and lacking the resources for more intensive enterprise reporting rely on notifications from the outside to craft their stories. This situation has inspired smaller organizations to improve their communications efforts to reach journalists.[12] At the same time, larger organizations are able to marshal their public relations resources to craft story ideas easily taken up by busy journalists under endless pressure to create content.[13] One study conducted in the United Kingdom found such a high degree of public relations–driven news content that it concluded "meaningful independent journalistic activity by the media is the exception rather than the rule."[14] This may make for efficient news work, but it complicates the ability of journalists to draw on norms of autonomy as an authoritative strategy.

The ethnographic evidence for routinized news sourcing practices is borne out in examinations of patterns emerging in news texts. An early significant account comes from Leon Sigal in his 1974 book *Reporters and Officials*. Sigal demonstrates the persistence of officials being called upon as sources and endeavors to explain the forces that make this happen. He argues that though sources, and usually official sources, supply journalists with their chief form of evidence, these routines become paradigmatic to the point where any deep consideration of these practices is unheard of.[15] The consequences of this pattern can be summed up in Sigal's of-ten-quoted statement: "News is not reality, but a sampling of sources' portrayals of reality, mediated by news organizations."[16] Journalists are not forced to adopt the claims of their sources, but they must rely on them for the very content of their stories.

In the intervening decades, others have built on Sigal's work, finding further evidence of officials being called upon as sources,[17] including the national security beat,[18] television news,[19] and local news.[20] Beyond sophisticated content analyses, the sourcing practices described here are readily visible in even a cursory glance at the home page of a news website. In most cases, elite sources regularly receive prominent foot-ing. But why does this matter? Answering this question requires attending to what may be called the problem of voice.

The Problem of Voice

From the standpoint of journalistic authority, a review of sourcing rou-tines and content patterns cannot satisfactorily answer the question of what it *means* for some sources and not others to get called upon to ap-pear in news stories. This is not only a material question but a symbolic one centered on the question of who may legitimately speak about the actions of others.[21] Although there are several ways to get to the ques-tion of voice, as the scholarship on sourcing attests, from the standpoint of journalistic authority it becomes an epistemic question above all else. Journalists' jurisdictional claims to produce knowledge about the world require legitimized patterns for gathering and presenting the news.[22] Care is needed to avoid an internalist view that accounts only for these patterns from the standpoint of the newsroom. Instead, journalists' claim to being considered legitimate chroniclers of the real world rests on knowledge work that commands authority from news audiences.

Faced with the epistemic problem of having to convince audiences of the legitimacy of their accounts, journalists regularly turn to the accounts of others to craft their stories. This is not to deny instances of firsthand news accounts, in which journalists tout their presence on the scene as verification of an account's accuracy and evidence of their abil-ity to gather information. News photographs mark the presence of the photojournalist in the space of occurring news.[23] However, the bulk of news accounts cobble together material attributed to sources, often directly through quotations or recorded interviews. The news account, in these instances, is an interpretation of interpretations. Even though journalists work with and transform this material into properly verified accounts according to set procedures, the news audience often receives only secondhand knowledge from journalists.

Treating sourcing not merely as a set of routines but as an epistemic argument for journalistic authority allows for a better view of why journalists favor *certain* sources over others. The tendency to attribute information directly is useful as an evidentiary strategy connecting information and interpretation to specific individuals, thus freeing the journalists from having to make such pronouncements. The close connection between factual assertions and their asserters leads Richard V. Ericson to label news as "a perpetual process of authorizing facts through official sources."[24] Gaye Tuchman sees this strategy as protective, indemnifying journalists from the follies of their sources.[25] What develops among journalists is a preference for already powerful actors—actors who possess a degree of administrative authority. As a result, the preference for attribution over other journalistic forms of evidence—e.g., firsthand accounts, research, argument—also handcuffs journalists by making them beholden to their sources.

The reluctance of journalists to stray outside the safe confines of elite source–based pronouncements has drawn ample criticism from journalism scholars. Daniel Hallin's study of the Vietnam War and W. Lance Bennett's indexing theory both find that the range of opinions appearing in news coverage trails the range of opinions expressed by elite actors. Hallin argues that the visibility of the antiwar movement had less direct an impact on changing the tone of news coverage of Vietnam than the public outcry from elected officials.[26] Once high-ranking political figures started speaking out against the war, the news coverage followed by playing up this conflict and giving more room for voices critical of America's actions in Southeast Asia. To use Bennett's term, the coverage is *indexed* to what these powerful speakers have to say.[27] The exclusion of opinions running counter to what elite sources express does not suggest that journalists are conniving. Rather, the tendency toward indexing indicates how journalists follow a set of sourcing rules that shape how they relate to—and select—sources to provide the evidence they require for their stories. This is not haphazard or merely efficient, but the epistemological premises on which journalistic authority have come to be based.

Given the tendency of journalists to stick close to elite opinion and observation, much of the criticism surrounding news-sourcing practices takes aim from a macrosocial perspective. These critics look beyond questions of routinization to the larger reproduction of dominant discourses. John Soloski makes this distinction when noting that journalists' use of sources "[determines] not only what information is presented to the public, but what image of society is presented."[28] This quote serves as a reminder that the news is not just information about incidents in the world but a discourse that gives particular meaning to these incidents, which is the basis of journalism's symbolic power.[29]

Scholarly concern over whose voices are being reproduced in news discourse and whose are not sprung up as a central concern when the classic newsroom ethnographies were being written at the end of the 1970s on both sides of the Atlantic.[30] Amid other critiques,[31] two important works emerged around the same time. In the United Kingdom, Stuart Hall and colleagues turned their attention toward sources in their classic book *Policing the Crisis*. The book's core argument holds that journalists' devotion to neutrality and their need to rely on officials creates an environment in which elite sources become "primary definers" whose proclamations about social life become normalized through their presence in news discourse.[32] By virtue of being listened to—the essence of authority—these sources command the power to set the frames of understanding for social phenomena, to which other actors are forced to respond. The book uses crime as an example to document how concern over muggings became a social crisis through this very process of elite definition. Although this model has been criticized for overly homogenizing elite sources and underplaying journalists' agency in crafting news stories,[33] it nonetheless compels scrutiny of journalism's role in giving voice to certain powerful actors—and denying voice for others.

The reciprocity between journalists and elite social actors also lies at the heart of Todd Gitlin's *Whole World Is Watching*. Gitlin's account of the how the US news media covered the anti–Vietnam War movement engages Antonio Gramsci's notion of hegemony in arguing for the power of news to shape frames of understanding. This is not conspiratorial but rather the result of entrenched patterns. Gitlin notes, "Simply by doing their jobs, journalists tend to serve the political and economic elite definitions of society."[34] Student antiwar activists, on the other hand, remained outside the terrain of acceptable coverage. Only when staging elaborate protests could these voices gain access to the news.

Although the studies cited above is mostly decades old, the dynamics they explore are still quite relevant. A prime example is the Occupy Wall Street movement. In September 2011, a diverse group of protestors took over Zuccotti Park in New York's financial district. The general theme of the protest was to target economic inequality, but there was intentionally no unified message. However, the nonhierarchical organizational structure that the Occupy protestors worked hard to maintain was very much at odds with journalists' expectations of a clearly delineated hierarchy in which certain high-ranking people are assigned to speak for the group.[35] Journalists just didn't know whom to quote. NPR media correspondent David Folkenflik commented on journalists' inability to deal with this ambiguity: "Reporters are trying to cram this nebulous new phenomenon into a more familiar template. Is it like the civil rights movement? The Tea Party? Something else altogether? And they are stumbling around to figure out how enduring and how consequential it will be."[36] Without familiar scripts or authorized spokespersons, journalists lacked readily available frameworks for covering the Occupy story. What's open to debate is the degree to which Occupy protestors' lack of conformity to standard sourcing practices damaged their ability to build a movement. Such is the entrenched nature of news structures.

The question of voice remains a vexing one when formulating expectations of journalism in pluralistic democratic societies. Normatively, news should deliver a thorough accounting of competing ideas about social life for the operation of a public sphere.[37] Yet, pragmatically, journalists are expected to quickly and efficiently relay the news of the day, much of it mundane and formulaic. Given space and time constraints, most stories can only document incremental happenings relayed to audiences with minimal details. To relate this to journalistic authority, a useful way forward is to get beyond the question of voice by itself to think relationally about what both sources and journalists gain by engaging in these entrenched practices.

AUTHORIZED KNOWERS AND JOURNALISTIC AUTHORITY

Study after study showing sourcing patterns favoring elite sources embedded within powerful institutions has led generations of critics to chastise journalists for granting too much power to a small sliver of sources and for restricting what journalists can say when *not* speaking through a source. But how do these sourcing patterns affect journalistic authority?

One argument is that the reliance on sources denigrates journalism by reducing reporters to the role of amplifiers for elites. No doubt, criticisms of journalists as overly obsequious carry some validity. An enduring example of how sourcing failures result in a black eye for journalism can be found in the reporting preceding the 2003 invasion of Iraq.[38] The front pages of US newspapers brimmed with unnamed source–laden stories detailing Iraq's secret stockpile of weapons of mass destruction, only to be discredited shortly after the start of war when no WMDs were found. *New York Times* reporter Judith Miller came to personify the reporting failures of this period. Following the invasion of Iraq, she quickly went from being lauded for choosing jail in defiance of a subpoena demanding she reveal an unnamed source to being pilloried for playing stenographer to the outlandish claims of the Bush administration.[39] Miller subsequently became a lasting symbol of sourcing gone wrong.[40] Yet, in this instance, it took the widespread failure of numerous reporters and editors within the US press followed by catastrophic consequences in the form of a decadelong and largely indecisive war for this critique of journalism to gain traction. This is not to deny the lasting significance of the reportorial shortcomings preceding the Iraq War. Rather, the point of invoking this episode is to single out its extraordinariness for parading journalists' reliance on elite sources in front of the public. Ultimately, the most depressing takeaway from the WMD reporting episode is that the journalistic sourcing practices involved were standard procedure.

Examining journalistic authority not from the perspective of journalists' extraordinary successes and failures but from ordinary practice requires acknowledging that, for the most part, the contemporary practices and narratives undergirding journalistic authority have grown up around the sourcing practices outlined above. Elite source–oriented articles are not the exception but standard. The persistence of these patterns forces the momentary bracketing of the above critiques in order to ask how the reliance on elite sources connects to journalistic authority. Failing to examine how journalists actually work increases the risk of mistakenly explaining journalistic authority only through journalistic norms. While norms matter in thinking about authority, so too do everyday patterns of news making.

Formulating a vision of the journalist-source authority relation starts with a recognition that sourcing routines favoring elites are not aberrant but deeply structured into news practice. Mark Fishman argues that journalists reproduce the "normative order of authorized knowers" by relying on sources with the requisite status to bolster their reporting.[41] In other words, journalists concerned with producing a legitimate account rely on particular sources viewed as already legitimately knowledgeable about a specific story. But this is a reciprocal relation, if journalism is assumed to have any legitimacy to produce accounts of the world. To be made a news source is to be considered knowledgeable about the topic of the reporting. And while journalism does not define social elites in and of itself, it does contribute to the reproduction of elite status through sourcing practices.

For a news story to include an individual or an organization as a source is not a neutral act but one that bestows authority through granting the source the right to be listened to. What arises is authoritative reciprocity, which Ericson and colleagues note in a Foucault-inspired passage in their book *Negotiating Control*: "In citing authoritative sources, news outlets not only underpin their sources' authority, they also reproduce their own authority. News organizations join with sources in representing the power-knowledge contours of organizational life, and thereby, the authoritative apparatus of society."[42]

Journalists in turn argue for their role as authorized knowers through their access and connection to these powerful sources. A news story encompasses both a recitation of sourced information and simultaneously a demonstration of the journalist's access to such sources. Access here is twofold: it both describes the competency of the journalist in being able to collect and organize information from diverse sources[43] and doubles as a display of proximity that illustrates journalism's connections to power. In this sense, connecting journalistic authority to the display of access to elite sources seems to contradict the normative commitment of maintaining distance bound up in the objective news paradigm. While journalists do not necessarily acquiesce to the powerful sources they rely on, they are rarely able to escape this dependency. Conspiracy is never as strong of an explanation as structural dependence.

The journalist-source authority relation is marked by mutual influence but is in the service of two different ideas of authority. Powerful sources pursue administrative authority in part through drawing on the symbolic authority of journalists to publicize their interests. This puts journalists in a situation of having to defend their independence from their sources while also constructing an account based on reproducing information openly attributed to these same sources. David Eason employs the term *disobedient dependence* to capture this precarious position of journalists as both reliant on and separate from their sources.[44] While journalists adopt a degree of skepticism—some would say cynicism[45]— and certainly can and do challenge the assertions their sources make, they also cannot escape their fundamental reliance on sources because of the need both for predictable work routines and for the epistemic authority of these sources. Eason places journalists between the extremes of being either handmaidens in league with their sources or independent actors completely free from external pressures in their search for truth. What lies in the middle is more complicated but also essential to acknowledge when explaining the journalist-source relation underlying arguments for journalistic authority.

The constant reproduction of elite voices in news content indicates a system of news that perpetuates its practices to the point where imagining alternative sourcing patterns is difficult. Yet the legitimacy of existing news forms depends on continued acquiescence from those outside of journalism. Journalism relies on authorized knowers while positioning itself as an authorized way of knowing, even if much of what is known is secondhand knowledge. Through their sourcing practices, journalists must reproduce the assertion that these relations—and not others—grant it authority to tell audiences the news about their worlds.

RETURN TO *SCOTUSBLOG*

While taking a bird's-eye view of the journalist-source relation by using content analysis to uncover sourcing patterns is manageable, gaining access to the microinteractions that take place daily between reporters and their sources is much harder. Journalists are often secretive about their sources as they seek to cultivate trust.[46] News audiences get the finished product, smoothed of its rough edges, with little insight into how any story came together. But every once in a while, some incident erupts to expose journalist-source relations in the same way that earthquakes sometimes expose rock formations otherwise hidden under our feet.[47] The fight over the credentialing of *SCOTUSblog* provides one such telling incident but in a particular way. *SCOTUSblog*'s repeated efforts to receive credentials and the subsequent denials may not reveal much about how sources and journalists work together, but the episode sheds light on the institutionalized constraints in which these interactions occur. It cracks open a door into how news work at the highest levels works, revealing broader insights into journalist-source relations.

SCOTUSblog pursued credentials mainly because of a practical need to gain a workspace in the Supreme Court building and to guarantee a seat at important hearings. In being denied, the site encountered the mishmash of uneven rules and hidden assumptions about journalism embedded in the credentialing process. This is not an isolated issue. A report from Harvard's Berkman Center for Internet and Society found that the rules governing credentials vary widely from location to location, with one out of five applicants having their applications denied at least once.[48] These rejections are not random. Freelancers and nontraditional news outlets face more barriers when seeking credentials. Many of the rules favor traditional news outlets while creating obstacles for individuals and emerging news organizations.

Press credentials are material in their outcomes—after all, credentials refer to the right to access physical places off-limits to the noncredentialed public. Moreover, credentials condition journalists' access to sources by allowing them to operate in the same space. But beyond the physical access they accord, credentials also have a symbolic dimension. They are a form of restricted recognition, conferring legitimacy to their possessors while also marking off their distance from the uncredentialed. Fights over credentialing are, at heart, proxies for larger fights over the definition of appropriate journalistic practices and actors. All of this makes the issue of credentialing important when considering journalistic authority. Yet the practice of credentialing is also often hidden or, at least, not on the minds of most news audiences. Credentialing decisions may dictate who has access and who doesn't, but they are not normally subject to public scrutiny.

SCOTUSblog's efforts to receive credentials did, for a moment, bring the issue of credentials into public view.[49] Had the Supreme Court itself rejected *SCOTUSblog*'s request, the resulting narrative would likely suggest that certain institutions have been slow to admit that new types of news outlets could be considered journalism. A flurry of complaints would have accused the Court's Public Information Office of being out of touch and demanded that it shouldn't decide what qualifies as journalism. But this was not the case at all. The Court defers to the Senate Press Gallery on credentialing to avoid thorny questions of demarcating who may be considered an appropriate journalist. And the Senate too avoids these quandaries by deferring to a panel of journalists to decide who is and who is not worthy of credentials. Even this panel operates according to codified rules. The vexing question here is why a panel of journalists decided to exclude *SCOTUSblog*.

Answering this question begins with the Standing Committee of Correspondents' own words, spelled out in a rejection letter *SCOTUSblog* made public. According to the committee, *SCOTUSblog* ran afoul of the following rule: "Applicants' publications must be editorially independent of any institution, foundation, or interest group that lobbies the federal government, or that is not principally a general news organization."[50] Because the committee equated advocating before the Supreme Court with lobbying, the presence of *SCOTUSblog* within the Goldstein & Russell law office meant this rule was being violated. Moreover, the committee argued that the blog was not truly editorially independent of the firm and still served a promotional role in drumming up business. The committee added that the close ties between the firm and the blog "[make] it hard to determine where one ends and the other begins." Because the blog could not be easily differentiated from the law firm, it could not meet the criterion of independence indispensable to being deemed worthy of a credential. In the committee's judgment, *SCOTUSblog* "fails the fundamental test of editorial independence."

Normatively, the committee remained steadfast in its protection of editorial independence as a bedrock principle for journalism. In its denial of *SCOTUSblog*, this institutional issue trumps questions of medium, outlet, or even voice. Independence is what needs protection above all else. This position stems from a larger commitment to journalistic autonomy emerging as a sine qua non for Western journalism in its break from partisan or state control.[51] The strict reading of this rule is meant to protect against unseen forces external to journalism imposing bias on news accounts concerning the highest levels of the federal government.

To say that *SCOTUSblog* founder Tom Goldstein did not agree with the committee's findings is to put it lightly.[52] He quickly fired back with a blog post questioning the conclusion that the blog and the law firm were inseparable by reiterating the policies and procedures in place to keep them independent of each other. But more telling than the squabble over this technical issue was the larger picture Goldstein painted of a changing media landscape:

> The members of the Standing Committee are traditional journalists who come from a proud and treasured tradition of complete independence from anything other than their craft. That is a fantastic model for journalism. But it is not the only one. And it is unfortunate that this is a decision in which members of the traditional media exercise their own power over access to the government to categorically exclude a wide swath of competitors.

In short, the rules as written and interpreted do not allow for journalistic plurality. They collapse independence as both a normative commitment and a structural arrangement endemic to traditional media organizations. And while *SCOTUSblog* certainly avers the importance of independence, it exists in a novel organizational setting. Move over, Goldstein argued that this setting was one of necessity rather than preference; despite its popularity and comprehensiveness, *SCOTUSblog* did not generate the necessary income to detach from the law firm and survive independently. It simply cannot earn enough revenue through its laser-like focus on the Supreme Court. In the end, the rules pertain to larger, profit-making media organizations while structurally excluding the rise of small, expert-driven news sites.

The question becomes whether *SCOTUSblog* is an aberration or a trendsetter. Goldstein opted for the latter by situating the blog within a larger phenomenon of expert-based news sites: "This scenario—specialists reporting on their respective fields of expertise—is going to grow, not diminish. Traditional media is contracting. Nontraditional, expert media is expanding, including because we have access to inexpensive distribution through the Internet. We do not need a printing press." This statement suggests several implications for how to think about journalistic authority. Foremost, it redefines journalistic expertise away from the ability to quickly collect, verify, and arrange information from sources into accurate accounts to the authority of the journalist as independently knowledgeable about the subject matter.[53] This is an important epistemological distinction between detached observation and engaged speculation.[54] It transforms the journalist-source relation as well by suggesting that the journalist becomes the source of information. It also detaches subject expertise from the moorings of journalistic institutions to support a wider range of organizational types.

The epistemic issue is bound up in the wider issue of paradigmatic competition to establish what might be considered appropriate—i.e., credential-worthy—journalism. One way to view the committee's rejection is to return to the concept of boundary work and its focus on symbolic contests among rival groups seeking to establish epistemic authority.[55] The committee takes as its mandate the task of establishing who should gain special access via a credential and who should be denied such access. This decision making cannot be arbitrary; it has to rest on a codified understanding of what qualifies as appropriate. The resulting guidelines then seemingly transcend the decision of any one individual to instead provide an objective reference point. However, these are not neutral guidelines. Instead, they embody deep-seated journalistic ideologies in their presentation of ways of thinking about journalism as concrete and immutable. As such, they endow the committee with the ability to engage in boundary work in both its rhetorical and material senses. The issuance or denial of credentials has consequences. While denying credentials does not prohibit an organization from reporting on Congress or the Supreme Court, it does hinder vital access to facilitate this coverage. But the denial is also a rhetorical act, as was seen in the explication of independence put forth to rationalize the denial of *SCOTUSblog*'s request. This action signals a belief in what journalism should be, and that belief gets translated into bright lines about who has access and who does not.

This episode should not be reduced to a struggle of journalistic new-comer *SCOTUSblog* against traditional news media. Days after the denial, the *New York Times*, the paragon of traditional US journalism, took up the cause of *SCOTUSblog* in an editorial titled "Give Scotusblog a Seat in Court," arguing: "Professional standards are necessary, but, by any measure, Scotusblog meets them. Its importance is demonstrated by its audience, which is not just top journalists and members of the public. According to the site's internal data, Scotusblog's single biggest user is the Supreme Court itself."[56] To the *Times*, the virtue of the site lies in its utility. In effect, *SCOTUSblog* is a source itself and not merely a journalistic outlet. The *Times*'s public support nullifies any suggestion of a united journalistic front against *SCOTUSblog*. Instead, the varying judgments suggest an increasingly complex emerging media landscape marked by a lack of agreement over basic definitions and boundaries.

SCOTUSblog's fight to receive credentials indicates how carefully journalists control their access to the elites they count on to produce the news. But sources work in concert with journalists to limit access by turning over credentialing to the journalists themselves. Both parties—the elite sources and the elite journalists—have an interest in limiting access to preserve their relationship. This is not to accuse them of overt collusion. No conspiracy is afoot. The explanation is much more ordinary in attempts to maintain an established belief system about what news should look like. The committee worked off of rules grounded in this system. It would be expected that the committee members would earnestly defend the legitimacy of its denial and reject charges that it was merely acting vindictively. Attributing its decision to beliefs rather than personal animus makes this episode that much more powerful of a statement about authority than had it just been simple jealously over the growing popularity of *SCOTUSblog*.

In the end, the journalist-source relationship should be recognized as the product of particular institutional workings that continuously shape the conditions in which the news is created. Journalists rely on sources as a basis for their authority, and authority is necessarily the product of legitimated restrictions. At the same time, *SCOTUSblog* has not backed down. And if Goldstein is correct that the site represents a harbinger of future news sites, then we ought to see new forms of the journalist-source authority relation in the future.

Presidents have long enjoyed direct access to the press through the ready ear of a reporter or the spotlight of a press conference.[57] Through speeches and even the quaint tradition of a weekly radio address, they find ways to reach the citizenry through the mass media. But what happens when the president no longer requires the microphones and cameras of journalists to reach a vast audience? This has become less and less a hypothetical question. At the time of this writing, Barack Obama could reach his 75 million Twitter followers directly without an intervening journalist. This is an astonishing number, considering Obama garnered 66 million votes in the 2012 election.[58] And Twitter is only one way the White House reaches citizens outside of traditional news channels. Obama's frequently updated Facebook page has nearly 49 million "likes," and his YouTube channel boasts over half-a-million subscribers, with slightly less for the White House channel. These numbers are not accidental. The Obama administration embraced nontraditional media and innovated with digital media channels to organize its two successful election campaigns.[59] In raising the bar for future campaigns, its aggressive pursuit of novel means for reaching the public directly will be emulated by both future presidential campaigns and administrations. Turning back to journalism, the rise of new communication channels underscores the need to look beyond news practices to larger changes in the media environment. From this broader perspective, the enhanced capabilities sources have to talk directly to the public alters the journalist-source relation and its connection to ideas of journalistic authority in fundamental ways.

In the past, journalists controlling broadcast and print channels accrued power, in part, through their control over the selection, creation, and dissemination of news to large audiences. The concern over agenda setting—long a staple of mass communication research[60]—has been predicated on a concern over the limited conduits for talking to the public. In this environment, to be a news source is to speak within this attenuated mediated space; being left out relegates a source to silence. However, these assumptions are now somewhat dated, as digital technologies have greatly expanded the terrain of mediated communication. With the move from an era of scarcity of mediated channels to one of abundance, journalists exercising their gatekeeping power do so in competition with sources able to speak to the public directly.[61] Spokespersons and public relations professionals have grown increasingly adept at locating digital media channels, even entirely circumventing the news.

For example, political campaigns obsess over how a candidate or race is understood. Even with copious news coverage, much campaign spending goes toward shaping the larger narrative by reaching voters directly through mailings and television advertisements.[62] Digital media offer another set of communication channels to bypass news. Most notably, Donald Trump tweets copiously to his millions of followers, and these tweets spark further news stories. But just because candidates have turned to digital channels does not mean we are in an era of enhanced participation.[63] Often, a one-way information flow originating with journalists comes to be replaced by a one-way flow from the campaign.[64] This is not to assume that journalists will be supplanted altogether, but these dynamics portend an enlarged media environment in which journalists control only one part.

Twitter also provides a useful venue to examine the changing news ecology. Alfred Hermida argues that Twitter should be understood as a hybrid space that "blurs long-standing distinctions between newsmaker, news reporter and news consumer."[65] The tweets of all three of these parties intermingle, and the ability to add followers and retweet messages allows for the amplification of messages. Optimistically, substituting the logic of the network for the logic of mass media allows for a wider variety of voices than would normally appear in news. Hermida cites Twitter for allowing protesters on the ground, from Egypt's Tahrir Square to Occupy Wall Street, to publicize their own narratives and facts.[66] Yet the ability to circumvent traditional news channels also benefits elite sources who already possess sophisticated communications resources.[67] In addition to using nonnews channels to circulate information, sources can also challenge and criticize how they are represented within news stories[68]

These developments signal the need to examine journalism in its wider communicative context. News stories exist in a complex ecosystem that increasingly includes news sources bypassing journalists to reach the public directly. The implications for journalistic authority are not clear. On one level, the ability of sources to speak directly to the public seems to weaken journalists' jurisdictional claims to chronicle events in the world. But on another, journalists are able to position themselves as trusted chroniclers amid a barrage of self-interested messages. Journalists can argue that they are always other-interested in basing their authoritative claims not in their own aggrandizement or self-interest but in benefiting their audiences. Regardless, the authority-source relation is being transformed by the shift from sources' dependence on news to their growing ability to speak to the public directly.

SPEAKING THROUGH THE VOICES OF OTHERS

The popular narrative around contemporary journalism is one of change and uncertainty in the face of new technologies for news gathering and news distribution. Yet routinized patterns of news production seem to endure—including a reliance on attributing information to sources.[69] From an epistemic perspective, journalism has grown up around attribution practices that pair information with specific sources. When imagining a generic news story, what comes to mind is an assemblage of information linked to nonjournalists.[70] What is forgotten is how, at heart, this is an evidentiary strategy as much as a production one. There is some irony, then, in journalistic authority being so closely associated with source-centric reporting practices: journalists speak through the voices of others as they seek to legitimate their own voice.

Journalists' reliance on sources acts as a legitimating strategy, but it also makes claims to journalistic authority deeply vulnerable. Appeals to professional autonomy—a cornerstone of epistemic authority—conflict with the need to connect every assertion with an attributed source. It is not surprising then that David Eason, in the first study to invoke *journalistic authority* as a specific term, devotes much attention to the problems that sourcing patterns pose for journalism.[71] Even as conventional sourcing patterns create this vulnerability, they are unlikely to unravel from the inside because they mutually benefit journalists needing attributed material for their stories and sources seeking attention for their positions. The practice of knowing through sources provides journalism with both an evidentiary strategy and a ritualistic enactment of the power-knowledge relations within society. This is not a shallow commitment, even if it perpetually exposes journalistic authority to the critique that journalists cannot live up to normative commitments they so stridently tout.

External changes will no doubt introduce new and different patterns of sourcing and knowledge production that embrace differing conceptions of journalistic authority. That such arrangements are often hard to imagine serves as a testament to how closely patterns of journalist-source relations are coupled to journalistic authority. At this point, the evidence for new models for news that alter journalism's entrenched knowledge practices is spotty. However, the model offered by *SCOTUSblog* is promising. Its authority derives not from access to elite sources but from subject expertise and comprehensive analysis. More broadly, *SCOTUSblog* is a net positive for journalism. It provides unparalleled knowledge about one of society's most important institutions. We are better off that it exists. Yet even as the site has become a valuable resource and a potential model for future news sites, *SCOTUSblog* faces intense challenges. Economically, it cannot generate the revenues needed to sustain itself as a standalone entity and must rely on its association with a law firm. Structurally, this lack of independence—as traditionally defined— doubly harms the site by also foiling its request for press credentials. Ironically, *SCOTUSblog*'s desire to avoid dependence on paid subscriptions or advertising—one can only imagine what Supreme Court clickbait would look like—negatively affects its ability to gain credentials. At the end of the day, the site presents promising new ways of doing journalism and perhaps will open the door for other experiments that could countermand the vulnerability that journalist-source relations pose for journalistic authority. For the time being, it lacks the institutional power of established news organizations and therefore is doomed to remain outside the boundaries of acceptable journalism imposed by other journalists—but for how long?

CHAPTER SIX

Mediating Authority

The Technologies of Journalism

Over time, technologies that were once new and wondrous fade into the background of everyday life. As they become part of the taken-for-granted infrastructure enabling contemporary practices, their familiarity cloaks their cultural significance and the ways they structure action.[1] The photocopier provides a useful example. Now a staple of the modern office (and bound up with printing, scanning, and even faxing capabilities), it was an entirely new piece of technology when Xerox introduced the first mass-produced copier, the 914, in 1959. Once its durability and ease of use became accepted, the photocopier quickly became an indispensable office device. As with any technology, arriving at a thorough understanding requires moving beyond the device itself to consider the myriad conventions—or protocols[2]—that develop around its use. The physical addition of a massive photocopier required offices to reconfigure their space and rethink workflow as well as the flow of bodies needing access to the machine.[3] The Xerox photocopier also altered work practices: what would have taken typists considerable time now could be done much more quickly and inexpensively. As an unthinking machine, it was also invested with the promise of exact duplication compared to the fallibility of human typing.[4] Aside from transforming labor, photocopiers also became social spaces as sanctioned points of congregation in offices.

Most importantly, the photocopier altered the very idea of the document.[5] Easy, exact duplication opened up new possibilities for the circulation and storage of documents, allowing for complex flows of information across bureaucratic networks. The photocopier became a tool to think with, and, as Lisa Gitelman argues, Xerox customers found many uses—and produced a far greater volume of copies—than what the company had imagined.[6] In all these ways, this example illustrates how technologies are more than mere objects that serve human needs. Tools shape practices, just as practices in turn shape tools.

The photocopier changed journalism by altering how documents could circulate. With instant and easy duplication, the boundaries of what could be kept secret irrevocably changed.[7] Most dramatically, copies of documents could be leaked to the press while the originals remained uncirculated. The most iconic example of this transformation took place in 1969, a decade after the release of the Xerox 914, when a photocopier played a crucial role in helping a young analyst at the RAND Corporation named Daniel Ellsberg smuggle out and copy the 7,000 pages composing the secret government-authored history of the Vietnam War that would become known as the Pentagon Papers.[8] The subsequent publication of the Pentagon Papers became a celebrated moment for journalism in holding power to account and setting legal precedence against prior restraint.[9] The episode remains prominent in the collective memory of journalistic accomplishment, and news workers continue to invoke it to support journalistic authority.

From a technological standpoint, the publishing of the Pentagon Papers contributed to a reshuffling of what could be kept private and what could be shared.[10] Following their release to the public, James Reston remarked in a *New York Times* column that the preponderance of leaks occurring during the Nixon administration owed more to the proliferation of copiers than to a spike in ill will. Reston conjured the following scenario to illustrate his hypothesis:

> Every copy going to any authorized person in the [National Security Advisor Henry] Kissinger meeting on the Indo-Pakistani war can easily and quickly be Xeroxed and circulated to the "responsible persons" in his own department, passing through aides and secretaries, who have other Xerox machines, and while most of them

merely pass the message along to it its intended receiver, anybody along the line can intercept and duplicate the message and circulate it at will, or so it seems.[11]

This scenario exposes the many points along a chain of document duplication where a stray copy may find its way to the outside and into the hands of a journalist. In turn, documents have special authority as a journalistic form of evidence. They are treated as something objective and concrete, as opposed to the subjective and partial interpersonal exchange with a human source.[12] The photocopier made available documents that were previously difficult to attain, which both increased journalists' pursuit of documentation and their use of these documents as evidence supporting their epistemic claims.

Copiers may not receive a second glance today until the paper jams, but recalling their effect on the reproduction and circulation of information—and how reproduction could be imagined—exposes the deep connections binding journalistic change with technological change.[13] Journalism, as a system of public communication, always involves technology—it operates through a complex media system to produce and distribute news. By extension, journalistic authority cannot be understood without thinking through this core role of technology. This chapter takes the issue of technology bubbling below the surface of the previous chapters and brings it out for inspection. It begins by assessing the larger discourses about technology that permeate contemporary talk about journalism. These discussions tend to treat the irruption of digital media as either harbingers of the death of news or its positive reinvention. But this discourse requires greater historical grounding to expose the deep-seated connections between the technologies of journalism and journalistic authority. This chapter tackles the issue of materiality by interrogating how the objects of journalism work in conjunction with narratives that support journalistic authority. Taking this view provides a perspective for analyzing emerging new practices, including the growing role of algorithms in news selection and, increasingly, the actual composition of news stories.

Technology dominates discussions of journalism in the twenty-first century. Journalists and academics expound on the ways digital media have upended the news industry while prognosticating about its future directions. This is not mere talk—the material consequences of technological changes have been acutely felt by the journalism industry.[14] Digital media have opened new means for news distribution and consumption, and the proliferation of new devices further complicates this environment. In these narratives, technological change becomes the driving force, leaving a variety of epiphenomena in its wake. For example, sharp declines in news revenues are attributed to the decline in print advertising as advertisers migrate to digital platforms. Mass advertising loses ground to targeted advertising relying on the wealth of personal data that can be attained from users, or it disappears thanks to free online classified services. Newspapers have responded by building robust websites, but advertising revenues continue to flag. Meanwhile, critics accuse the preponderance of low-quality clickbait and the repackaging of news content by online aggregators of further diminishing quality journalism. All of this takes place against the backdrop of an expanded array of media content competing for public attention. Jobs have been lost, and some newspapers have even ceased daily printing, if not closed altogether. Journalists labor to produce news, but a cloud of uncertainty hangs over the viability of news as an industry, particularly at the local level. From this perspective, the tale of technology becomes the tale of a diminished press.[15]

Countering such tales of woe, other observers highlight how new platforms have democratized public communication. Digital media radically lower the barriers to entry, enabling individuals and organizations that had been previously relegated to the reception side of mass communication to become active participants. From individual bloggers to wholly new digital news organizations, technology is heralded for extending the news in ways never before possible.[16] A new generation of journalists touts itself as entrepreneurs ready to reinvent the industry.[17] Nonjournalists have gained digital avenues to supply firsthand accounts or even challenge what journalists report.[18] New forms of interaction and engagement are now possible that could not have existed in any meaningful way through the one-way flows of mass communication. This tale of technology is that of the augmented press.

These are thumbnail sketches, to be sure, but they are also familiar ones. Is one of them correct? Or more correct? Certainly, narratives of pessimism and optimism have both their merits and shortcomings, and adjudicating these claims is beyond the scope of this book. Instead, the focus here tilts from the visible differences manifested in these interpretations to their core contention that technology is the key driver for making sense of the overall state of journalism and its future directions. In this sense, these opposing narratives share a common understanding of digital upheaval. Technological change has become an organizing principle for understanding journalism; it acts as a metanarrative, even if it inspires divergent interpretations.

The attention to change is hardly surprising given the prominent transformations occurring across the news landscape. After all, continuity is rarely news. Yet the influence of stasis gets less attention than it deserves, as it is often confused with its near synonym *inertia* or even lethargy. Stasis should instead be recognized as indicating both entrenched practices often tacitly reproduced and an active attachment to these practices as a source of legitimacy. Endurance provides a key source of institutional strength by maintaining the authority relations on which legitimacy depends. This conceptualization of stasis connects to an older sense of authority grounded in longevity. The past provides support for the present because it generates recognition among the different social actors involved in the creation of authority. As individuals and even specific organizations change, institutional continuity supports claims to authority. Static formations are familiar and do not need to be reintroduced anew.

Digital media may usher in rapid change, but many engrained aspects of journalism are slow to change. This latter dynamic can be seen in the normative investment in professionalism explored in chapter 1, recurring formal patterns discussed in chapter 2, the stories journalists tell about themselves recounted in chapter 3, and news-making practices related to entrenched sourcing practices detailed in chapter 5. Ways of thinking about journalism, the practices that produce news, and its textual forms all persist and become inseparable from the epistemic claims supporting journalistic authority. An emphasis on innovation may outshine the resilience of the old, but the tenacity of journalistic patterns across time deserves recognition for its role in legitimating the continued production of news.

If focusing solely on newness overlooks the role of deep-seated patterns in supporting journalistic authority, then focusing only on resilient structures diminishes the contextual pressures that shape journalism in a particular time and place. The conceptualization of journalistic authority developed here accounts for the historical relationship between journalistic practice and technology while also remaining sensitive to how technological innovations affect journalistic authority. This balance between what is new and what is resilient rests on counteracting two tendencies that creep into conversations about journalism and technology.

First, the murkiness inherent in language results in a bias that equates technology with newness. The use of *technology* as a synonym for the vague referents *new media* or *digital media* indicates the lexical difficulty of trying to corral a mess of different devices, networks, protocols, and practices into a single unifying term. Encompassing all of this stuff within a single phrase creates a challenge that is difficult to avoid when selecting an adequate noun to capture various interrelated phenomena. Beyond descriptive ambiguity, this usage turns into a problem when *technology* becomes a linguistic wedge referring only to recent technological developments while ignoring—and even naturalizing—existing technologies. It then dehistoricizes journalism's relationship with technology.

A second issue arises when technologies of journalism become invisible except when introduced or challenged. A television may no longer seem that interesting or even relevant to thinking about news in the twenty-first century compared to a smart phone—even if local television news continues to be tremendously popular.[19] This blindness limits our understandings of technological adoption. In a study covering four decades of technological innovations in news work, Matthew Powers pushes beyond current disruptions to reengage earlier moments of transition—such as the computerization of the newsroom—that are now so taken for granted as to escape any consideration.[20] Mirroring current discourse on the digitization of news, past generations of news workers confronted the implementation of new newsroom technologies with an array of contradictory reactions, from the assuredness of continuity to fear of disruption to the hopefulness of reinvention, before they eventually became an unnoticed part of how the news is created. Barbie Zelizer notes similar patterns with the arrival of photojournalism. Once an outcast drawing suspicion, images have attained sacrosanct status as news objects, particularly in the realm of witnessing discussed below.[21] Even the telegraph, extinct (or evolved) as it is, occasioned both new practices and new ways of imagining journalism.[22] Dredging up journalists' long history of discomfort with technological change is not meant to belittle or dismiss contemporary technological concerns. Material changes are deeply felt in any age. Instead, these examples indicate the need to view technology as indispensable to journalism rather than superfluous or an issue unique to the present.

Historicizing the tension between institutional stasis and technological change as an incumbent issue for journalism provides a foundation for examining how narratives around new technologies become moments of explicit meaning making.[23] Through metajournalistic discourse, actors publicly negotiate emergent practices and their relationship to journalistic authority.[24] In this sense, the materiality of new technologies is paired with interpretive discourse seeking to explain, refine, and legitimate their use in relation to existing ideas of journalism. News norms and practices, the foundations of journalistic authority, are never merely transferred to new communication technologies. Nor are they invented whole cloth without reference to previous technologies. Instead, what needs to be recognized is how news norms and practices are rethought, adapted, and even transformed by shifts in technology.[25]

This conflict between stasis and change has been examined in a rich body of recent research on news production.[26] For example, Jane Singer shows how the advent of online journalism problematized notions of journalistic professionalism, transforming a weak yet relatively stable self-conceptualization of journalistic professionalism into one that had to address the threat of unfamiliar technological practices and their accompanying forms.[27] At the time she was writing in the early 2000s, bloggers were beginning to emerge as an alternative voice within the mediated public sphere in ways that made journalists uncomfortable. These blogs presented alternative modes of address and a networked configuration unlike what journalists understood to be correct. These diverse potential models of journalistic work and understandings of what it means to be a journalist become more visible, driving journalists to reconsider their roles in ways that had previously been more marginal. Put simply, the community had to confront itself. What such examples indicate is the dual nature of technology as a force of stability undergirding claims to journalistic authority and as a force of disruption upending these very claims. The relationship between technological innovation and journalistic authority can be a messy one, and making it clearer necessitates looking more closely at how the objects of journalism relate to its authority.

OBJECTS OF JOURNALISM

A common weakness plaguing ordinary thinking about journalistic authority occurs when technology is assigned an ancillary role in the creation of news. Scholars interrogating the news as a legitimated cultural form often query journalists' normative commitments, their interpersonal news-gathering practices, and the textual strategies they employ. All of these are vital and have been much discussed throughout this book, but they overlook the particular role of technology. After all, the term *press* refers both to an institution and its machinery. This linguistic double referent of the practices and means of communication needs to be retained to theorize about journalistic authority.[28]

Journalistic work always involves technologies, from the mundane reliance on pencils, note pads, tape recorders, and telephones to the complex reliance on video-editing software, computer servers, printing presses, and satellites.[29] From the earliest stages of news gathering through to the dissemination and consumption of the finished news product, journalism cannot be meaningfully detached from technology.[30] To capture this sense, C. W. Anderson and Juliette De Maeyer argue for the need to include "objects of journalism"—the technological apparatus through which journalism creates a public discourse—as an integral component of news making.[31] Doing so, they argue, "opens us up to a relational understanding of technology rather than a deterministic one, an understanding that sees the material aspects of objects as inevitably imbricated in a web of human and non-human relations."[32] By eschewing determinism and adopting the analytical assumptions of actor-network theory, technology becomes an actor itself, one that both is shaped by social and technical processes and that in turn shapes the actions of human users.

Starting with objects of journalism on their own terms allows for greater sensitivity to the constraints and patterns that dictate news work. For example, newsrooms are often thought of in terms of hierarchy and the coordinated division of labor across a news organization, from executive editor to assistant copy editor. What get lost in the flowcharts are the technologies that undergird these systems—telephones, e-mail, floor plans, office doors, elevators, and so on. Most notably, newsrooms rely on content management systems to facilitate workflow. These systems, which combine software interfaces with networked hardware, are not a neutral technology born from nowhere and malleable to the whims of reporters and editors. Instead, they are artifacts with a developmental history and are shaped by the struggles of competing actors with a variety of divergent interests while also structuring how journalists work and interact.[33] They are intentionally rigid to cope with the temporal demands of news work and require conformity from the journalists who rely on them. Content management systems make news work possible while simultaneously imposing constraints on what is possible.

Taking seriously the objects of journalism contributes to a robust view of journalistic authority as encompassing not only journalist-audience and journalist-source relations but also journalist-technology relations. The production and distribution of authoritative utterances takes place within sociotechnical systems comprising complex communicative networks. As these arrangements solidify, they come to have great power in shaping news as a form of public knowledge by facilitating certain possibilities while proscribing others. In making such a claim, it needs to be said that foregrounding objects of journalism does not equate to technological determinism. As Pablo Boczkowski's study of early online news adoption at newspapers demonstrates, technological systems shape and are shaped by economic and professional forces.[34]

The relationship between objects of journalism and journalistic authority is also visible through the attachment of symbolic value to ordinary news objects. Journalists use material objects to create "the 'mark' of authority,"[35] which in the wider literature on authority is generally associated with such objects as a judge's gavel and robe. Even objects that are not pure adornment, such as a stethoscope, become part of the apparatus that structures the particular authority relation between the doctor and the patient. Marks of authority are no less important for journalism. In possessing mediated authority rather than an interpersonal variety, journalists have created a diverse range of recognizable symbols that contribute to their authoritative performance, from the dangling press pass to the local television news crew live at the scene with camera, lights, and microphone emblazoned with the station logo. Textual patterns and visual objects, from the Gothic lettering of a newspaper name to the carefully constructed television news set, are intentionally created to establish a particular mode of authority relation with audiences.[36] Such choices are not merely aesthetic; they reveal durable understandings of how news actors pursue legitimacy.

THE TECHNOLOGY OF AUTHORITATIVE WITNESSING

Technology not only makes journalistic mediation possible, it structures what this mediation can look like and how journalists can imagine their work in pursuit of authority. The intermeshing of journalistic authority and technology can be made clear through journalism's exaltation of the reporter as witness—a situation in which bodily presence underpins claims to journalistic authority.[37] The history of journalistic witnessing is long, predating both the conventions of the interview and the development of familiar recording technologies associated with modern witnessing. The epistolary origins of the term *correspondent* hint at the longer tradition of firsthand accounts in newspapers. With witnessing, the authority of the in-person account takes precedence over the assemblage of journalistic knowledge through authorized knowers discussed in the previous chapter on news sources. Journalistic witnessing is a cultural practice infused with meaning that supports journalistic authority. Bearing witness involves both authorial presence to observe something and the subsequent recounting of what was witnessed to audiences at a distance. Journalism's right to be listened to becomes the right to be listened to *at a distance* in moments where the audience cannot be a direct witness itself.

This duality of journalistic witnessing as both present and distant occurs through the intervention of objects of journalism without which journalistic witnessing cannot occur. Witnessing shows that authority is not synonymous with experience; it also necessitates the mediation of experience through technology. Over time, technologies of witnessing have changed drastically, from written accounts taking weeks or months to arrive to digital video instantaneously relayed through a satellite. These shifts are not only about expediency or improved efficiency. What needs to be recognized is how the changing technology of witnessing alters the norms, values, and expectations of journalistic witnessing that, in turn, affect the development of arguments supporting journalistic authority.

Witnessing as both presence and relay has a long iconic history in journalism. Examples include Herbert Morrison's radio description of the Hindenburg disaster, Edward R. Murrow's rooftop reporting from the Battle of Britain, the 1965 Bloody Sunday attack on civil rights marchers in Selma, Alabama, and police brutality at the 1968 Democratic National Convention in Chicago.[38] The successive development of media technologies—photography, film, wire services, satellite transmission, video, digital imaging—have been touted as enhancing journalists' ability to relay their accounts to distant audiences. The letter is replaced by the voice, the written account by the photograph, the delayed account by the immediate one. Once impossible or extremely limited, live witnessing eventually became a hackneyed slogan, particularly for local television stations offering a diet of eyewitness news. Technological improvements have made distant witnessing a commonplace occurrence, further feeding the association between geographic presence and journalistic authority. The process of conveying news accounts across time and space collapses "the distinctions between report, role, and technology."[39] To speak of journalistic witnessing requires exploring, for example, how the presence of the camera in the space of witnessing and the technologies that bring images to audiences in their own spaces become woven into arguments for journalistic authority.

Technologies of mediation are not reserved for journalism. This emphasis on objects of journalism also helps examine tensions developing around the ability of citizen witnesses to mediate experience at a distance outside of news channels.[40] Just as the photocopier altered what could be kept secret and what could be shared for an earlier generation, camera-equipped smartphones capable of taking a picture or video and then uploading it online to be instantly shared with others has transformed witnessing. The proliferation of photographs has been astounding.[41] And this is not a hypothetical argument: a survey of protestors in Egypt's Tahrir Square in 2011 found half of them shared pictures of the protests.[42] New improvements point to the even greater proliferation of recording devices, including such wearable recorders as Google Glass.[43]

In the end, it bears repeating that journalistic authority cannot be understood from normative commitments and organizational forms alone. Discussions of authority must also include how technologies of journalism are used, how they shape these uses, and how the patterns and structures that emerge attain power as legitimated means for relaying experience.

TECHNOLOGICAL INNOVATION AND JOURNALISTIC AUTHORITY

Despite the historical codevelopment of journalism and technology, discussions of the contemporary news environment are dominated by technology. As either an agent of creative destruction or simply destruction—depending on one's outlook—this emphasis on technology shapes how journalism, and therefore journalistic authority, can be thought about. This section brings together discursive and material perspectives to examine the case of a new class of journalists who work for very little, never waste time by the watercooler, and follow directions without any grumbling: robots. More precisely, the focus is on natural language generation software utilizing algorithms to convert existing data into news stories mimicking the work of humans.[44] A raft of start-ups has emerged, led by Narrative Science (originally dubbed StatsMonkey) and Automated Insights (originally StatSheet). To date, the software has been used primarily for writing collegiate sports stories and summaries of financial filings for corporations. Automated Insights rose to prominence when Yahoo Fantasy Football began using the software to offer automated breakdowns of users' weekly performances. The Associated Press now uses this same software to author stories about the earnings reports of publicly traded companies.

News organizations have partnered with these technology companies to produce automated journalism, or the creation of news texts via computer programs that exclude the human author from the newswriting process.[45] This mechanized newswriting begins with the creation of an appropriate lexicon and a list of possible news narratives or frames. For example, the precise language of business writing differs from the color of sports writing, just as what is newsworthy for a business story contrasts with sports stories. Once unleashed, the software takes available data—box scores and SEC filings, for example—and generates an original news story organized around narrative principles concocted through the software's algorithm. The final story emerges fully formed out of the decision-making processes built into the natural language generation software. To date, the potential for this technology lies chiefly in extending the total range of available news stories to take advantage of the long-tail market for news. A collegiate swim meet or earnings report of a smaller Fortune 500 company may not attract the readers necessary to warrant the resources of a human journalist to craft a story, but the technology easily and cheaply produces a passable news story for the small number of readers who may be interested. In theory, these small audiences add up to sizable ones in aggregate, leading to increased advertising revenue.

Although automated journalism resides on the margins of journalism, appearing more as a supplement than a threat, the technology has advanced enough to elicit a closer look at the technological and journalistic assumptions embedded in its emerging practices. Automated journalism develops through a network of interrelated systems arising out of a confluence of technological innovations, design decisions, commercial motives, and contextual media factors. Computer scientists have made sufficient advancements in artificial intelligence and natural language generation to make the software possible, organizations increasingly make available data able to be analyzed, and online publishers seeking both more content and reduced costs becoming willing customers.[46] What's also needed is an audience willing to accept automated journalism as a legitimate mode of cultural production. In this way, automated journalism fits within a larger cultural shift in which humans regularly interact with nonhumans or automated systems in everyday life. All of these technological, economic, and cultural factors coalesce in particular ways to shape the practices of automated journalism. There is no predetermined outcome.

Automated journalism comprises not only a set of technological practices but also ways of understanding and thinking about journalism and what makes for an authoritative account. These understandings are expressed in the discourse accompanying the expansion of robot news, primarily by the proponents of the technology in their efforts to popularize it and by human journalists trying to interpret what this means for them. Just as the technology develops, so does discourse about the technology. Automated journalism, which begins as an unfamiliar practice outside of existing discourses of journalistic authority, is made familiar.

Proponents of the technology embed automated journalism in narratives of innovation. All new products require the creation of an explicit problem or deficit to be ameliorated.[47] In particular, new services—like automated writing—directed at long-standing practices—like news—have to overcome entrenched institutional patterns to convince potential customers of their worthiness. Such is the case for Chicago-based Narrative Science, a company that developed out of a partnership between the journalism and computer science programs at Northwestern University. While its initial target was news, the company now positions its product as a general automated-writing service useful to a number of information-based industries. Its marketing materials emphasize its Quill software as providing both a coherent story structure and the ability to extract meaning: "Quill uncovers the key facts and interesting insights in the data and transforms them into natural language. The result? Narratives that rival your best analyst or writer, produced at a scale, speed and quality only possible with automation."[48] North Carolina–based competitor Automated Insights describes its services through similar language: "Automated Insights' patented Wordsmith platform transforms Big Data into narrative reports by spotting patterns, correlations and key insights in the data and then describing them in plain English, just like a human would."[49] Both companies stress three factors: cost-effective efficient processes, the ability to extract and explain patterns in data, and a mimetic quality imitating human thinking and writing.

Executives at Narrative Science and Automated Insights have been quite vocal in explaining the value their products bring to journalism. Narrative Science CEO Stuart Frankel defined a vision of automated journalism as providing a collaboration between humans and machines: "We can generate parts of a story from the data that a computer is better at pulling, and a human can add the color or interviews conducted to broaden the appeal."[50] This involves assigning tasks to the automation software that are easier for a computer to do so as to create excess time for humans to engage in more in-depth stories. As Automated Insights founder Robbie Allen predicted, "We'll look back years from now and think it's funny that we ever had people doing that stuff."[51] This language of cooperation is accompanied by bolder predictions. Frankel boasted about the flexibility of his service: "If the data is there, and a human can write that story using the data, then we can write that story."[52] Allen went further in envisaging how improvements in artificial intelligence will erode the division of labor between human and computer authors: "Because it's algorithmic, it can only get better over time. . . . Within five years, our writing will be as good as the best sportswriters out there. And it's going to be difficult for humans to compete."[53] Forecasts of quick progress in automated journalism also came from Narrative Science founder Kris Hammond, who told the *New York Times* that in five years "a computer program will win a Pulitzer Prize—and I'll be damned if it's not our technology."[54] Although these are inherently self-promotional statements coming from executives vying to grow their businesses, the future they present should not be overlooked. They reflect both an understanding of automated journalism as augmenting traditional news and a vision for surpassing the work of human journalists. This latter scenario did not go unnoticed by journalists.

The arrival of automated journalism raises obvious questions about human labor.[55] Modern work is replete with stories of humans being replaced by machines, from factory workers to travel agents.[56] Given the economic state of journalism and the imperative for journalists to do more with less, it is not surprising to find fear that these algorithms will result in smaller newsrooms instead of freeing up reporters to do other projects. As *Pando Daily* speculated, publishers will "realize that an algorithm is cheaper than an actual reporter. That's when news stories become commodities: easy to produce, easy to replicate, easy to distribute. Combine those factors with the decline of digital ad dollars and newsroom layoffs, and it's no wonder that we are seeing a crisis in journalism."[57] *Wired*'s Steven Levy posited a similar concern in a profile of Narrative

Science: "As the computers get more accomplished and have access to more and more data, their limitations as storytellers will fall away. It might take a while, but eventually even a story like this one could be produced without, well, me."[58] The history of journalism is filled with examples of human labor replaced through automation (e.g., typesetting) or rendered obsolete via new technologies (e.g., photographic darkrooms) that inspire apprehension over any particular innovation that might lead to fewer workers. But automated journalism strikes at the heart of journalistic work in unprecedented ways.

Viewing the emergence of automated journalism through the lens of journalistic authority raises questions regarding its impact on journalism as a particular epistemic practice. Pursuing this argument requires taking a broader view of simmering tensions regarding what makes journalism authoritative. Chapter 2 depicted the long-running division between conceptions of news writing as a mechanistic process steeped in a foundational commitment to objectivity and as a creative act drawing on the qualities of narrative, language, and aesthetics to convey a story.[59] The first sense reflects the informational view of journalism,[60] which has been codified in presentational practices and techniques (e.g., the news lede, the inverted pyramid, quotation usage). This mechanistic style of news also has come to occupy a normative role as the symbol of what news writing looks like.[61] By contrast, the creative mode reflects journalism's literary roots and the appeal to noninformational ideals like emotion.[62] This duality moves from questions of form to larger questions regarding the origins of journalistic authority. The informational mode connects to an ideal of journalism as a mirror reflecting society back to itself through the news. The intervention of the journalist is to collect and convey information to audiences. Conversely, the creative mode reflects an understanding of the journalist as an author presenting an interpretation that gives meaning to events in the world. Another way of looking at this tension is to consider the informational mode as externalizing insight, which is then discovered and rendered into news. Meanwhile, the creative mode situates insight as the internal product of human interaction with the physical world of events. These positions are presented as a stark rift, but in practice they blur together to a great degree. News reporters seeking to communicate a faithful account of events in the world also add color to make their stories more memorable. Newspapers and news sites seek clever writing and television journalists prefer pleasing visual arrangements.

What automated journalism does is cleave these two sides apart by perpetuating the ideal of algorithmic writing as able to overcome human barriers to objective reporting. Understanding this argument requires stepping back to examine the broader role of algorithms as the preeminent decision-making technologies of contemporary life. An algorithm is an inscribed procedure that produces an output based on inputs—for example, a search engine returns an ordered set of pages based on a user's query (along with other contextual factors), or an online shopping site recommends a product based on past behavior and preferences.

Algorithms permeate many sectors of contemporary life, often in invisible ways.[63] In the realm of knowledge production, supporters herald algorithms for purportedly objective decision making that avoids the cognitive biases that plague humans.[64] Yet care must be taken not to confer upon algorithmic processes the quality of inherent neutrality. Like any technology, algorithms have politics.[65] And the degree to which this handover of tasks previously confined to humans occurs requires an engagement with the politics underlying these algorithmic processes.[66] All algorithms contain what Tarleton Gillespie calls a "knowledge logic" governing issues of inclusion and relevance.[67] They are encoded with particular criteria that are not value-free. For example, the decision of an algorithm to select stories with a familiar political viewpoint while obscuring stories with opposing views stems from a particular judgment about how one should act as a citizen.[68] However, these embedded logics are regularly hidden from view—often justified on competitive grounds.[69] Users receive only the end product, which precludes easy accountability.[70]

Automated journalism shifts the role of algorithms from the selection and presentation of news stories to their actual creation. In doing so, existing narratives of algorithmic neutrality get attached to nonhuman-authored stories. This discourse in turn contributes to journalists' fears that automated journalism will replace them because the news account, as a basic reflection of external events, is not the product of the individual but the events depicted. And mirrors are easy to replace. The ultimate irony is that the mechanistic writing that journalists tout in supporting claims for their authority is increasingly susceptible to being taken over by machines. Meanwhile, the creators of automated journalism technologies are able to draw on preexisting arguments for journalistic authority when peddling the value of their software for news production.

The discourse surrounding automated journalism indicates a bifurcated imagination as to what constitutes journalistic authority. On the one hand, the authority of the algorithm to produce accurate accounts is based on an assumption regarding the inherently objective nature of machines. While this view elides the human origins of the algorithms and all the nonneutral decisions embedded within their discourse-making practices, it is nonetheless a powerful discourse that weds beliefs about the unemotional operation of technology with the epistemic foundation of objective journalism. Yet the adoption of automated news processes—or even its specter—has led journalists to differentiate themselves from robot news by arguing for the authority of the individual journalist as a creative force irreplaceable by algorithmic writing. On the CNN website, journalism educator Greg Bowers put it this way: "If you're writing briefs that can be easily replicated by a computer, then you're not trying hard enough."[71] Similarly, digital news innovator Steve Buttry told the *American Journalism Review*, "If professional journalists say 'we add value in our writing and reporting,' then we really need to bring value."[72] From this perspective, the rise of automated journalism as a new material form leads the journalistic community to assess its practices in ways that were previously unnecessary before journalists faced robotic challengers. Automated journalism repositions human creativity within discourses of journalistic authority. As Farhad Manjoo made clear in *Slate*: "If we define human creativity as a kind of invention meant to please other human beings, machines would seem ill-suited for the task—computers are good at copying, not at coming up with wholly new things."[73] This viewpoint reduces automated journalism to its mimetic core before holding up the originality of human thinking as an alternative. In the end, these are visions of journalism as both feeling and unfeeling, with foundational arguments emerging on both sides.[74] Any resolution in the near term is unlikely, but the contours of these arguments will continue to take shape in the years to come.

The example of automated journalism, still in a nascent stage, provides a vantage point for examining both shifts in practice and the discourse accompanying technological change. I argue that algorithms should not be reduced to neutral programs executed by unthinking, objective computers but considered as subjective human-made instruments encoded with the particular biases of their creators. As algorithms increasingly become part of news selection and writing, they demand critique for their social and political implications. In particular, the growing role of algorithms in journalism means that journalistic authority can no longer be discussed without referring, in part, to the automated processes that affect what gets produced and what gets seen. Nor should a stark line be drawn between human and algorithmic actors; they are increasingly imbricated in a hybrid sociotechnological system.[75] Understanding journalistic authority in the twenty-first century requires examining the shape of this hybridity in the overall circulation of news as accounts of the world aimed at wide audiences who recognize, on some level, their legitimacy.

RECOGNIZING THE MATERIALITY OF JOURNALISTIC AUTHORITY

Efforts to conceptualize the connection between technology and journalism should begin with Patricia Dooley's observation that the technologies of journalism, from print to broadcasting to online media, were not invented with journalism in mind.[76] Gutenberg did not envision the *New York Times*, Marconi conceived of radio as wireless telegraphy, and Twitter's initial launch stressed mobile status updates instead of eyewitness coverage of breaking news. Rather, the mutual adaptation of journalism to technology and technology to journalism has occurred over centuries. Yet the familiarity of journalism's technological forms obscures this process except when the arrival of new material forms disrupts established modes. Once a technology becomes familiar, its power in shaping news becomes less recognizable. After decades of television, mediated distance seems illusory rather than an accomplishment.

This cannot do if we want to understand journalistic authority. Most conceptions of authority do not focus on technology, even as journalism does not exist without technologies of production and distribution. Disregarding or simplifying the role of technology in how journalism works diminishes understandings of journalistic authority. Instead, we must add the use of material objects to create and distribute news to ideas of journalism as a set of knowledge-producing practices and ways of thinking about these practices.

I argue for the need to assess the journalism-technology authority relation alongside journalism's relations with its sources and its audiences. Technologies shape the possibilities of news practices, and the journalistic use of these technologies shapes their meaning and their incorporation into arguments supporting journalism's legitimacy. Objects of journalism become objects of journalistic authority. This process can be seen in the long history of how technologies of witnessing shape the meanings of witnessing. From written letters to early photojournalistic practices to present-day satellite phones, journalists incorporate these objects into their news-making practices as well as narratives situating their reportage as a legitimate means of communicating events from a distance. Technology is not ancillary to this but integral.

Recognizing and historicizing the journalist-technology relation is a necessary precursor to formulating a critical position to assess the dominant position technology occupies in discourses about contemporary journalism and its future. Great care needs to be taken to avoid falling into the forgetful trap of presentism and its ironic counterpart in which various actors divorce technology from journalism by viewing technology as a separate, external force. Likewise, studies of journalistic innovation need to avoid getting bogged down in the intricacies of a specific technology that may be outdated in a few years. The greater challenge for scholars and practitioners alike is to examine the larger connection between widespread technological change and changing ideas about journalism. As the case of automated journalism demonstrates, technologies become vehicles for expressing the hopes and fears surrounding emerging news forms. Ultimately, we need to attend to the materiality of these technologies as well as the discourses in which they are embedded. The negotiation of new technologies produces moments of introspection that double as public sites in which the various practices, organizational arrangements, and normative commitments that inform journalistic authority become open to debate and renewal.

CHAPTER SEVEN

Challenging Journalistic Authority

The Role of Media Criticism

When President Barack Obama took the dais to deliver the commence-ment speech at Barnard College in 2010, he extolled the graduating students for their creativity and optimism before issuing a hackneyed challenge for the new graduates to use their talents to make their mark on the world. In making this appeal, Obama zeroed in on a familiar target:

> No wonder that faith in our institutions has never been lower, par-ticularly when good news doesn't get the same kind of ratings as bad news anymore. Every day you receive a steady stream of sensa-tionalism and scandal, and stories with a message that suggests change isn't possible, that you can't make a difference, that you won't be able to close that gap between life as it is and life as you want it be. My job today is to tell you don't believe it.[1]

In his rhetorical indictment of journalism as a negative social force ad-versely affecting the actions of others, Obama lambastes news for its bias toward negativity and for emphasizing the shocking over the substan-tive. The suggestion that such choices are guided by ratings further chal-lenges the autonomy of newsworthiness by imputing that commercial imperatives drive journalistic decision making. What is also notable is how familiar this accusation is, which is evident in its succinctness. Obama does not need to explain or provide examples in order for his audience to understand the critique he is making. Instead, he activates a deeper cultural narrative about journalism. Attacking news coverage provides Obama with a popular, preexisting sentiment he can then use as a wedge to promote optimism as a remedy. From the standpoint of journalistic authority, what matters is not the merits of Obama's critique but its persistence.

Media criticism, by which this chapter means publicly mediated critiques of journalism,[2] pervades discourse about journalism. Whether or not these critiques are insightful or sustained,[3] their presence cannot be ignored if journalism is to be considered a culturally embedded form of production charged with creating knowledge about the world. A consistent theme in this book has been to work against treatments of news texts or practices as isolated to instead stress sensitivity to the context in which news is created and circulated. Each news story does not arrive fresh, sui generis, but is embedded in a complex cultural landscape that shapes how news stories are created, circulated, understood, and even challenged. An analysis of journalistic authority would be incomplete without confronting what these discourses look like and how they affect journalism. To this end, this chapter takes up the journalist-critic authority relation.

Treating journalistic authority as the right to be listened to—that is, as a relational quality—necessitates accounting for what discourses *about* journalism do. Chapter 3 invoked the term *metajournalistic discourse* to indicate the arguments journalists make in public on their behalf. But journalists are not alone in their efforts to define journalism and the grounds for its authority.[4] Instead, they are only one set of voices in a complicated rhetorical environment. To the growing heterogeneity of news forms in the postindustrial news landscape, we must be add the heterogeneity of narratives about journalism occurring inside and outside of the news.[5] Metajournalistic discourse should be recognized as a complex space of struggle over the grounds of journalistic authority.

Although the terrain of media criticism contains a broad array of different actors speaking in different places about journalism, this chapter narrows slightly to focus on negative appraisals of the press. The central concern of this chapter is what it means for journalism's authority to be subject to pervasive scrutiny. In particular, the familiar charge of liberal bias will be explored, as it has become deeply embedded in discussions of contemporary journalism. The chapter also considers how digital media extend the landscape of media criticism in new ways.

WHERE DOES MEDIA CRITICISM COME FROM?

Taking up media criticism as an object of inquiry requires starting with the assertion that all criticism comes from somewhere. It is not detached discourse whose meaning can be understood through analyzing its textual traces alone but rather the product of the social practices of particular actors. Beyond examining the text itself, analyses of media criticism should address three contextual aspects: the normative grounds on which criticism rests, the strategic aims and institutionalized settings of the critics, and the communicative means through which criticism is created and circulated. This wider perspective better illuminates the intentions behind media criticism as a purposive discursive act aimed at affecting news practices.

To criticize is to express disapproval, which leads to a primary analytical need to query the explicit or implicit bases on which such disapproval is rendered. Accusations of deficient performances require the enunciation of a corresponding ideal that is not being met. Any evaluative judgment rests on criteria, and these criteria are social products to be examined. With journalism specifically, much criticism lobbed at the news is predicated on democratic normative preconceptions that are themselves rarely an object of reflection. The primacy of normativity over other dimensions (aesthetics or effectiveness, for example) dictates how journalism is judged. But journalistic normativity itself should be seen as an object of inquiry.[6] Norms are not natural objects but ideological constructions that organize and constrain the actions of various social actors. For example, the prevailing objectivity norm operating in much of Western journalism connects to larger ideas of liberal democracy.[7] Beyond epistemological questions of objectivity, attending to embedded assumptions concerning the communicative roles for journalists and their audiences as rational political actors is vital. To utilize this normative position to assess the news becomes an exercise in arguing on behalf of the social value of this position. From this perspective, media criticism carries with it entrenched ideas of how society should operate.

A second element of media criticism involves the strategic aims of its creators.[8] Critical assessments emerge from situated actors, and what their positions indicate about the intentions of this criticism needs attention. This inquiry includes not only individual goals but institutionalized forms of media criticism that have developed. A number of organizations operate with the sole purpose of critiquing news coverage from a particular perspective.[9] In the United States, the right-leaning Media Research Center declares that its "sole mission is to expose and neutralize the propaganda arm of the Left: the national news media."[10] This statement contains both a core assumption—journalists not only harbor political bias but actively work on behalf of liberal policies—and a remedy—amelioration through public revelation. The Media Research Center carries out the latter through continuous media monitoring, including with its NewsBusters website and the syndicated columns of its founder, L. Brent Bozell III. On the left, Fairness and Accuracy in Reporting and Media Matters for America—and Media Lens in the United Kingdom—argue that the news media too often present elite opinions or fall prey to influence from advertisers. The intent of these groups is twofold: to pressure journalists into altering their coverage and to cater to their own interpretive communities.[11] For example, the website HonestReporting.com, which "monitors the news for bias, inaccuracy, or other breach of journalistic standards in coverage of the Arab-Israeli conflict," promotes news coverage from a pro-Israel perspective by chastising major news outlets that fail to do so.[12] One lead story indicative of this mission criticized the *New York Times* for its reluctance to include the hostile actions of Palestinians in its coverage of peace talks.[13] Through such concerted efforts to shape news coverage, these organizations simultaneously reinforce narratives about the power of journalism to influence audiences' understandings of the world while lodging critiques that threaten journalists' arguments for authority.[14]

A third aspect of media criticism to be examined concerns the channels through which criticism is created and distributed. The focus in this chapter is on public criticism distributed through various media channels.[15] These media should be seen as more than just neutral conduits through which criticism passes. Instead, the affordances of any medium affect the barriers to being a communicator, the shape and attributes of messages, and the conditions of reception and response. Cable television news, talk radio, and online sites all differ as media for the expression of discontent with media discourse.[16]

In sum, viewing media criticism as a product of preconceived normative assumptions carried out by actors with strategic aims through a media channel lays the foundation to assess its relationship with journalistic authority. All accusations of illegitimacy contain a case for what legitimate practices look like. To be in a position to establish this duality is to occupy a position of power to demarcate the boundaries of acceptable action.[17] This is true for journalism, as critiques of particular news practices and arguments about quality call into question the legitimacy of journalism.[18] At the same time, definitional control over journalism can never be total. Instead, contestation swirls around efforts to state what is good or bad journalism in any time or place. Media criticism, both in its internal iterations and its external varieties, exposes the fault lines running through public arguments for journalistic authority. To add clarity to the diffuse discursive terrain of media criticism, we can turn to one of its most prominent forms: the assumption of widespread liberal bias.

CHARGES OF LIBERAL BIAS

In the simplest terms, charges of liberal bias accuse journalists of harboring an internalized leftist political worldview that warps news coverage through the inclusion of either unchecked assumptions or purposive covert attempts to distort news stories. Charges of such outright bias rarely gain much credence in academic circles, as journalism scholars correctly point to other entrenched biases that push news toward conflict, oversimplification, sensationalism, and acquiescence to powerful officials.[19] Often accusations of liberal bias get dismissed as either naive oversimplifications or conniving attempts by conservatives to affect news coverage. Yet the degree to which these claims persist in discourses about news warrants a closer look. This section will not argue on behalf of those who make claims of liberal bias but instead reflects on what decades of sustained allegations of liberal bias mean for journalistic authority. Understanding journalism to be embedded within a social context necessitates thinking through what these bias claims look like and what their function is.

For starters, accusations of liberal press bias connect to the difficult negotiation of authority and antiauthoritarianism within contemporary US conservative politics. Although embracing patriotism and militarism, conservatives articulate a simultaneous disdain for the state and advocate for smaller government. The political turn to neoliberalism emphasizes individual rights and unfettered economic functioning over the centralizing tendencies of government. Although journalists lack ruling authority, they do function as a centralizing communicative power in that they purport to represent the real back to the public—a weighty social purpose. Charges of liberal bias focus specifically on the symbolic power wielded by journalists—also a familiar topic within the academic study of journalism through such foundational concepts as gatekeeping, agenda setting, and framing. In a shared sense, scholars deploying these terms and critics alleging liberal bias express concern over the concentration of representational power into the hands of the few. These arguments rest on juxtaposing journalism's own normative ideals with the actual news products the public receives.[20] As a salve, many in both camps champion the democratizing potential of digital media forms to diversify media content and allow new voices to participate.

But from this point, these two critical paths sharply diverge. Those that indict the media for its leftward tendencies begin from the assumption of a chasm pitting an elite news media (with *media* often used as a singular noun) with its leftist slant against an unseen victimized audience subjected to an endless stream of biased news. Bias claims cleave communicators from their audiences, with journalism rendered illegitimate by its prejudices. This argument requires the existence of both of these groups—elite leftist journalists and unseen masses subjected to their work—to offer a coherent critique. At a fundamental level, the values of urban, coastal, and educated journalists are held to be different—and not in a positive sense—from the majority of the nation. As with any antielitist argument, journalists are accused of holding themselves to be superior to the public they are meant to serve.

Right-wing media criticism has become a central component of conservative political identity. Commonly held assumptions about news bias strengthen interpretive communities by providing a point of opposition that becomes a shared rallying point.[21] In their analysis of conservative media content, Kathleen Hall Jamieson and Joseph Cappella demonstrate how the term *liberal media* functions as an example of semantic priming that conjures up a common enemy in mainstream journalism.[22] Interpretations of bias appear frequently across conservative media, which gives rise to "a shared vocabulary for dismissing mainstream interpretations of the news."[23] Accusations of liberal bias appear across conservative media in political talk radio, blogs, magazines, books, editorial pages, and cable news. These sites are not discrete, but deeply intertwined across conservative media. Bernard Goldberg provides one example of the interconnectedness of actors engaged in constant, one-sided accusations of liberal bias. Aside from authoring the bestselling books *Bias: A CBS Insider Exposes How the Media Distort the News* and *Arrogance—Rescuing America from the Media Elite*, Goldberg regularly appears on Fox News Channel's *The O'Reilly Factor* to comment on news. He also runs a blog and has over 100,000 Twitter followers. As a pundit, Goldberg has attained the stature to build a career largely focused on the niche issue of liberal bias.

To this community, even the invocation of the *mainstream media* carries with it the connotation of leftward bias. Such is the power of the link between *mainstream* and *liberal* that the two are often used synonymously in critiques of the news. As a frame, bias becomes a way of understanding the news. It is a decoder ring that bestows on audiences the effect of feeling savvy for seeing through journalistic bias.[24] In the end, Jamieson and Cappella argue, conservative media become an echo chamber of like opinions while simultaneously framing mainstream news as hostile to conservatives and, therefore, deserving of constant suspicion. This double move of creating a public arena for unquestioned conservative opinion while nurturing interpretive strategies for dismissing nonconservative news creates a space devoid of disconfirming viewpoints.

Finally, charges of liberal bias need to be connected to larger political battles. Within the conservative media landscape, critiques of mainstream media liberal bias are imbricated with larger political critiques of the Democratic Party, liberalism, and specific policies. The fluidity of boundaries among the press, a political party, and a set of ideas works strategically to construct the perception of an interlinked, dominant left-wing ideology permeating life in the United States. In these arguments, examples of the liberal media–bias critique are not hard to come by. But understanding how these arguments unfold requires delving into claims of media bias to explore their inner workings and their significance for journalistic authority

MEDIA CRITICISM AND "BEHIND THE BIAS"

Liberal media bias is a regular target for Sean Hannity, host of the eponymous *Hannity* prime-time program on the Fox News Channel. Hannity, who began as a right-wing talk radio host, routinely peppers his attacks on the political left with jabs at journalists for their biases. But on April 22, 2011, Hannity dedicated his entire hour-long program to the topic in a documentary-style episode bearing the title "Behind the Bias: The History of the Liberal Media." The title itself gives away the program's strategy of interspersing historical and contemporary examples to go beyond isolated invocations of the media-bias frame described above by Jamieson and Cappella. The special narrativizes bias by constructing a historical framework that weaves an all-encompassing story rooting contemporary accusations of liberal media bias in a postwar journalistic mentality. Its goal is to provide the audience with more reasons not to trust what they read, see, and hear—unless it is through conservative media.

To make this argument stick, "Behind the Bias" turns to a parade of speakers that itself reinforces the echo chamber critique of right-wing commentary. The program shifts among interviews with former members of the George W. Bush administration (Karl Rove, Dana Perino), a former Republican National Committee chairman (Ed Gillespie), a right-wing academic associated with the conservative American Enterprise Institute think tank (Gerard Alexander), the founder of a right-wing media criticism organization (Brent Bozell), and several Fox News commentators (Sarah Palin, Juan Williams, Byron York, Doug Schoen, Dana Perino). The episode also includes commentators, bloggers, and radio hosts from across the conservative media spectrum (Michelle Malkin, John Hinderaker, Hugh Hewitt, John Fund, William McGowan, Dorothy Rabinowitz), which connects *Hannity* to various conservative media outlets, including the *Wall Street Journal* editorial page, *Newsmax*, the

Washington Examiner, the *Weekly Standard,* and talk radio. In short, the episode makes its case through an array of political and media voices united by their conservative beliefs. This common vision reinforces the unified message running throughout the hour-long program.

There is nothing subtle about the accusations lobbed at the news media in "Behind the Bias." Right at the top of the program, Hannity introduces the special with two inbuilt assertions that extend through the entire hour. First, liberal-media bias exists and, second, it produces victims:

> And welcome to this special edition of *Hannity*, "Behind the Bias," a close-up look at the Obama-mania media's liberal bias. Now, it is common knowledge that the mainstream media from the major television networks to the country's most influential newspapers are biased against the GOP. Tonight, we'll examine some of the major scandals that resulted from this bias, and the victims that it has left in its wake.[25]

The attachment of "common knowledge" to the initial assertion sets the tone; the special does not take a prosecutorial angle of employing evidence to convince viewers. Instead, it starts from the assumption of a shared conviction that bias exists and then takes up the task of providing an overview with a historical gloss. Hannity's next statement after the opening takes this tack: "Republicans may have learned to live with media bias and even to fight against it. But, to many the roots of this bias remains a mystery." The assertion of enmity toward the press is then followed by a shift to a historical frame. Hannity adds, "The media's hostility towards the GOP first emerged as a bizarre tendency to apologize for America's enemies," which serves as a lead-in to a historical segment portraying the American news media after World War II as working against US policy interests.

Apart from this opening segment, the majority of the special deviates from the promise of a historical accounting of liberal bias to instead rehash a series of recent incidents that have become emblematic of systemic bias to those on the right. These include the retracted 2004 *60 Minutes* story on George W. Bush's National Guard service, Katie Couric's interview with Sarah Palin in 2008, and Fox News commentator Juan

Williams's termination from NPR in 2010. The special also paid particular attention to the *New York Times*, which has long been a conservative target. Hannity channels this critique by arguing that bias has caused the paper to decline: "The *New York Times*, long revered as the gold standard in print journalism, lost its lofty position as a result of bias." Later, the special includes quotes from Michelle Malkin criticizing the *Times* for working against conservatives: "They're explicit overt agenda was to try and chill conservative thought and criminalize conservative speech." This statement is immediately followed by media critic Brent Bozell questioning the newspaper's independence: "The *New York Times* lost its journalistic mind. It went from being an unquestioned left-of-center newspaper to a radical left-wing newspaper. It might as well be produced by the Obama administration." These claims connect to critiques of specific stories, but their expansiveness envelops the whole of the news organization in a manner that inoculates against any other claims made by the newspaper. Everything it publishes—now and in the future—becomes suspect.

Beyond identifying incidents of political slant, "Behind the Bias" links the perpetration of left-wing news bias to the victimization of conservatives. These narratives permeate the episode, rising to the top in the final segment that Hannity introduces through portraying bias as incontrovertible: "Now based on all the evidence that you have seen so far not many would dare to dispute the existence of a liberal bias in today's so-called mainstream media. But perhaps no one is more acutely aware of this and that bias than those who have been adversely affected by it." This segment goes on to include George W. Bush, John McCain, Sarah Palin, and Juan Williams, who was given the final word of the program: "If you stop and review these items, this kind of media bias in this country, then you can see how pernicious it is and how extensive and cancerous it can be. I sit here as a victim of it." The language of victimization shifts the focus from the mere slanting of stories toward a leftist viewpoint to deliberate acts of journalistic subterfuge to manipulate public opinion and silence nonconformists. This viewpoint provides viewers with reasons not only to dismiss news portrayals but also to work against them.

To solidify this last point, the episode explicitly situates news audiences as also victims, albeit with a newfound savviness for deflecting liberal media bias. Hugh Hewitt makes this claim overt by noting: "The

American voter is beginning to develop a sense of sophistication that they are no longer so easily manipulable by media narrative that they used to be." He adds that in contrast to leftist media manipulation, conservative opinion will prevail: "We still win anyway, conservatives do, because we've got facts and truth on our side more often than not." This sentiment further entrenches the victimization narrative by presenting journalists as purposively eliding or attacking conservative policies that would undoubtedly benefit society. It also goads viewers into seeing themselves as victims of liberal-media bias who can respond with greater distrust of the news and increased support for conservative causes.

Writing off Hannity's coordinated attack on journalists would not be difficult. Most notable is what "Behind the Bias" omits to make its case. Historically, it attacks the press for undermining US policy while ignoring the complicity of journalists in abetting McCarthyism in the 1950s or the Vietnam War in the 1960s.[26] It confronts the *New York Times* for its liberal bias under editor Howell Raines but omits the newspaper's role in ginning up the government's flimsy case for invading Iraq in 2003 during his editorship.[27] It plays up the role of blogs in bringing down CBS News's Dan Rather for his *60 Minutes* reporting on Bush's National Guard service without referencing the aggressive reporting of other mainstream news outlets challenging CBS. It invokes the Valerie Plame scandal but ignores the Bush administration's own involvement in prosecuting the case. The omissions could go on and on, but the point is not to pick apart the factuality of the episode. To do so would distract from attending to what it does to further entrench the mythos of liberal-media bias. In the end, Hannity's special must be recognized for its sustained effort to undermine the legitimacy of much of the news media.

The attacks of Hannity and others provide a public narrative for how to see the press outside of how the press presents itself. The bias trope offers an organizing principle that condenses perceptions about individual journalists or individual stories into a master narrative about journalism. This trope also gives rise to narratives of victimization by the Right, provoking calls for a shift in news coverage. For example, Fox News Channel's longtime slogan of "Fair and Balanced" has long been derided as absurdly false considering the right-wing slant of its programming. But this critique misses the point; the insistence that Fox

News is fair and balanced is itself an act of media criticism positioning other news as leftist. Such positioning also encourages new streams of conservative media to be built on the mythology of left-wing bias. This latter development gains further traction with new waves of media criticism via digital media, discussed below.

What "Behind the Bias" ultimately illustrates is the broad range of discourses about journalism that circulate alongside the news and shape how it is understood. The work of journalists to construct public narratives about their work must be contextualized within a broader discursive field of competing forces. Even differentiating between internal or external accounts is difficult; Hannity waffles on the question of whether he is a journalist,[28] while the Fox News Channel clearly defines itself as journalism even as many deride it as not news. Recognizing this messy discursive space in which persistent critiques occur broadens understandings of the cultural processes through which journalistic authority arises and is questioned. Journalistic authority is not static or unified but a matrix of practices and meanings responsive to the larger context in which the news is created and consumed. The relational view of journalistic authority situates this contestation as an indelible component of how news is made culturally meaningful. Criticism shapes the context in which audiences consume news, and audiences have become increasingly skeptical.[29] Hannity certainly seeks to fuel this skepticism through the lens of liberal-media bias. And, increasingly, audiences are gaining communicative tools to make their opinions known.

AN ERA OF CONSTANT CRITICISM

Away from the copious reporting on national and international affairs occupying its front pages, the *New York Times* regularly produces fashion-trend stories attuned to the latest sartorial innovations springing up around New York. When the newspaper published a story on the return of the monocle as trendy eyewear, "One Part Mr. Peanut, One Part Hipster Chic,"[30] online ridicule was swift. On social media, groans and parodies quickly appeared. Twitter users vied to outdo each other with humorous riffs, with even Mr. Peanut lending his support for the eyewear on the official Planters account. Aside from pointing to the absurdity of monocle mania, these commentators used the incident to dissect the larger phenomenon of *Times* trends articles. This discussion led back to the *Times* when public editor Margaret Sullivan took up the issue in a column celebrating the inanity of the piece, whose silliness was already recognized by the style section staff.[31] This response from Sullivan spawned yet another set of reactions critical of her response to critics. Discussion of the newspaper's editorial judgment in its lifestyle reporting led to questions ranging from the overreliance on ludicrous fads to elitist tendencies in its culture reporting. For example, the *Gothamist* blog chided Sullivan for ignoring deeper issues in how the newspaper discerns trends: "Sullivan misses one very important characteristic of these trend stories: the fact that an inordinate amount of them are essentially puff lifestyle pieces about the absurdly wealthy for the absurdly wealthy."[32] What began as self-parody turned into substantive critique. But beyond its idiosyncrasies, the monocle incident helps illustrate two central aspects of how media criticism works in the digital era: the expanded terrain of mediated criticism and the collapse of boundaries between news consumption and external commentary.

Along with nearly every form of mediated communication, the rise of digital networked technologies has greatly expanded the terrain of metajournalistic discourse. Previously, participation in the mediated public sphere—at least as independent from established media institutions—required access to expensive equipment and channels of distribution, be it a newsstand or broadcast spectrum space. In the era of mass communication, this could be enormously expensive. New technologies—e.g., the copy machine—enabled the spread of underground publications, but this was nearly insignificant in a larger sense of what audiences were exposed to. Some nonelite voices appear in the news to talk about the news, for example, through newspaper letters to the editor. While highly curated, letters pages provide a space for voices from outside of journalism to directly respond to news content, including negative critiques. In print form, the selection of letters results from a process overseen by an editor who has her own understanding of what qualifies as an acceptable letter and how such letters complement the overall paper.[33] In addition, newspaper readers' voices also appear through ombudsmen, public editors, and reader representatives, although they are often condensed to fit with the narrative needs of the column. In turn, the allegiances of reader representatives vary from being independent advocates for readers to being representatives or ambassadors of newspapers.[34]

These forms of journalist-controlled criticism differ from the discourses produced outside news. Given the diversifying ability of digital news consumers to become producers, or "produsers,"[35] journalism scholars have rightfully devoted a great deal of attention to studies of citizen journalism, participatory culture, and user-generated content.[36] Less studied has been how these means of content creation also become new means for media criticism.[37] Social media, blogs, and comments sections make possible a whole conversation around news reporting existing alongside the reporting itself. This gives rise to the "crowd-criticism" of the news media through competition over appropriate frames and accusations of bias.[38] While the diversification of voices makes it more difficult for any one voice to be amplified,[39] social media sites facilitate the multiplication of voices through sharing the posts of others.

At a grassroots level, the audience as news sentinel is perhaps best summarized in the statement "We can fact-check your ass." The "we" in this sentence is telling. In his history of blogging, Scott Rosenberg labeled this quote, attributed to blogger Ken Layne in 2001, "a war cry" for the nascent blogosphere.[40] Years before Facebook and Twitter arrived, blogging offered an accessible structure for building networks of amateur media critics able to contest news stories.[41] The technological interface facilitated challenges to the "monovocality" of contemporary news, to use Barnhurst and Nerone's term,[42] by stressing the partiality of any news account.

The combative nature of digital media criticism should not be overlooked. A wide range of voices encompassing everything from angry individuals to well-funded organizations utilizes digital media channels to challenge news content and place pressure on journalists to alter their future coverage. Through the dynamic of advocatory gatekeeping pressure,[43] actors engaged in media criticism work strategically—and often in concert—to effect change in news coverage patterns. This concept rests on the ongoing assumption of journalism's symbolic power to select and frame news. To contest this power, a community of critics attacks news practices to force a shift in the tone of the coverage of a particular story or to get journalists to amplify or dampen coverage.

A second issue, which has received far less attention, results from the growth of social media as sites for sharing and consuming digital news. In contrast to direct access to news—e.g., going to the home page of a news site, searching for stories via Google News, attaining stories via RSS, etc.—users confront news stories within a situation in which often an extra layer of meaning has been added to the story by the sharer.[44] The cocirculation of news stories and criticism has become a fixture of social media. Twitter or Facebook users sharing the link of a news story can attach commentary or explanation—whether positive or negative—to encourage their followers or friends to interact with a story. Even within news sites, the inclusion of space for user comments immediately following a news account blurs the boundaries between journalist and reader.[45] Although comments sections are often hampered by incivility,[46] they indicate new formations in which journalists and their audiences come into contact in the same textual space.[47]

Both social-media sharing and online comments result in news stories circulating within the same space as their critiques.[48] News stories are enveloped in extratextual meaning that frames for the reader why content is shared. Given the popularity of the *New York Times*'s monocle story as a target of online ridicule, many readers likely first came across the story as enmeshed in mockery, thus providing a preexisting interpretive lens shaping how the story was read. The consequence of the collapse of the space between criticism and the target of criticism is the further erosion of the news story as a standalone text. It problematizes efforts to pinpoint a fixed beginning and end for any news story.

Even if journalists continue to provide the bulk of what may be considered news, the context in which their stories appear is rife with external, mediated commentary interpreting their meaning. News stories are met with instant feedback, fact-checking, and challenges to their veracity and even their honesty—all of which circulate in the same digital spaces as the stories themselves. These developments present a challenge to journalistic authority in so far as they function as forms of metajournalistic discourse questioning news content. They extend the ability to define news to voices outside of journalism as well as offer sites to laud novel media forms that challenge traditional news channels. These voices require the acknowledgment of how journalists supporting their claims to journalistic authority must contend with and account for an audience that can speak back to them.

ENFORCING ACCOUNTABILITY OR ESTABLISHING SUSPICION?

What role does trust in journalism play in sustaining journalistic authority? Public opinion surveys show trust in journalism to be declining, and earlier I argued skepticism has become the culturally acceptable perspective when confronted with questions about believing the news. These trends suggest widespread recognition of news accounts as partial products of human retelling rather than a mirror of something that happened. This is not a negative development. Given the power of journalism in creating public knowledge, news audiences are expected to possess the critical analytical skills to be informed assayers of society's chief information providers.[49] Yet this chapter indicates something else going on that has received too little attention in the conversations about journalism and journalistic authority. The news, as a discourse, is always embedded within other discourses about the news. This metajournalistic discourse shapes how news is received and interpreted. External media criticism, as one fragment of this larger terrain, should be recognized as a discursive form with its own underlying normative assumptions, strategic aims, and means of circulation.

In portraying cultural authority to be a relational concept forged between those who lay claim to authority and those who lack authority, the suspicion of intentional or unintentional inaccuracy undermines the cultural authority of journalists. A powerful discourse about journalism is that it is hopelessly biased on behalf of the Left and actively works against conservative beliefs. Some critics go so far as to conflate the news media with the Democratic Party. This is certainly an exaggeration, but the larger question is how persistent accusations of bias affect understandings of journalistic authority. The lexical equivalence of mainstream media with leftist bias serves as a priming mechanism that allows news audiences to discount information they disagree with. Accusations of liberal-media bias cast news stories as dubious if not deceitful. This is a powerful argument countering the narratives undergirding journalism's own arguments for legitimacy.

Media criticism continues to grow in both centralized and decentralized ways. The special episode of *Hannity* on liberal news bias demonstrates the dense network of actors and institutions involved in espousing these bias claims—from popular right-wing news organizations to high-ranking government officials. Media watch groups employ sophisticated content analysis operations to promote accusations of systemic bias— from both the Right and the Left. At the same time, decentralized forms of media criticism have proliferated through digital media channels with low barriers to entry and potentially strong network effects. This digital criticism may take the form of a meticulously crafted blog post or an off-hand Twitter comment. Looking across these forms, one is struck by the diversity of media criticism as well as its persistence. Making sense of this diffusion of criticism requires sensitivity to the context through which news circulates and is recirculated by audiences. Coupled with the growing heterogenization of news,[50] this complex environment points to greater confusion in the future.

Divining what this means for journalistic authority is difficult, as the growth of media criticism propels the spread of both positive and negative narratives. Optimistically, media criticism increases the accountability of news and places journalists in conversation with their audiences about how the news is created and how it errs.[51] Armed with media literacy skills, the public assesses news with a critical eye. Corrections occur faster, and journalists engaging their critics produce better stories. Pessimistically, media criticism, particularly from the Right, continues to be a communicative weapon used to instill suspicion in much of journalism for self-serving ends of altering news coverage patterns or driving audiences away to other news sources. In this vein, media criticism drives political polarization or, in the worst case, leads to a much higher susceptibility to media demagoguery.

Given these potential scenarios, it is clear that there is a lot at stake for journalistic authority beyond how it affects journalists. The discourse of accountability promises better news, but the criticism surveyed in this chapter indicates a suspicion so deep it forestalls collective attempts at skepticism to instead invite outright dismissal of contemporary news as legitimate. This is often by design by self-interested parties engaged in a wider political struggle, but its impact can be felt by all.

Conclusion

The Politics of Journalistic Authority

In March 2004, the Project for Excellence in Journalism published its inaugural *State of the News Media* report.[1] As an extensive online-only text, the report coupled a wide array of metrics about the news industry with commentary on what these trends meant for journalism. In its attempt to prognosticate about where news was heading, the overview included the following passage:

> The journalists' role as intermediary, editor, verifier, and synthesizer is weakening, and citizens do have more power to be proactive with the news. But most people will likely do so only episodically. And the proliferation of the false and misleading makes the demand for the journalist as referee, watchdog, and interpreter all the greater.[2]

These sentences capture a growing anxiety toward an unknown future in the face of a more varied media environment, but they also calm fears by reassuring readers that news audiences will continue to cling to legacy news as an arbiter of the real. Amid the cacophony of a boundless mediated public sphere, journalism will prevail.

At the time these sentences were written, I worked as a researcher at the Project for Excellence in Journalism, poring through decades of news industry data to assemble the trend lines that would be turned into narratives about US journalism for the report. The picture that emerged was clear. Legacy news organizations had been shedding audiences for many years: newspaper circulation faced decline, the major news magazines were losing readers, and the network television news broadcasts drew far fewer viewers than in the past. The future of news obviously lay in digital platforms, but in ways that were still murky.[3] Original online news content remained scarce, and while blogging was grabbing attention as a potential future for news, it was still a very novel form. Revisiting the report from the vantage point of 2016, it is easy to see that many of the trends that would accelerate in later years were already in place—legacy news owners privileged profit over reinvention, growing cable news and talk radio options contributed to audience polarization, and a spirit of innovation (and investment) drove developments in information and communication technologies.[4]

Change was assured, yet the speed and severity with which the news industry would have to adapt over the next decade was difficult to foresee. Most strikingly, the dramatic drift of advertising dollars away from subsidizing mass communication channels, the rise of free classifieds, and the shock of the Great Recession all would lead to unprecedented decline for newspapers. In 2004, when the first *State of the News Media* report appeared, the US newspaper industry earned $46.7 billion from print advertisements; a decade later, that number had shrunk to $16.4 billion.[5] What was also not understood was what the future of native digital news would look like beyond efforts by legacy media organizations to fortify their online presence and a few early trendsetters like *Salon* and *Slate*. In March 2004, Facebook was a month old, Twitter, BuzzFeed, and iPhones were a few years away, and Google News was barely more than a side project. Rereading the report serves as a portal to another time, even if it is little more than a decade ago.

This time traveling illustrates how shifts in journalism comprise both long-term developments occurring over decades of incremental change and brisk disruptions in which news practices can spring up and established forms can fall apart in only a few years. These dramatic lurches grab attention, but such trends need to be situated within a host of interconnected factors that are both endemic and external to journalism.[6] Changes in technology, communication infrastructure, organizational imperatives, advertising strategies, media ownership, and cultural preferences all matter. These circumstances do not escape attention but become ensnared in accompanying discourse offering explanations, predictions, lamentations, and so forth about the future of news. As the *State of the News Media* report (now more than a decade in the running) attests, change occurs alongside its public interpretation.

These claims lead back to the central question underpinning this book: how is it that news comes to provide legitimate knowledge about the world? No easy answer will do. As a particular cultural practice, journalism exists within a complex and variable set of social relationships. Understanding journalistic authority requires sensitivity to how these relations are configured to legitimate news, as well as to how changes in these relations alter the cultural conditions in which journalism must operate. Journalism requires authority in the sense of obtaining a right to be listened to, but how authority relations manifest themselves is fluid and context dependent. Legitimate journalism looks different in different places and different times.

The introduction laid out two tasks that this book hoped to achieve: the formation of a general theoretical framework for analyzing journalistic authority and the deployment of this framework as a tool for assessing the state of journalistic authority. Although this divide suggests a duality pitting generality against specificity, in practice these tasks are intrinsically related. Throughout the chapters of this book, the analysis of journalistic authority has continually pivoted back and forth between the general and specific, bringing them into mutual conversation. Nonetheless, the following sections pull them apart to present a framework for a relational model of journalistic authority abstracted from its concrete expressions. The first half revisits the previous chapters to present an overview of the relational model of journalistic authority. But because models are useful only for the insight they provide in ordering the messy world of practice, the second half dives back in with an analysis of the present politics of journalistic authority.

A RELATIONAL MODEL OF JOURNALISTIC AUTHORITY

Laying out a relational model begins with a return to the definition offered in the introduction: journalistic authority is a contingent relationship in which certain actors come to possess a right to create legitimate

TABLE 7.1

The Relational Model of Journalistic Authority

Authority components	Authority relations
Group identity	Journalist–audience
Textual practices	Journalist–source
Metadiscourse	Journalist–technology
	Journalist–critic

discursive knowledge about events in the world for others. In its simplest sense, noncoercive authority is a right to be listened to. This definition accentuates the connection among three necessary elements: actors who create knowledge, the discursive shape of this knowledge, and the relationships through which knowledge is created and circulated. These elements illuminate the interrelatedness of journalistic authority. No single aspect of journalistic authority can explain the others. Instead of any easy simplification, acknowledging a complex of interrelated factors encourages a comprehensive view that places social actors in context. Journalistic authority does not name a single determining force but a constellation of interrelated forces. This multifaceted approach helps avoid a reductionist reading privileging the determinant power of any one factor. With this claim in mind, table 7.1 lays out the relational model of journalistic authority. Each entry corresponds to a chapter in the book, and the columns mirror the division between part 1 and part 2.

Group identity pertains to both how journalists construct shared belief systems and how they demarcate who may be included as a legitimate knowledge producer. Chapter 1 examined this component through the centripetal force of professionalism and its enduring hold on defining how journalists ought to behave and how they ought to understand their work. In the United States, journalistic professionalism is made tricky by the lack of structural practices for marking off who is and who is not a journalist. Yet even if the definition of journalism as a profession has its deficiencies, the assertions that journalists make about their unique social contribution and the importance of their work takes on a professional character. The core arguments supporting journalism are deeply normative and predicated on the provision of a valuable social service that benefits more than just journalists. But how do these internal group dynamics and normative commitments lead to an external claim on authority? Certainly, the creation of news involves numerous interpersonal encounters with news sources, management, other journalists, and contact with news audiences. However, journalists must be recognized, at core, as embedded in relationships of mediated authority. Recognizing journalists' authority as one inherently defined by distance requires examining two forms of outputs that constitute the remaining two components: the production of discourse—news texts—and the production of metadiscourse about what news does.

News texts hew closely to familiar patterns. This formulism makes the creation of news a practical undertaking given the unrelenting time constraints, competitive pressures, and uncertainty of newsworthy events that journalists contend with each day. Journalism students learn how to emulate this discourse, and the persistence of templates across news outlets allows journalists to switch organizations without fundamental retraining. Chapter 2 argued that beyond making news doable, these forms concretize modes of journalistic authority. Any news text is not a neutral means of knowledge transfer but a deliberate set of practices that contain within them arguments for the legitimacy of what is being conveyed and who is doing the conveying. News texts contain epistemological and narrative qualities—e.g., source attribution, inverted pyramid, summary ledes, etc.—that are calibrated in particular ways to be identifiable as reliable accounts to news audiences. Journalists perform their authority through the texts they create.[7] At the same time, news discourse cannot be reduced to the external manifestation of internal journalistic norms. News texts contain an excess of meaning, including elements that connect to aesthetic values and emotional registers.

The third component centers on the narratives journalists create about journalism. In contrast to the naturalization of news forms and structures, narratives about journalism are explicit in how they imagine journalism. Journalism exists not only in practice but in the narratives that get told and retold about these practices. A whole metadiscourse surrounds news, shaping how it is to be understood through the creation of meaning about journalism as a cultural practice. Through public discourse about their work, journalists construct stories that support their claims to be authoritative knowers and draw boundaries marking off others. These narratives may include tacit assumptions about what makes for good journalism, or they may be more overt in examining the social role of journalism.

Examining how journalists construct group identity, textual practices, and metanarratives provides only a partial view of journalistic authority. As a socially embedded practice, journalism cannot be neatly rent from its context, nor can journalists be assumed to exercise total control over the perceptions and practices of journalism. Instead of walling off journalism, the model of journalistic authority advanced in this book situates it as a cocreation involving various actors—both human and technological—arranged across social space. This view reinforces the argument that authority is not a thing but an effect that emerges relationally.[8] One cannot lay claim to the mantle of authority without recognition from others already considered to be authoritative as well as recognition from those outside the boundaries of authority. The authority relation rests on the recognition of socially sanctioned legitimacy. Privileging the relational qualities of journalistic authority moves the focus outside of the newsroom or news texts to the symbolic and material interactions through which journalism is legitimated—as well as contested. Four such relations—journalist-audience, journalist-source, journalist-technology, and journalist-critic—were examined in the preceding chapters.

The journalist-audience authority relation is perhaps the thorniest. Being an authority necessitates an asymmetric relationship of acquiescent dependence from those who lack it.[9] The forms and strategies through which this separation takes place spill out beyond defining what in-group members should do to include expectations for those on the outside as well. These relations are crystallized in particular textual practices. A news text, whatever the medium, contains within it both an account of an event and meaning about why this account should be considered legitimate. But to be *authoritative* rather than *persuasive*, these patterns become naturalized as the correct means for knowledge transferal. They invite tacit recognition from the audiences that consume them. The form itself is the heuristic. Yet news audiences are certainly not acquiescent to this authority in any straightforward way. Surveys indicate a public increasingly wary of the performance of news organizations (along with other public institutions). As outward displays of skepticism toward news have become the norm, it is important to differentiate credibility from authority. The former indicates a local assessment often tied to specific news actors, whereas the latter encompasses a deeper cultural formation. However complicated the journalist-audience authority relation may be, it remains the central relationship on which the recognition of journalistic authority is built.

By contrast, the journalist-source relation is much more visible in the cocreation of news. The primary method journalists use to legitimate any bit of information is to explicitly connect it to a source. Within news texts, journalists deploy overt quoting practices in print and recorded utterances in broadcasting to accentuate the connection between assertion and the source of these assertions. This is an evidentiary strategy as much as a textual practice. In promoting patterns of particular sources as authoritative, news discourse provides a symbolic map of society's authorized knowers. Ultimately, the journalist-source relationship is marked by a mix of contrasting and overlapping needs. Even as they may have different motives, sources come to rely on journalists for access to the public while journalists need sources to complete their work. Yet, increasingly, social media alter this relationship by providing sources direct access to the public, even allowing sources to contest how they have been represented in news texts.

Although technology permeates these other relations, singling out the journalist-technology relation underscores the interrelatedness of journalism with technology. The main argument is that the relationship between journalism and technology should not be reduced to journalists' reliance on media technology as tools used to create and distribute news at the whim of journalists. Following the tenets of actor-network theory, technology can be understood as an actor in the sense that different technologies shape what the news can look like. As technology changes, so does journalism practice and, ultimately, the arguments for journalistic authority that relate to these practices. Journalists attain mediated authority through the interplay of these three elements.

Finally, the journalist-critic relation extends the definition-making work of metadiscourse to actors outside of journalism. News production, circulation, and consumption occur within a complex discursive arena in which competing ideas about journalism also circulate. Journalists laying claim to providing authorized knowledge engender criticism from various stakeholders taking aim at journalism's entrenched strategies.[10] In this way, the consumption environments of news coexist with a terrain of metajournalistic discourse taking aim at news content. This discourse is not abstract commentary but an inextricable component of the context of news work in which a variety of actors seek to shape gatekeeping practices, proffer alternatives, or affect how audiences understand the news they receive.

These four sets of relations are not exhaustive. An important fifth relationship—journalist-state—has received scant attention in this book but certainly deserves further explanation. Journalists operate within legal boundaries set by the state with regard to such matters as libel, prior restraint, and gag rules. The state also dictates who, if anyone, qualifies for special rights in matters of source confidentiality. On a broader level, media policies and regulations affect the operation of journalism by creating barriers or subsidies. An additional relationship of journalist-market also needs mentioning. The ideals of journalistic professionalism coupled with a structural division between the newsroom and management have tended to write market pressures out of understandings of journalism. This has never been a perfect divide,[11] but it has been increasingly strained by the recent economic struggles of news. For example, the growing awareness of real-time metrics for news traffic accentuates considerations of the market in the provision of news.[12] Moreover, a stress on entrepreneurship for digital news start-ups further elides this division.[13] These developments help bring to the forefront attention to how journalists negotiate their authority alongside pressures to secure appropriate funding to sustain their work.

The model of journalistic authority offers a schematic for tracking various components and relationships, but it is built upon a fundamental assumption of dynamism. Modes of group identity, textual practices, types of supporting narratives, and webs of relations between actors vary across time and space, even within a media ecosystem.[14] The importance of this observation lies in avoiding concrete pronouncements that unduly homogenize journalistic authority. We simply cannot say,

"Here is what journalistic authority looks like" in any general way. Eschewing permanence instead focuses analytical attention on how unique combinations of forces act on journalistic authority and ultimately shape the practices through which the news is made and circulated.

The assertion of dynamism makes possible the duality of journalistic authority as indicating both a generalized type of relationship necessary for the generation of social knowledge and a very specific set of enacted practices. Authority is always a core facet of journalism, but the practices and arguments that underlie this authority vary in response to cultural, political, economic, and technological shifts. Journalistic authority exists in a tension between stability and change, and the material objects and social processes that support or undermine stability and change require more attention within journalism studies. Even as much of journalism research is committed to a forward-looking perspective, journalism history remains vital as a means of understanding the contingency of journalistic practice across a wider temporal milieu. For the same reason, comparative work sheds light on the connections among journalistic authority, news practices, and political context. Any study of journalistic authority provides a snapshot—an artifact that makes a moment knowable by freezing time and demarcating space. This does not diminish the value of such studies, but acknowledging their contingency helps avoid either an atemporality that collapses the past into the present or a false universality.

Looking across these elements, a relational model of journalistic authority presents a nonreductive perspective that calls attention to the associations among different components and actors that make journalistic authority possible in any time and place. It accentuates the need to account for how these parts work together as well as the conflicts that arise among and within them. To develop what is hoped to be a useful—and fundamentally adaptable—analytical tool, this section has divorced the model from its application. But how can its usefulness be judged? Instead of stopping with theoretical abstractions, we can now turn to a broader view of the present politics of journalistic authority.

Any grand statement about the state of journalistic authority is sure to be met with a chorus of disapproving critics armed with lists of exaggerations and omissions. A glance across the body of work falling under the umbrella of news reveals a great deal of diversity, and accounting for the larger web of relationships reveals an extensive variety of people and practices. Within this milieu, one can always find supporting examples for claims about journalism, just as one's critics can locate dissenting cases. Further questions abound about the trajectory of news: Are these journalism's darkest days? Or its grand rebirth? Is change being overstated or underappreciated? Will society suffer? Or will it even notice? The approach here is to refrain from providing answers (plenty of books and essays already do so) to instead look more closely at how the questions being asked matter.

The danger in representing journalism to be x or y is not the fallacy of oversimplification but a lack of recognition of the interpretive position from which such claims spring. Persistent questions surrounding the boundaries of journalistic practice make clear that words like *journalist*, *journalism*, or *news* lack fixed meanings. What matters is careful attention to how actors create, justify, and promulgate their particular usage of these terms. Talk about journalism must be situated with the context of its production—and the modes by which it strives to establish legitimacy or delegitimize particular practices or forms.[15] Any assertion concerning the rise of new technologies, emergent news forms, or accusations that journalism is experiencing institutional crisis involves a particular interpretation that strives both to define the situation at hand and to support its speaker's own interpretive legitimacy.[16]

To make a public pronouncement about journalism is to engage in the politics of journalistic authority. Politics here refers both to the practice of governing the actions of others and the competition to attain the right to govern legitimately. The first sense denotes visions of the social order at the heart of political pronouncement; it is the normative suggestion of what ought to be that animates the concrete proposal for how to achieve it. But the second sense is just as important: politics requires gaining the necessary support to put into place actions meant to achieve these visions.

Within the domain of journalism, actors promoting particular visions of news simultaneously promote their legitimacy to offer such interpretations to their audience. This process occurs in mundane ways through the simple choice of what words to use to describe which actors. When a speaker refers to journalists, who is being included and excluded? What is being conjured when one speaks of mainstream news? It also occurs through more explicit efforts at persuasion, a discursive mode of motivating action that is generally considered anathema to the tacit workings of authority.[17] Authority, at least in the knowledge-based view, works through inbuilt assumptions regarding legitimacy that surround certain patterns of communicative practice and the practitioners entrusted to this work. By contrast, persuasion involves explicit attempts to convince others through altering or reinforcing beliefs and practices. It is an appeal to argument rather than to social location of the speaker.

The competition to define journalism is a public competition to define appropriate practices and to dictate how practices are to be understood. To expand or constrict shared conceptions of journalism to include certain practices, norms, or actors requires arguments that justify this inclusion. Actors engaging in metajournalistic discourse peddle these arguments but in ways that extend beyond personal gain or loss to instead engage with social gain or loss. Reductions in newspaper staffs have led to thousands of layoffs, and while the loss of anyone's income is certainly lamentable, journalists present the larger effect as a diminishment of news and a loss of information. News is made to be important beyond itself. The competition to define journalism—that is, the politics of journalistic authority—is the struggle to define how news matters. This argument leads to the question of power.

Despite the sustained focus on authority, questions of power have been largely absent in this book. There are analytical reasons for this: *power* and *authority* have become closely intertwined in English, and the introductory chapter argued for separating authority from power to avoid the former from muscling out the nuances of authority. Power is most obvious in its coercive mode, but, as discussed in the introduction, journalism lacks such blunt mechanisms of control. Instead, discussions of journalistic authority engage a specific form of social power separate from persuasion or coercion that accentuates the various relationships that need to be in place for journalism to be authoritative. We can read power back into the outcome of these relationships—journalism's discursive function of creating legitimate knowledge about the world. More precisely, journalists possess two interrelated yet distinct forms of power: *representational power* and *relational power.*

Representational power is quite familiar within journalism studies. By presenting audiences with accounts of events argued to be accurate depictions, journalists attain control over the circulation of meaning. Concern over these depictions is the chief motivator for the study of journalism. Generations of researchers have elucidated the myriad endogenous and exogenous factors that shape news accounts while developing intricate arguments for why news forms matter. A concern with such effects can be found in the seminal literature on gatekeeping,[18] framing,[19] and agenda setting,[20] as well as in cultural studies theories of power.[21] This book has shown how the authority underlying representational power corresponds to a highly developed method of knowing, both through established practices that create news and the predictable forms of news itself. Representational power rests on the social recognition that a news account is legitimate. But where does representational power come from?

Answering this question requires conceptualizing journalism's relational power. The basis of this power lies in the necessary relationships that need to be in place for representational power to exist. A persistent theme in this book has been how journalistic forms that support journalism's legitimacy as a knowledge-making practice—its normative ideals, textual patterns, and metanarratives—also structure the social roles of sources, owners, advertisers, and audience members. Relational power refers to the ability of journalists to dictate the nature of these associations. In doing so journalists make assumptions about the various roles, behaviors, and cultural understandings that exist across these relations. This argument reinforces the perspective that forms of knowledge should not be reduced to their textual characteristics but should also include how such forms contain within them claims about who should have this knowledge and what should be done with it. Journalistic forms reflect and shape the relationships in which they are embedded. Representational power requires relational power.

In contributing to representational and relational power, journalistic authority gives rise to the power to legitimately describe reality and to dictate the grounds by which others accept the legitimacy of the methods, forms, and roles through which this reality is produced. How this is accomplished is always particular to context and open to change. For example, journalism predicated on what may be called the professional model naturalizes this power through normative commitments to objectivity, impartiality, distance, and so forth that position news as a discourse of factuality. This naturalization diverts attention from the contingency of news practices by emphasizing instead incidents as the drivers and shapers of news, not the journalists themselves. Sources are used to convey information, and audiences are positioned as receivers of neutral accounts that they can then use to formulate opinions. This is clearly a particular vision of journalism, but it is necessarily also a vision of how nonjournalistic actors ought to behave as well.

Of course relational power is not exclusive or monolithic; journalists present differing visions of news, and extrajournalistic actors shape journalism through their interactions and in speaking publicly about journalism. In this discursive environment, the politics of journalistic authority become apparent when core ideas of what makes news legitimate become the subject of public contestation. The emerging debates may be geared to surface critiques questioning journalistic performance, or they may strike at the basic arguments supporting journalistic authority. To conceptualize the stakes of this latter position, we can return to what Peter Dahlgren calls the struggle over "definitional control" of journalism. What is being defined is not just what qualifies as news but, more importantly, the forms of knowledge production—and the relationships they produce—that are considered legitimate. To make this discussion more concrete, we can interrogate what these conflicts look like though examining the rise of the polyvocal press.

THE POLITICS OF A POLYVOCAL PRESS

The politics of journalistic authority is, at heart, a struggle over the basic norms and practices that legitimate news. These conflicts vary in time and place, with differing levels of intensity, and at present the principal conflict involves the expansive consequences of digital media. In fits and starts, the digitization of the news ecosystem has created new opportunities for a wider range of voices to participate in or interact with news; sparked innovation through digital native news sites; altered distribution practices; and changed how advertisers reach their targets. This may not be a uniform or unidirectional shift, but it is a pervasive one.

The inevitable question—and one addressed repeatedly throughout the preceding chapters—is how these developments alter the conditions of journalistic authority. What are the politics of journalistic authority in the digital era? A way to condense this question is to situate it as a division between arguments for news as fundamentally monovocal or the acceptance of a polyvocal press. The notion of a monovocal press arose in chapter 2 through the work of Kevin Barnhurst and John Nerone on the history of newspaper design.[22] As newspapers moved from the nineteenth century into the twentieth century, the front pages of newspapers morphed from a patchwork din of disparate happenings to an orderly presentation of neatly and hierarchically arranged stories. News stories came to employ a singular authoritative voice to imply the accuracy of the news account. In the mode of monovocality, every news product is a single map of what is worth knowing assembled for a diverse audience through journalists' methodical selection practices. The "page one" meeting, still the lynchpin of newspaper production,[23] exemplifies journalistic monovocality. Beyond news form, the monovocal press coincides with the ideals of a professionalized press adhering to set rules of practice, normative commitments, and organizational forms to produce news.[24] Monovocality is not just an internalized professional attitude but just as importantly a way of understanding journalism that extends outward to define journalists' relationships with sources, audiences, critics, and even the market.

By contrast, visions of a polyvocal press emphasize journalists' inescapably subjective position. It is not synonymous with opinion but a more fundamental acceptance of the partiality of any representation of the real. Given this epistemic complexity, polyvocality should not be construed as diametrically opposed to the ethos of monovocality. Instead, it is used here to corral an assortment of practices and norms embracing collaboration, fluidity, and the acceptance of news as limited knowledge. From this perspective, the uncertainty lurking in the representation of any event can be mitigated by the inclusion of multiple perspectives, be it a smartphone-enabled witness, an expert's blog, crowdsourced data, or even another journalist's account. Instead of a singular fixed story, news may arise across a variety of sources in real time, such as can be seen on Twitter during breaking news. With polyvocality the means and relations through which journalistic authority can be achieved shift toward a collaborative process stressing transparency and a multiplicity of views as much as following a set of procedures.[25]

In short, the division between monovocality and polyvocality is not just about news forms or who should be allowed to make news but a deeper rift concerning what news knowledge ought to look like. The usefulness of this framework can be see in how it enables a reassessment of the core claims of journalistic authority offered in this book. Consider, for example, the concept of asymmetry with regard to the establishment of an authority relation. Journalism's asymmetry with its audiences has traditionally been built into modes of knowledge creation as well as restrictions of access to mediated communication. Journalists gather information from sources, package it into a news story, and then present it to audiences with the hope that they will take it as legitimate information that can be acted upon. But this is not the only available model. With democratized access to communication technology, the expansion of available information, and the opening up of expressive forms, asymmetry has to find its grounding through other boundary-making means.[26] The roles separating producers and consumers have become less secure. The extent to which this has happened is debatable;[27] much of what we call news is still produced by journalists. But the changing conditions of possibilities with regard to the circulation and production of knowledge should not be ignored. The ability of witnesses located in the right place at the right time to gather and disseminate information or of experts to analyze events from an informed yet subjective viewpoint signals the occasional fluid transference of authority in ways that had just not been possible in the past without the intervention of a monovocal press as mediator.

Polyvocality alters journalists' control of knowledge within the overall media environment. Proponents of polyvocal forms of news support alternative means of establishing authority, including enhanced participation, decreased boundaries between news producers and consumers, subjective voice, a commitment to advocacy, and networked reporting. These elements have appeared at various points in the book:

chapter 4 concluded its exploration of journalist-source relations by discussing the ability of nonjournalists to utilize communication tools in new ways. This is also true of elites who can reach publics outside of news, as chapter 5 noted. Elite sources have long enjoyed access to the public through the news, but they can only ever partially control their representation through the news. New technologies, especially in the realm of social media, open new avenues for communicating with the public. The public relations industry, to take one example, has begun to shift from affecting press coverage to circumventing news altogether. This is not all external to journalism; the practices of native advertising blur the boundaries between editorial and commercial expression in the space of news.[28]

Polyvocality is also fueled by the preponderance of media criticism examined in chapter 7. The goals of much media criticism are instrumental in seeking to alter news coverage to be more or less favorable to certain political perspectives. But, on a deeper level, the textual universe of media criticism points back to the context of news consumption. News audiences experience news in a complicated media environment in which news texts increasingly come wrapped in external interpretations, be it remarks accompanying a link to a news story on Facebook and Twitter or the comments sections appended to news stories. These examples point to polyvocality not as a textual characteristic but as a broader concept applicable to a wider range of extratextual practices that also deserve attention.

If proponents of a monovocal press emphasize adherence to shared norms and practices to achieve the best possible representation of events, then a polyvocal press stresses the acknowledgment of a multiplicity of situated accounts. Advocates of monovocality fear a diversified media environment will increase political polarization, fragment audiences, leave demagoguery unchecked, and result in filter bubbles.[29] These concerns raise important potential negative consequences, but they also illustrate how entrenched the ideology of monovocality has become in thinking about journalism. Polyvocality has its own ideological biases, albeit its still emergent character belies singular interpretations.

In the end, no single trajectory accounts for the changes taking place across the landscape of news. A likely outcome for the future is a heterogeneous journalism ecosystem marked by the coexistence of news outlets relying on different sets of practices and relations to argue for their authority.[30] This future owes much to the uncertainty surrounding how to fund journalistic ventures given shifts in advertising that no longer privilege the mass communication model to the same degree as in the past.[31] The monovocality-polyvocality divide helps illustrate some of the major trends that are reshaping the premises through which journalism acquires legitimacy. But these developments are uneven, occurring in different ways and in different places. Nor can the situation be reduced to an old-versus-new divide, as legacy media busily experiment with novel formats in the face of business models that are no longer viable. Instead of seeking to condense these differences, they can be understood within the framework offered by the politics of journalistic authority as attempts at shaping the representational power of news as well as the relational power bound up in dictating how social actors should interact with the news.

RECONSTRUCTING JOURNALISTIC AUTHORITY

Is journalistic authority weak or strong? The massive amount of news generated around the clock all over the world in a variety of media provides some evidence for the successful retention of authority. Yet the fault lines are plainly visible, and the past is no guarantee of the future. Concern is rampant, as it should always be when it comes to matters of how the news works. But instead of lamenting the headwinds that challenge journalistic authority, the way to end this book is by repositioning its inherent malleability as an opportunity. The contemporary media environment is awash in experiments with new journalistic forms taking place both within legacy news organizations seeking to stay relevant and digital start-ups building organizational models from the ground up. These actions are further meditated through discussions about the so-called future of news that openly debate what journalism ought to look like. Some new directions will take root, while others will simply not be viable. Evaluating this era remains an important task for journalism studies, but it doesn't need to end there. In this moment in which much discussion explicitly addresses the forms and relations that ought to undergird journalistic authority, we need to recognize our own role. The pronoun *we* is meant to be inclusive, as none of us stand outside of journalism. Just by living in a society in which news is expected to support democratic processes and create community, we are not external to these discussions and these relations. We all have a stake in the news.

The critiques of traditional modes of journalism are well known: sourcing patterns favor elite sources, reproduce social hierarchies, and suppress certain voices; an omniscient tone oversimplifies issues and tends to focus on surface problems; journalists' detached position casts audiences as passive spectators; and commercial imperatives drive coverage decisions in ways that work against the greater public good. These problems cannot be dismissed as sloppiness or poor adherence to practice. After all, they are so entrenched precisely because they are bound up within the ideas of professional journalism and in accompanying arguments and practices supporting journalism's legitimacy. The irony is that these negative trends arise as side effects from news practices adhering to the core arguments journalists use to support their authority.

The way forward is to first understand the elements that connect together to produce journalistic authority. Taking authority for granted only masks a fuller understanding of the power of journalism and the relational associations through which the news is made possible as a cultural practice. To this end, we should push aside any a priori explanatory role for normative arguments to instead situate journalism as suspended in a web of social relations. From this perspective, norms play an instrumental role in journalistic authority, not a determinant one. This proposition is not meant to denigrate norms or to doom journalism to a relativistic morass. Rather, thinking carefully about norms not as natural or fixed but as deliberate inventions containing the hopes of what communication can do presents an opening to protect certain visions, contest others, and advocate for new visions of journalism.

In pursuing the dynamics of journalistic authority, questions about journalism can be reframed to interrogate how certain legitimating practices become institutionalized, the assumptions bound up in these practices, and the boundaries that get placed around them. We face many novel questions. When do mobile communication technologies create new opportunities for witnessing travesties that demand a response, and when do they facilitate an excess of information that distracts from learning of such travesties? When does digital news benefit us with unimagined depths of information on specific topics, and when do news algorithms steer our attention toward topics or opinions that we already know? How do new organizational forms invigorate newsrooms, and when do they further restrict the range of stories and voices in the news? We have no shortage of questions concerning the present and future of news, and we need to remain attentive to the forms that develop and how they relate to the larger issue of what makes journalism authoritative.

Beyond questions of explanation lie strategies of intervention. The relational view of journalistic authority stresses the cocreation of journalism and the importance of attending to metadiscourse. Yet we are not ourselves detached from this process. Instead, this model should shift us from observers to participants within the conversation of what news should look like. Put simply, the motivating question to ask is: what forms should journalistic authority take? Answering this question is vital in moving journalism forward. It carries within it an acknowledgment that journalism is a constructed and malleable cultural practice and therefore an adaptable one. We are not idle spectators relegated to watch this process from the sidelines but rather active stakeholders concerned about the quality of news and the public that it will serve in the generations to come.

Notes

INTRODUCTION: THE MANY RELATIONSHIPS OF JOURNALISM

1. Bill Keller, "Henry Luce, the Editor in Chief," *New York Times*, April 22, 2010, Sunday Book Review, http://www.nytimes.com/2010/04/25/books/review/Keller-t.html?pagewanted=all&_r=0.

2. For recent research employing journalistic authority, see Sue Robinson, "'Someone's Gotta Be in Control Here': The Institutionalization of Online News and the Creation of a Shared Journalistic Authority," *Journalism Practice* 1, no. 3 (2007): 305–21; Sue Robinson, "The Mission of the J-Blog Recapturing Journalistic Authority Online," *Journalism* 7, no. 1 (2006): 65–83; Matt Carlson, "Blogs and Journalistic Authority: The Role of Blogs in US Election Day 2004 Coverage," *Journalism Studies* 8, no. 2 (2007): 264–79; Michael Karlsson, "The Immediacy of Online News, the Visibility of Journalistic Processes and a Restructuring of Journalistic Authority," *Journalism* 12, no. 3 (2011): 279–95; Geoffrey Baym, "Emerging Models of Journalistic Authority in MTV's Coverage of the 2004 US Presidential Election," *Journalism Studies* 8, no. 3 (2007): 382–96; Thomas E. Ruggiero, "Paradigm Repair and Changing Journalistic Perceptions of the Internet as an Objective News Source," *Convergence* 10, no. 4 (2004): 92–106; David W. Park, "Blogging with Authority: Strategic Positioning in Political Blogs," *International Journal of Communication* 3, (2009): 24; Kimberly Meltzer, "The Hierarchy of Journalistic Cultural Authority: Journalists' Perspectives according to News Medium," *Journalism Practice* 3, no. 1 (2009): 59–74.

3. Seth C. Lewis, "The Tension Between Professional Control and Open Participation: Journalism and Its Boundaries," *Information, Communication & Society* 15, no. 6 (2012): 836–66.

4. This question is an adaptation from H. M. Höpfl, "Power, Authority and Legitimacy," *Human Resource Development International* 2, no. 3 (1999): 219.

5. Alex Jones, *Losing the News: The Future of the News That Feeds Democracy* (New York: Oxford University Press, 2009).

6. Todd Gitlin, "A Surfeit of Crises: Circulation, Revenue, Attention, Authority, and Deference," in *Will the Last Reporter Please Turn Out the Lights*, ed. Robert W. McChesney and Victor Pickard (New York: New Press, 2011), 97–98.

7. Barbie Zelizer, *Covering the Body: The Kennedy Assassination, The Media, and the Shaping of Collective Memory* (Chicago: University of Chicago Press, 1992), 8.

8. Ibid., 65.

9. Two other foundational works are David L. Eason, "On Journalistic Authority: The Janet Cooke Scandal," in *Media, Myths, and Narratives*, ed. James W. Carey (Newbury Park, CA: Sage Publications, 1988), 205–27, and C. W. Anderson, "Journalism: Expertise, Authority, and Power in Democratic Life," in *The Media and Social Theory*, ed. David Hesmondhalgh and Jason Toynbee (New York: Routledge, 2008), 248–64.

10. Bill Kovach and Tom Rosenstiel, *The Elements of Journalism: What Newspeople Should Know and the Public Should Expect* (New York: Three Rivers Press, 2001). In full disclosure, the author formally worked with Kovach and Rosenstiel at the Project for Excellence in Journalism.

11. Ibid., 17.

12. Eason, "On Journalistic Authority."

13. Michael Schudson, *The Power of News* (Cambridge, MA: Harvard University Press, 1995), 3.

14. Bruce Lincoln, *Authority: Construction and Corrosion* (Chicago: University of Chicago Press, 1995).

15. Hannah Arendt, "What Is Authority?" in *Between Past and Future: Eight Exercises in Political Thought* (New York: Penguin Books, 1958).

16. R. P. Wolff, "The Conflict Between Authority and Autonomy," in *Authority*, ed. Joseph Raz (New York: New York University Press 1990), 21.

17. Max Weber, *The Theory of Social and Economic Organization*, ed. Talcott Parsons, trans. A. M. Henderson and Talcott Parsons (New York: Free Press, 1947).

18. Ibid., 329.

19. R. B. Friedman, "On the Concept of Authority in Political Philosophy," in *Authority*, ed. Joseph Raz (New York: New York University Press 1990), 57.

20. Ibid., 57.

21. Höpfl, "Power, Authority and Legitimacy," 219.

22. Ibid., 222, 226.

23. *Potestas* refers to legitimate power invested in a clearly demarcated position or office—this is closest to Weber's bureaucratic authority. A judge may rule over a courtroom but has no special powers in the cafeteria. By contrast, *potentia* refers to power through force, or coercive power, as in *scientia potentia est* (knowledge is power).

24. Höpfl, "Power, Authority and Legitimacy," 220. For example, the political authority of the ancient Roman Senate did not derive from its power (*potentia*) or even its office (*potestas*) but through the timelessness of the body itself stretching back to the founding of Rome. Its members spoke from the collective wisdom not only of those present but also through the long tradition of the governing body. It was to be respected.

25. Arendt, "What Is Authority?" 120–28.

26. Höpfl, "Power, Authority and Legitimacy," 223.

27. Lincoln, *Authority: Construction and Corrosion*, 3.

28. Friedman, "On the Concept of Authority," 76.

29. Richard Sennett, *Authority* (New York: Knopf, 1980).

30. Friedman, "On the Concept of Authority," 71. For Weber, this dynamic of "a willingness to obey" expressed through "a belief by virtue of which persons exercising authority are lent prestige" forms the core of legitimate authority. See Weber, *Theory of Social and Economic Organization*, 382.

31. Frank Furedi, *Authority: A Sociological History* (Cambridge: Cambridge University Press, 2013), 187.

32. Sennett, *Authority*, 19.

33. James Boyd White, *Acts of Hope: Creating Authority in Literature, Law, and Politics* (Chicago: University of Chicago Press, 1995), 306.

34. Lincoln, *Authority: Construction and Corrosion*, 10–11.

35. Paul Starr, *The Social Transformation of American Medicine* (New York: Basic Books, 1982).

36. Ibid., 13.

37. Keith M. Macdonald, *The Sociology of the Professions* (London: Sage, 1995), 134.

38. Andrew Abbott, *The System of Professions: An Essay on the Division of Expert Labor* (Chicago: University of Chicago Press, 1988).

39. Ibid.

40. Thomas F. Gieryn, *Cultural Boundaries of Science: Credibility on the Line* (Chicago: University of Chicago Press, 1999).

41. Ibid., 1.

42. Friedman, "On the Concept of Authority," 68.

43. Jay Rosen, "The 'Awayness' Problem," *Columbia Journalism Review*, September 3, 2013, http://www.cjr.org/cover_story/the_awayness_problem.php.

44. In the mid-1970s, at a time when a few mass communication channels dominated the news, Sandra Ball-Rokeach and Melvin DeFleur observed that the "dependence on media information resources is an ubiquitous condition in modern society" and as such should be implemented into theorizing about media effects. See Sandra J. Ball-Rokeach and Melvin L. DeFleur, "A Dependency Model of Mass-Media Effects," *Communication Research* 3, no. 1 (1976): 3–21.

45. Michael Schudson, *Discovering the News: A Social History of American Newspapers* (New York: Basic Books, 1978).

46. "Code of Ethics," Society of Professional Journalists, September 24, 2013, http://www.spj.org/ethicscode.asp.

47. John Soloski, "News Reporting and Professionalism: Some Constraints on the Reporting of the News," in *Media, Culture & Society* 11, no. 2 (1989): 207–28. See also Michael Schudson and C. W. Anderson, "Objectivity, Professionalism, and Truth Seeking in Journalism," in *Handbook of Journalism Studies*, ed. Karin Wahl-Jorgensen and Thomas Hanitzsch (New York, Routledge, 2008), 88–101; Silvio Waisbord, *Reinventing Professionalism: Journalism and News in Global Perspective* (Cambridge: Polity Press, 2013).

48. Lewis, "The Tension Between Professional Control"; Steven Maras, *Objectivity in Journalism* (Cambridge: Polity Press, 2013).

49. Anderson, "Journalism: Expertise, Authority, and Power."

50. This does not mean that the structure of the text determines its consumption, only that it has a powerful influence over it. This idea has been most famously put forth in Stuart Hall, "Encoding, Decoding," in *The Cultural Studies Reader*, ed. Simon During (London: Routledge, 1993), 90–103.

51. James Boyd White, *Acts of Hope: Creating Authority in Literature, Law, and Politics*, (Chicago: University of Chicago Press, 1994), 304.

52. Friedman, "On the Concept of Authority," 65.

53. Teun A. Van Dijk, *News as Discourse* (Hillsdale, NJ: Lawrence Erlbaum Associates, 1988), 83. However, Van Dijk does consider news to be rhetoric using a looser definition than the author.

54. Gaye Tuchman, "Objectivity as Strategic Ritual: An Examination of Newsmen's Notions of Objectivity," *American Journal of Sociology* (1972): 660–79.

55. Of course, opinion writing does build arguments and even attempt to persuade, but this does not carry over to news accounts. In many ways, the differences between news and opinion writing illuminate the different approaches to knowledge.

56. Allan Bell, *The Language of News Media* (Oxford: Blackwell Publishers, 1991), 147.

57. Jo Bogaerts, "On the Performativity of Journalistic Identity," *Journalism Practice* 5, no. 4 (2011): 399–413. See also Marcel Broersma, "The Unbearable Limitations of Journalism on Press Critique and Journalism's Claim to Truth," *Inter-*

national Communication Gazette 72, no. 1 (2010): 21–33; Sandrine Boudana, "A Definition of Journalistic Objectivity as a Performance," *Media, Culture & Society* 33, no. 3 (2011): 385–98.

58. Marcel Broersma, "Journalism as Performative Discourse: The Importance of Form and Style in Journalism," in *Journalism and Meaning-Making: Reading the Newspaper*, ed. Verica Rupar (Cresskill, NJ: Hampton Press, 2010), 15–35. Broersma adds on page 19: "The authority of a news item is established through the way it is represented in language, the reputation of the journalist, the medium the item is published or presented in and the profession as a whole."

59. Ibid., 30.

60. S. Elizabeth Bird and Robert W. Dardenne, "Myth, Chronicle, and Story," in *Media, Myths, and Narratives*, ed. James W. Carey (Newbury Park, CA: Sage Publications, 1988), 67–86; Broersma, "Journalism as Performative Discourse."

61. Matt Carlson, "Rethinking Journalistic Authority: Walter Cronkite and Ritual in Television News," *Journalism Studies* 13, no. 4 (2012): 483–98.

62. Michael Williams, *Problems of Knowledge: A Critical Introduction to Epistemology* (New York: Oxford University Press, 2001), 14, 17.

63. The classic text for this point is Gaye Tuchman, *Making News: A Study in the Construction of Reality* (New York: Free Press, 1978).

64. Robert E. Park, "News as a Form of Knowledge: A Chapter in the Sociology of Knowledge," *American Journal of Sociology* 45, no. 5 (1940): 669–86.

65. Mats Ekström, "Epistemologies of TV Journalism: A Theoretical Framework," *Journalism* 3, no. 3 (2002): 259–82. Italics in original.

66. Donald Matheson, "Weblogs and the Epistemology of the News: Some Trends in Online Journalism," *New Media & Society* 6, no. 4 (2004): 446.

67. Ekström, "Epistemologies of TV Journalism," 262.

68. See Starr, *The Social Transformation*.

69. As a way to move past comparisons with scientific and technical expertise, Zvi Reich argues that journalistic expertise lies in balancing the management of news sources while simultaneously managing relations with audiences—a skill set he labels "bipolar interactional expertise." See Zvi Reich, "Journalism as Bipolar Interactional Expertise," *Communication Theory* 22, no. 4 (2012): 339–58.

70. Matheson, "Weblogs and the Epistemology of the News." See also David M. Ryfe, *Can Journalism Survive? An Inside Look at American Newsrooms* (Malden, MA: Polity Press, 2013).

71. Matheson, "Weblogs and the Epistemology of the News," 458.

72. For an update on Park, see Rasmus Kleis Nielsen, "Digital News as Forms of Knowledge: A New Chapter in the Sociology of Knowledge," in *Remaking the News*, ed. Pablo J. Boczkowski and C. W. Anderson (Cambridge, MA: MIT Press, forthcoming).

73. It is tempting to put the word *journalism* in quotes throughout this book to mimic Evgeny Morozov's deft move of accounting for the imprecision of the word *Internet* by placing it in quotes throughout the entirety of his book, *To Save Everything, Click Here: The Folly of Technological Solutionism* (New York: PublicAffairs, 2013). That may be a tad too excessive for this work, but the sentiment that the term *journalism* cannot be applied to an agreed-upon fixed object should be understood.

74. Michael Schudson, "The Politics of Narrative Form: The Emergence of News Conventions in Print and Television," *Daedalus* 111, no. 4 (1982): 97–112.

75. Gwenyth L. Jackaway, *Media at War: Radio's Challenge to the Newspapers, 1924–1939* (Westport, CT: Praeger, 1995); Zelizer, *Covering the Body*; Pablo J. Boczkowski, *Digitizing the News: Innovation in Online Newspapers* (Cambridge, MA: MIT Press, 2004); Matthew Powers, "'In Forms That Are Familiar and Yet-to-Be Invented:' American Journalism and the Discourse of Technologically Specific Work," *Journal of Communication Inquiry* 36, no. 1 (2012): 24–43.

76. Jay Rosen, *What Are Journalists For?* (New Haven: Yale University Press, 1999).

77. Michael Schudson, *Discovering the News*. Enumerating definitional ambiguities is not meant to imply the unimportance of efforts to construct boundaries. On the contrary, boundary work is a constant for journalism, even if agreed-upon, universal boundaries for the term *journalism* can never be decisively set or sustained. See Matt Carlson and Seth C. Lewis, *Boundaries of Journalism: Professionalism, Practices and Participation* (New York: Routledge, 2015).

78. For the application of institutionalism in journalism studies, see Wilson Lowrey, "Institutionalism, News Organizations and Innovation," *Journalism Studies* 12, no. 1 (2011), 64–79.

79. Ryfe, *Can Journalism Survive?* 140–41.

80. C. W. Anderson, Emily Bell, and Clay Shirky, *Post-Industrial Journalism: Adapting to the Present* (New York: Tow Center for Digital Journalism, 2012), 116, http://towcenter.org/wp-content/uploads/2012/11/TOWCenter-Post_Industrial_Journalism.pdf.

81. Matt Carlson and Nikki Usher, "News Startups as Agents of Innovation: For-Profit Digital News Startup Manifestos as Metajournalistic Discourse," *Digital Journalism* 4, no. 5 (2016), 563–81.

82. Robinson, "'Someone's Gotta Be in Control Here.'" Also Jane B. Singer et al., *Participatory Journalism: Guarding Open Gates at Online Newspapers* (Malden, MA: Wiley-Blackwell, 2011).

83. Stuart Allan, *Citizen Witnessing* (Cambridge: Polity Press, 2013).

84. Lewis, "The Tension Between Professional Control."

85. Park, "Blogging with Authority."

86. Abbott, *The System of Professions*.

87. Anderson, "Journalism: Expertise, Authority, and Power"; Lewis, "The Tension Between Professional Control."

88. Andy Williams, Claire Wardle, and Karin Wahl-Jorgensen, "'Have They Got News for Us?' Audience Revolution or Business as Usual at the BBC," *Journalism Practice* 5, no. 1 (2011): 85–99.

89. Lincoln, *Authority: Construction and Corrosion*, 11.

90. This point is made in Eason, "On Journalistic Authority."

91. Henry Jenkins, *Convergence Culture: Where Old and New Media Collide* (New York: New York University Press, 2006).

1. PROFESSIONALISM AS PRIVILEGE AND DISTANCE: JOURNALISTIC IDENTITY

1. David Weigel, "In Trump vs. Ramos, Conservatives Pick a Side," *Washington Post*, http://www.washingtonpost.com/news/post-politics/wp/2015/08/26/in-trump-vs-ramos-conservatives-pick-a-side/.

2. Henrik Örnebring, "Anything You Can Do, I Can Do Better? Professional Journalists on Citizen Journalism in Six European Countries," *International Communication Gazette* 75, no. 1 (2013): 35–53.

3. For this argument, see C. W. Anderson, "Journalism: Expertise, Authority, and Power in Democratic Life," in *The Media and Social Theory*, ed. David Hesmondhalgh and Jason Toynbee (New York: Routledge, 2008), 248–64.

4. Mark Deuze, "What Is Journalism? Professional Identity and Ideology of Journalists Reconsidered," *Journalism* 6, no. 4 (2005): 442–64.

5. Michael Schudson and C. W. Anderson, "Objectivity, Professionalism, and Truth Seeking in Journalism," in *The Handbook of Journalism Studies*, ed. Karin Wahl-Jorgensen and Thomas Hanitzsch (New York: Routledge, 2008), 94.

6. Jeremy Tunstall, *Journalists at Work: Specialist Correspondents, Their News Organizations, News Sources, and Competitor-Colleagues* (London: Constable Press, 1971).

7. David H. Weaver et al., *The American Journalist in the 21st Century: U.S. News People at the Dawn of a New Millennium* (New York: Routledge, 2006).

8. Henrik Örnebring, "Reassessing Journalism as a Profession," in *The Routledge Companion to News and Journalism*, ed. Stuart Allan (London: Routledge, 2010), 568.

9. Everett C. Hughes, "Professions," *Daedalus* 92, no. 4 (1963): 655–68.

10. Keith M. Macdonald, *The Sociology of the Professions* (London: Sage, 1995), 6.

11. See ibid., for a useful overview.

12. Magali Sarfatti Larson, *The Rise of Professionalism: A Sociological Analysis* (Berkeley: University of California Press, 1977).

13. Another way to view professionalization efforts is as a struggle over jurisdiction among competing groups. See Andrew Abbott, *The System of Professions: An Essay on the Division of Expert Labor* (Chicago: University of Chicago Press, 1988); Paul Starr, *The Social Transformation of American Medicine* (New York: Basic Books, 1982).

14. Silvio R. Waisbord, *Reinventing Professionalism* (Cambridge: Polity, 2013).

15. Schudson and Anderson, "Objectivity, Professionalism, and Truth Seeking," 90.

16. Meryl Aldridge and Julia Evetts, "Rethinking the Concept of Professionalism: The Case of Journalism," *British Journal of Sociology* 54, no. 4 (2003): 547–64.

17. Örnebring, "Reassessing Journalism," 568.

18. In the United Kingdom, journalists have a similar relationship with the National Union of Journalists. See Howard Tumber and Marina Prentoulis, "Journalism and the Making of a Profession," in *Making Journalists: Diverse Models, Global Issues*, ed. Hugo de Burgh (London: Routledge: 2005), 66.

19. Aldridge and Evetts, "Rethinking the Concept," 558. They also note that there is a stronger sense of professionalism in the United States than the United Kingdom.

20. Dan Berkowitz, "Doing Double Duty Paradigm Repair and the Princess Diana What-a-Story," *Journalism* 1, no. 2 (2000): 125–43.

21. Deuze, "What Is Journalism?," 446.

22. John Soloski, "News Reporting and Professionalism: Some Constraints on the Reporting of the News," *Media, Culture & Society* 11, no. 2 (1989): 207–28.

23. Risto Kunelius and Laura Ruusunoksa, "Mapping Professional Imagination: On the Potential of Professional Culture in the Newspapers of the Future," *Journalism Studies* 9, no. 5 (2008): 662–78.

24. Mark Coddington, "Defending a Paradigm by Patrolling a Boundary: Two Global Newspapers' Approach to WikiLeaks," *Journalism & Mass Communication Quarterly* 89, no. 3 (2012): 377–96.

25. Jenny Wiik, "Identities under Construction: Professional Journalism in a Phase of Destabilization," *International Review of Sociology* 19, no. 2 (2009): 351–65.

26. See Thomas Jefferson to Edward Carrington (document 8), 16 January 1787, in "Amendment I (Speech and Press)" in *The Founders' Constitution*, vol. 5, ed. Philip Kurland and Ralph Lerner (Chicago: University of Chicago Press, 1986). Available at http://press-pubs.uchicago.edu/founders/documents/amendI_speechs8.html.

27. See Alex Jones, *Losing the News: The Future of the News that Feeds Democracy* (New York: Oxford University Press, 2009).

28. Peter Dahlgren, introduction to *Journalism and Popular Culture*, ed. Peter Dahlgren and Colin Sparks (London: Sage, 1992), 1–23.

29. Michael Schudson, *The Good Citizen: A History of American Civic Life* (New York: Free Press, 1998).

30. Dahlgren, introduction to *Journalism and Popular Culture*.

31. Wolfgang Donsbach, "Journalists and Their Professional Identities," in *The Routledge Companion to News and Journalism*, ed. Stuart Allan (London: Routledge, 2010), 38–48.

32. Soloski, "News Reporting and Professionalism," 213. Soloski follows Larson in showing professionalism to be embedded in a profit-seeking market system. Professionalism is not the antithesis to bureaucratized commercialism but a form of control that developed within a capitalist framework.

33. Daniel Hallin, *We Keep America on Top of the World: Television Journalism and the Public Sphere* (London: Routledge, 1994), 171.

34. Aldridge and Evetts, "Rethinking the Concept," 555. This idea comes from Fournier's conception of professionalism leading to "control at a distance through the construction of 'appropriate' work identities and conducts." Valérie Fournier, "The Appeal to 'Professionalism' as a Disciplinary Mechanism," *Sociological Review* 47, no. 2 (1999): 280–307. See also Nikolas Rose, *Powers of Freedom: Reframing Political Thought* (Cambridge: Cambridge University Press, 1999).

35. It also makes possible flexible work situations, which has always been a part of journalism.

36. C. W. Anderson, Emily Bell, and Clay Shirky, *Post-Industrial Journalism: Adapting to the Present* (New York: Tow Center for Digital Journalism, 2012), http://towcenter.org/wp-content/uploads/2012/11/TOWCenter-Post_Industrial_Journalism.pdf.

37. Waisbord, *Reinventing Professionalism*, 93.

38. Autonomy also works on an individual level, which was discussed in the previous section with regard to professionalization as a disciplining force.

39. Waisbord, *Reinventing Professionalism*, 115.

40. Thomas F. Gieryn, *Cultural Boundaries of Science: Credibility on the Line* (Chicago: University of Chicago Press, 1999).

41. Stephen J. A. Ward, *Invention of Journalism Ethics: The Path to Objectivity and Beyond* (Montreal: McGill-Queen's University Press, 2005), 102.

42. Michael Schudson, "Autonomy from What," in *Bourdieu and the Journalistic Field*, ed. Rodney Benson and Erik Neveu (Cambridge: Polity, 2005), 214–23.

43. For examples, see Ben H. Bagdikian, *The Media Monopoly*, 6th ed. (Boston: Beacon Press, 2000); John H. McManus, *Market-Driven Journalism: Let the Citizen Beware?* (Thousand Oaks, CA: Sage, 1994); Robert D. McChesney, *The Problem of the Media: US Communication Politics in the Twenty-First Century* (New York: New York University Press, 2004); and Vincent Mosco, *The Political Economy of Communication* (London: Sage, 2009).

44. J. Herbert Altschull, "Boundaries of Journalistic Autonomy," in *Social Meanings of News: A Text-Reader*, ed. Dan Berkowitz (Thousand Oaks, CA: Sage, 1997), 259.

45. Matt Carlson, "Dueling, Dancing, or Dominating? Journalists and Their Sources," *Sociology Compass* 3, no. 4 (2009): 526–42.

46. David L. Eason, "On Journalistic Authority: The Janet Cooke Scandal," in *Media, Myths, and Narratives*, ed. James W. Carey (Newbury Park, CA: Sage, 1988), 205–27.

47. Matt Carlson and Seth C. Lewis, eds., *Boundaries of Journalism: Professionalism, Practices and Participation* (New York: Routledge, 2015).

48. Michael Schudson, "The Objectivity Norm in American Journalism," *Journalism* 2, no. 2 (2001), 165.

49. Dahlgren, introduction to *Journalism and Popular Culture*, 1–23.

50. Henry Jenkins, *Convergence Culture: Where Old and New Media Collide* (New York: New York University Press, 2006).

51. Stuart Allan, *Citizen Witnessing: Revisioning Journalism in Times of Crisis* (Cambridge: Polity, 2013); Kari Andén-Papadopoulos and Mervi Pantti, "Reimagining Crisis Reporting: Professional Ideology of Journalists and Citizen Eyewitness Images," *Journalism* 14, no. 7 (2013): 960–77.

52. Given the lofty connotations of knowledge, Robert Park distinguishes between two forms of news knowledge: *knowledge about* and *acquaintance with*. The former indicates a greater level of depth, while the latter pertains to the shared notice of events. This distinction circumvents comparisons with scientific or in-depth modes of knowledge creation to instead shine light on the particular types of knowledge journalists produce. Robert E. Park, "News as a Form of Knowledge: A Chapter in the Sociology of Knowledge," *American Journal of Sociology* 45, no. 5 (1940): 669–86.

53. For a thorough survey of this literature, see Steven Maras, *Objectivity in Journalism* (Cambridge: Polity, 2013).

54. Edward J. Epstein, *News from Nowhere: Television and the News* (New York: Vintage Books, 1973). Robert M. Entman, "Framing: Toward Clarification of a Fractured Paradigm," *Journal of Communication* 43, no. 4 (1993): 51–58.

55. Theodore L. Glasser, "Objectivity and News Bias," in *Philosophical Issues in Journalism*, ed. Elliot D. Cohen (New York: Oxford University Press, 1992), 176–85.

56. W. Lance Bennett, *News: The Politics of Illusion* (New York: Longman, 1983), 81.

57. Jay Rosen, "The View from Nowhere: Questions and Answers," *Press Think*, November, 10, 2010, http://pressthink.org/2010/11/the-view-from-nowhere-questions-and-answers/.

58. Maras, *Objectivity in Journalism*, 84.

59. Bill Kovach and Tom Rosenstiel, *The Elements of Journalism: What Newspeople Should Know and What the Public Should Expect* (New York: Three Rivers Press, 2001).

60. Ward, *Invention of Journalism Ethics*.

61. Dan Schiller, *Objectivity and the News: The Public and the Rise of Commercial Journalism* (Philadelphia: University of Pennsylvania Press, 1981).

62. Michael Schudson, *Discovering the News: A Social History of American Newspapers* (New York: Basic Books, 1978).

63. Walter Lippmann, *Public Opinion* (New York: Macmillan, 1922).

64. Schudson, "The Objectivity Norm," 163.

65. Ibid., 161.

66. Ibid., 157.

67. Abbott, *The System of Professions*.

68. Gieryn, *Cultural Boundaries of Science*.

69. Hannah Arendt, "What Is Authority?" in Arendt, *Between Past and Future* (New York, Penguin Books, 1958), 108.

70. R. B. Friedman, "On the Concept of Authority in Political Philosophy," in *Authority*, ed. Joseph Raz (New York: New York University Press, 1990), 56–91.

71. Schudson and Anderson, "Objectivity, Professionalism, and Truth Seeking," 96.

72. Tumber and Prentoulis, "Journalism and the Making of a Profession," 63.

73. This point was made forcefully by Anderson, "Journalism: Expertise, Authority, and Power," 258.

74. Carolyn Marvin, *When Old Technologies Were New: Thinking About Electric Communication in the Late Nineteenth Century* (New York: Oxford University Press, 1988).

75. Dennis Overbye, "For Nobel, They Can Thank the 'God Particle,'" *New York Times*, October 8, 2013, http://www.nytimes.com/2013/10/09/science/englert -and-higgs-win-nobel-physics-prize.html.

76. One could only imagine if academic research were treated the same way.

77. Schudson and Anderson, "Objectivity, Professionalism, and Truth Seeking," 94.

78. Waisbord, *Reinventing Professionalism*, 83.

79. Tumber and Prentoulis, "Journalism and the Making of a Profession," 58.

80. Örnebring, "Reassessing Journalism," 571; Waisbord, *Reinventing Professionalism*, 135.

81. Tammy Boyce, "Journalism and Expertise," *Journalism Studies* 7, no. 6 (2006): 889–906; Susan Herbst, "Political Authority in a Mediated Age," *Theory and Society* 32, no. 4 (2003): 481–503.

82. Zvi Reich, "Journalism as Bipolar Interactional Expertise," *Communication Theory* 22, no. 4 (2012): 339–58. Italics in the original.

83. Waisbord, *Reinventing Professionalism*, 227.
84. Ibid., 130. This argument is similar to Karin Knorr-Cetina, *Epistemic Cultures: How the Sciences Make Knowledge* (Cambridge, MA: Harvard University Press, 1999).
85. Mats Ekström, "Epistemologies of TV Journalism: A Theoretical Framework," *Journalism* 3, no. 3 (2002): 259–82.
86. Waisbord, *Reinventing Professionalism*, 135; for Bourdieu's meaning of *doxa*, see Pierre Bourdieu, *Outline of a Theory of Practice*, trans. Richard Nice (Cambridge: Cambridge University Press, 1977).
87. Dan Berkowitz, "Non-Routine News and Newswork: Exploring a What-a-Story," *Journal of Communication* 42, no. 1 (1992): 82–94. By contrast, proponents of mediatization would argue that news sources shape their presentations to best fit the news-gathering needs and schedules of journalists. See Gianpietro Mazzoleni and Winfried Schulz, "Mediatization of Politics: A Challenge for Democracy?" *Political Communication* 16, no. 3 (1999): 247–61.
88. Gaye Tuchman, *Making News: A Study in the Construction of Reality* (New York: Free Press, 1978).
89. Marie R. Haug, "The Deprofessionalization of Everyone?" *Sociological Focus* 8 (1975): 197–213.
90. Of course, search engines are not a neutral technology. See Alexander Halavais, *Search Engine Society* (Cambridge: Polity, 2009).
91. Tamara Witschge and Gunnar Nygren, "Journalism: A Profession Under Pressure?" *Journal of Media Business Studies* 6, no. 1 (2009): 37–59.
92. Ibid., "Journalism," 55.
93. David M. Ryfe, *Can Journalism Survive: An Inside Look at American Newsrooms* (Cambridge: Polity, 2012).
94. This was also noted in Pablo J. Boczkowski, *Digitizing the News: Innovation in Online Newspapers* (Cambridge, MA: MIT Press, 2004).
95. Sue Robinson and Cathy DeShano " 'Anyone Can Know': Citizen Journalism and the Interpretive Community of the Mainstream Press," *Journalism* 12, no. 8 (2011): 963–82.
96. See C. W. Anderson, *Rebuilding the News: Metropolitan Journalism in the Digital Age* (Philadelphia: Temple University Press, 2013). The clash between old and new will be examined in chapter 6.
97. Waisbord, *Reinventing Professionalism*, 224, 214.
98. John O'Sullivan and Ari Heinonen, "Old Values, New Media: Journalism Role Perceptions in a Changing World," *Journalism Practice* 2, no. 3 (2008): 357–71.
99. Örnebring, "Reassessing Journalism," 568–69.
100. Waisbord, *Reinventing Professionalism*, 212.
101. Anderson, "Journalism: Expertise, Authority, and Power," 259.

102. Nick Couldry, *Media Rituals: A Critical Approach* (London: Routledge, 2002).

103. Seth C. Lewis, "The Tension Between Professional Control and Open Participation: Journalism and its Boundaries," *Information, Communication & Society* 15, no. 6 (2012): 836–66.

104. Gieryn, *Cultural Boundaries of Science*; Carlson and Lewis, *Boundaries of Journalism*.

105. For a study on how this occurs with news production, see Richard V. Ericson, Patricia Baranek, and Janet B. L. Chan, *Visualizing Deviance: A Study of News Organization* (Milton Keynes, UK: Open University Press, 1987).

106. Maras, *Objectivity in Journalism*, 58.

2. TEXTS AND TEXTUAL AUTHORITY: FORMS OF JOURNALISM

1. Mackenzie Weinger, "Congressman Links to *Onion*," *Politico*, February 7, 2012, http://www.politico.com/news/stories/0212/72507.html#ixzz2iUEWru21.

2. "Planned Parenthood Opens $8 Billion Abortionplex," *The Onion*, May 18, 2011, http://www.theonion.com/articles/planned-parenthood-opens-8-billion-abortionplex,20476/.

3. See "Literally Unbelievable," http://literallyunbelievable.org/.

4. Jonathan Weisman and Jeremy W. Peters, "Government Shuts Down in Budget Impasse," *New York Times*, September 30, 2013, http://www.nytimes.com/2013/10/01/us/politics/congress-shutdown-debate.html.

5. "U.S. on Verge of Full-Scale Government Hoedown," *The Onion*, September 30, 2013, http://www.theonion.com/articles/us-on-verge-of-fullscale-government-hoedown,34057/.

6. Robert K. Manoff and Michael Schudson, *Reading the News: A Pantheon Guide to Popular Culture* (New York: Pantheon, 1986).

7. Michael Schudson, *Discovering the News: A Social History of American Newspapers* (New York: Basic Books, 1978).

8. Paul Starr, *The Social Transformation of American Medicine: The Rise of a Sovereign Profession and the Making of a Vast Industry* (New York: Basic Books, 1982).

9. Diana C. Mutz, *Impersonal Influence: How Perceptions of Mass Collectives Affect Political Attitudes* (New York: Cambridge University Press, 1998). Also Zvi Reich, "Journalism as Bipolar Interactional Expertise," *Communication Theory* 22, no. 4 (2012): 339–58. This is not to deny greater contact between journalists and their audiences, but the defining character of news is still the mediated story.

10. An alternative path would be to look deep inside the construction of a particular news story to parse the authoritative strategies embedded within. One

classic example of this strategy is Stuart Hall, Chas Critcher, Tony Jefferson, John Clarke, and Brian Roberts, *Policing the Crisis: Mugging, the State, and Law and Order* (London: Macmillan, 1978).

11. Kevin G. Barnhurst, and John C. Nerone, *The Form of News: A History* (New York: Guilford Press, 2001), 3.
12. Barnhurst and Nerone, *The Form of News*, 7.
13. Barbie Zelizer, *Taking Journalism Seriously: News and the Academy* (London: Sage, 2004).
14. An exchange between Bill Keller and Glenn Greenwald highlights these distinctions: "Is Glenn Greenwald the Future of News?" *New York Times*, October 27, 2013, http://www.nytimes.com/2013/10/28/opinion/a-conversation-in-lieu-of-a-column.html.
15. Even the idea of what constitutes an event is imposed by journalists or other actors.
16. John Hartley, *Understanding News* (London: Methuen, 1982).
17. Gaye Tuchman, *Making News: A Study in the Construction of Reality* (New York: Free Press, 1978).
18. It would also be enormously difficult for news audiences if no set forms existed.
19. Walter R. Fisher, "Narration as a Human Communication Paradigm: The Case of Public Moral Argument," *Communications Monographs* 51, no. 1 (1984): 1–22.
20. This anecdote also indicates the degree to which the inverted pyramid has become synecdochic of all news writing despite the plethora of forms that exist.
21. Michael Schudson, "The Politics of Narrative Form: The Emergence of News Conventions in Print and Television," *Daedalus* 3, no. 4 (1982), 97–112.
22. Bruno Latour, "Technology Is Society Made Durable," *Sociological Review* 38 (1990): 103–31.
23. Michael Schudson, *The Power of News* (Cambridge, MA: Harvard University Press, 1995).
24. Elizabeth S. Bird and Robert W. Dardenne, "Myth, Chronicle, and Story," in *Media, Myths, and Narratives*, ed. James W. Carey (Newbury Park, CA: Sage, 1988), 78.
25. Stuart Allan, *News Culture*, 2nd ed. (Maidenhead, UK: Open University Press, 2004).
26. Allan Bell, *The Language of News Media* (Oxford: Wiley-Blackwell, 1991).
27. This topic is treated at length in chapter 4.
28. Robert Darnton, "Writing News and Telling Stories," *Daedalus* 104, no. 2 (1975): 175–94.
29. Ibid.
30. Bird and Dardenne, "Myth, Chronicle, and Story," 67.

31. Matt Carlson, *On the Condition of Anonymity: Unnamed Sources and the Battle for Journalism* (Urbana: University of Illinois Press, 2011).

32. Matt Carlson, "Dueling, Dancing, or Dominating? Journalists and Their Sources," *Sociology Compass* 3, no. 4 (2009): 526–42. The topic of news sources is covered in chapter 5.

33. Stuart Hall, "The Rediscovery of Ideology: Return of the Repressed in Media Studies," in *Culture, Society, and the Media*, ed. Michael Gurevitch et al. (London: Routledge: 1982), 52–86.

34. Peter Dahlgren, introduction to *Journalism and Popular Culture*, ed. Peter Dahlgren and Colin Sparks (London: Sage, 1992).

35. Jürgen Habermas, *The Structural Transformation of the Public Sphere: An Inquiry into a Category of Bourgeois Society*, trans. Thomas Burger (Cambridge, MA: MIT Press, 1991).

36. Daniel C. Hallin, *We Keep America on Top of the World: Television Journalism and the Public Sphere* (London: Routledge, 1994).

37. Zelizer, *Taking Journalism Seriously.*

38. Key readings include: Hall et al., *Policing the Crisis*; Glasgow University Media Group, *Bad News* (London: Routledge and Kegan Paul, 1976); W. Lance Bennett, *News: The Politics of Illusion*, 2nd ed. (New York: Longman, 1988).

39. Rob Pollard, "Adam Curtis: We Don't Read Newspapers Because the Journalism Is So Boring," *New Statesman*, February 4, 2014, http://www.newstatesman.com/culture/2014/02/adam-curtis-interview.

40. John J. Pauly, "The Politics of New Journalism," in *Literary Journalism in the Twentieth Century*, ed. Norman Sims (New York: Oxford University Press, 1990), 110–29.

41. Chris Atton and James F. Hamilton, *Alternative Journalism* (London: Sage, 2008).

42. Tanni Haas, *The Pursuit of Public Journalism: Theory, Practice, and Criticism* (New York: Routledge, 2007).

43. Donald Matheson, "Weblogs and the Epistemology of the News: Some Trends in Online Journalism," *New Media & Society* 6, no. 4 (2004): 443–68; David W. Park, "Blogging with Authority: Strategic Positioning in Political Blogs," *International Journal of Communication* 3 (2009): 250–73.

44. Schudson, *The Power of News*, 21.

45. Barnhurst and Nerone, *The Form of News*, 22.

46. Ibid., 222.

47. This language has been echoed by Mark Zuckerberg in his understanding of what social media do.

48. Barnhurst and Nerone, *The Form of News*, 303.

49. The ability of journalists to select and arrange news has been codified in the media effects literature through the concept of agenda setting. In its most basic

sense, the research on agenda setting indicates that the interpretive selections journalists make about issue importance tend to be reproduced by news audiences. Over decades, this research has become increasingly savvy in detailing this effect, but looked at from above, agenda setting provides further evidence for the presentational authority of journalists. Setting the news agenda is central to the claims journalists make in selecting and presenting the news. Journalists justify this power through an appeal to professional norms.

50. Zvi Reich, "Constrained Authors: Bylines and Authorship in News Reporting," *Journalism* 11, no. 6 (2010): 707–25.

51. Barnhurst and Nerone, *The Form of News*, 248–51.

52. Hartley, *Understanding News*.

53. Allan, *News Culture*, 37.

54. Matt Carlson and Daniel A. Berkowitz, "Twilight of the Television Idols: Collective Memory, Network News, and the Death of Walter Cronkite," *Memory Studies* 5, no. 4 (2012): 410–24.

55. Torunn Selberg, "Television and Ritualization of Everyday Life," *Journal of Popular Culture* 26, no. 4 (1993): 3–10.

56. The website of the UK newspaper *Daily Mail* has become one of the leading English-language news sites in the world through a site mainly consisting of a single home page with new content continually added at the top.

57. C. W. Anderson, *Rebuilding the News: Metropolitan Journalism in the Digital Age* (Philadelphia: Temple University, 2013); Nikki Usher, *Making News at the New York Times* (Ann Arbor: University of Michigan Press, 2014).

58. Alexis Sobel Fitts, "When Metrics Drive Newsroom Culture," *Columbia Journalism Review*, May 11, 2015, http://www.cjr.org/analysis/how_should_metrics _drive_newsroom_culture.php.

59. Matt Carlson, "When News Sites Go Native: Redefining the Advertising–Editorial Divide in Response to Native Advertising," *Journalism* 16, no. 7 (2015): 849–65.

60. Mark Coddington, "The Wall Becomes a Curtain: Revisiting Journalism's News-Business Boundary," in *Boundaries of Journalism*, ed. Matt Carlson and Seth C. Lewis (New York: Routledge, 2015), 67–82.

61. Matt Carlson, "Order Versus Access: News Search Engines and the Challenge to Traditional Journalistic Roles," *Media, Culture & Society* 29, no. 6 (2007): 1014–30.

62. Stefaan G. Verhulst, "Mediation, Mediators, and New Intermediaries: Implications for the Design of New Communication Policies," in *Media Diversity and Localism: Meaning and Metrics*, ed. Philip Napoli (Mahwah, NJ: Lawrence Erlbaum, 2007), 122.

63. Matt Carlson, "The Robotic Reporter: Automated Journalism and the Redefinition of Labor, Compositional Forms, and Journalistic Authority," *Digital Journalism* 3, no. 3 (2015): 416–31.

64. C. W. Anderson, "What Aggregators Do: Towards a Networked Concept of Journalistic Expertise in the Digital Age," *Journalism* 14, no. 8 (2013): 1008–23.

65. Matt Carlson, "Embedded Links, Embedded Meanings: Social Media Commentary and News Sharing as Mundane Media Criticism," *Journalism Practice* 17, no. 7 (2016): 915–24.

66. Zachary M. Seward, "The Homepage Is Dead, and the Social Web Has Won—Even at the New York Times," *Quartz*, May 15, 2014, http://qz.com/209950/the-homepage-is-dead-and-the-social-web-has-won-even-at-the-new-york-times/.

67. This section uses the term *news image* primarily with reference to photography, although there are other image practices that persist in news content.

68. Dona Schwartz, "To Tell the Truth: Codes of Objectivity in Photojournalism," *Communication* 13, no. 2 (1992): 95–109.

69. Lorraine Daston and Peter Galison, *Objectivity* (New York: Zone Books, 2007).

70. John Ellis, *Seeing Things: Television in the Age of Uncertainty* (London: I. B. Tauris, 2000).

71. Sarah Kember, "The Shadow of the Object: Photography and Realism," in *The Photography Reader*, ed. Liz Wells (London: Routledge, 2003), 202–17.

72. Loup Langton, *Photojournalism and Today's News: Creating Visual Reality* (Malden, MA: Wiley-Blackwell, 2009).

73. Schwartz, "To Tell the Truth," 96–97.

74. Michael Griffin, "The Great War Photographs: Constructing Myths of History and Photojournalism," in Bonnie Brennen and Hanno Hardt, eds., *Picturing the Past: Media, History, and Photography* (Urbana: University of Illinois Press, 1999), 122–57.

75. Stuart Hall, "The Determination of News Photographs," in *The Manufacture of News*, ed. Stanley Cohen and Jock Young (Beverly Hills, CA: Sage, 1973), 226–43; Roland Barthes, *Image/Music/Text*, trans. Stephen Heath (New York: Hill and Wang, 1977).

76. John Berger, *About Looking* (New York: Pantheon, 1980).

77. Karin E. Becker, "Photojournalism and the Tabloid Press," in *The Photography Reader*, 291–308.

78. Stuart Allan, *Citizen Witnessing: Revisioning Journalism in Times of Crisis* (Cambridge: Polity, 2013).

79. Andrew Beaujon, "Chicago Sun-Times Lays Off Its Photo Staff," *Poynter*, May 30, 2013, http://www.poynter.org/news/mediawire/214837/chicago-sun-times-lays-off-its-photographers-photo-staff/.

80. This is hardly a deviant action. In my institution, learning to manipulate images in Photoshop has become a standardized part of our curriculum.

81. Matt Carlson, "The Reality of a Fake Image: News Norms, Photojournalistic Craft and Brian Walski's Fabricated Photograph." *Journalism Practice* 3, no. 2 (2009): 125–39.

82. Jenni Mäenpää and Janne Seppänen, "Imaginary Darkroom: Digital Photo Editing as a Strategic Ritual," *Journalism Practice* 4, no. 4 (2010): 454–75.

83. Julianne H. Newton, "Photojournalism: Do People Matter? Then Photojournalism Matters," *Journalism Practice* 3, no. 2 (2009): 233–43.

84. Matt Carlson, "Rethinking Journalistic Authority: Walter Cronkite and Ritual in Television News," *Journalism Studies* 13, no. 4 (2012): 483–98.

85. Zelizer, *Taking Journalism Seriously*, 177.

86. James W. Carey, *Communication as Culture: Essays on Media and Society* (London: Routledge, 1992).

87. Carey, *Communication as Culture*, 17.

88. Bird and Dardenne, "Myth, Chronicle, and Story," 69.

89. Jack Lule, *Daily News, Eternal Stories: The Mythological Role of Journalism* (New York: Guilford Press, 2001).

90. For another example, see Richard Campbell, *"60 Minutes" and the News* (Urbana: University of Illinois Press, 1991).

91. Zelizer, *Taking Journalism Seriously*, 189.

92. John Fiske and John Hartley, *Reading Television* (London: Routledge, 1978).

93. Elihu Katz and Daniel Dayan, *Media Events: The Live Broadcasting of History* (Cambridge, MA: Harvard University Press, 1992).

94. Karin Becker, "Media and the Ritual Process," *Media, Culture & Society* 17, no. 4 (1995): 629–46.

95. Philip Elliott, "Press Performance as Political Ritual," *Sociological Review Monograph* 29 (1980): 141–77.

96. Simon Cottle, "Mediatized Rituals: Beyond Manufacturing Consent," *Media, Culture & Society* 28, no. 3 (2006): 411–32.

97. Matt Carlson, "Rethinking Journalistic Authority," 483–98.

98. Barry Richards, "News and the Emotional Public Sphere," in *The Routledge Companion to News and Journalism*, ed. Stuart Allan (London: Routledge, 2010), 301–11.

99. Richards, "News and the Emotional Public Sphere," 303.

100. Karin Wahl-Jorgensen, "The Strategic Ritual of Emotionality: A Case Study of Pulitzer Prize-Winning Articles," *Journalism* 14, no. 1 (2013): 129–45.

101. Norman Fairclough, "Political Discourse in the Media: An Analytical Framework," in *Approaches to Media Discourse*, ed. Allan Bell and Peter Garrett (Malden, MA: Blackwell, 1998), 142–63; see Matt Carlson and Eran Ben-Porath, "'The People's Debate': The CNN/YouTube Debates and the Demotic Voice in Political Journalism," *Journalism Practice* 6, no. 3 (2012): 302–16.

102. Carolyn Kitch and Janice Hume, *Journalism in a Culture of Grief* (New York: Routledge, 2008). See also Mervi Pantti and Johanna Sumiala, "Till Death Do Us Join: Media, Mourning Rituals and the Sacred Centre of the Society," *Media, Culture & Society* 31, no. 1 (2009): 119–35.

103. Barbie Zelizer, *Covering the Body: The Kennedy Assassination, the Media, and the Shaping of Collective Memory* (Chicago: University of Chicago Press, 1992).

104. Carlson, "The Reality of a Fake Image."

105. See Barbie Zelizer and Stuart Allan, *Journalism After September 11* (New York: Routledge, 2011).

106. Robert Hariman and John Louis Lucaites, *No Caption Needed: Iconic Photographs, Public Culture, and Liberal Democracy* (Chicago: University of Chicago Press, 2007).

107. Michael Griffin, "The Great War Photographs," 122–57; Barbie Zelizer, *Remembering to Forget: Holocaust Memory Through the Camera's Eye* (Chicago: University of Chicago Press, 1998).

108. Matt Carlson, "The Reality of a Fake Image."

109. Marita Sturken, *Tangled Memories: The Vietnam War, the AIDS Epidemic, and the Politics of Remembering* (Berkeley: University of California Press, 1997).

110. Carlson, "Rethinking Journalistic Authority."

111. See Matt Carlson and Nikki Usher, "News Startups as Agents of Innovation: For-Profit Digital News Startup Manifestos as Metajournalistic Discourse," *Digital Journalism* 4 no. 4 (2016): 563–81.

112. See Park, "Blogging with Authority"; Matheson, "Weblogs and the Epistemology of the News."

3. TELLING STORIES ABOUT THEMSELVES: JOURNALISM'S NARRATIVES

1. Christine Haughney, "Times Wins Four Pulitzers; Brooklyn Nonprofit Is Awarded a Reporting Prize," *New York Times*, April 15, 2013, http://www.nytimes.com/2013/04/16/business/media/the-times-wins-four-pulitzer-prizes.html?_r=0.

2. Paul Tash, "Remarks" (speech delivered at the 2013 Annual Pulitzer Luncheon, Columbia University, New York, NY, May 30, 2013).

3. Although one notable difference was the prize for national reporting given to the news site *Inside Climate News*, which was the first Pulitzer awarded to an online news organization.

4. Peter Dahlgren, introduction to *Journalism and Popular Culture*, ed. Peter Dahlgren and Colin Sparks (London: Sage, 1992), 1–23.

5. Actors outside of journalism also engage in public discourse defining what journalism is, and this specific topic will be taken up in chapter 7.

6. For a fuller theoretical treatment, see Matt Carlson, "Metajournalistic Discourse and the Meanings of Journalism: Definitional Control, Boundary Work, and Legitimation," *Communication Theory* (forthcoming). For empirical examples, see Matt Carlson, *On the Condition of Anonymity: Unnamed Sources and the Battle for Journalism* (Urbana: University of Illinois Press, 2011); and Carlson, "Gone, But Not Forgotten: Memories of Journalistic Deviance as Metajournalistic Discourse," *Journalism Studies* 15, no. 1 (2014): 33–47.

7. This argument is explored in more detail in Carlson, "Metajournalistic Discourse and the Meanings of Journalism."

8. For example, the growing practice of native advertising is accompanied by robust discussion regarding its merits and detriments. See Matt Carlson, "When News Sites Go Native: Redefining the Advertising-Editorial Divide in Response to Native Advertising," *Journalism* 16, no. 7 (2015): 849–65.

9. Meryl Aldridge and Julia Evetts, "Rethinking the Concept of Professionalism: The Case of Journalism," *British Journal of Sociology* 54, (2003): 547–64.

10. Tanni Haas, "Mainstream News Media Self-Criticism: A Proposal for Future Research," *Critical Studies in Media Communication* 23, no. 4 (2006): 350.

11. Barbie Zelizer, *Covering the Body: The Kennedy Assassination, the Media, and the Shaping of Collective Memory* (Chicago: University of Chicago Press, 1992); Peter Dahlgren, introduction to *Journalism and Popular Culture.*

12. This section is adapted from Matt Carlson, "'Where Once Stood Titans': Second-Order Paradigm Repair and the Vanishing U.S. Newspaper," *Journalism* 13, no. 3 (2012): 267–83.

13. Matt Carlson, "Telling the Crisis Story of Journalism: Narratives of Normative Reassurance in Page One," in *The Crisis of Journalism Reconsidered: Democratic Culture, Professional Codes, Digital Future*, ed. Jeffrey C. Alexander, Elizabeth Butler Breese and Maria Luengo (New York: Cambridge University Press, 2016), 135–52.

14. Rob Reuteman, "Rocky and I Made It Our Business to Be Useful," *Rocky Mountain News*, February 27, 2009.

15. Debra J. Saunders, "Cutting Off Your News to Spite Your Face," *San Francisco Chronicle*, February 26, 2009, http://www.sfgate.com/opinion/article/Cutting-off-your-news-to-spite-your-face-3170870.php.

16. Pablo J. Boczkowski, *Digitizing the News: Innovation in Online Newspapers* (Cambridge, MA: MIT Press, 2004); David Ryfe, *Can Journalism Survive? An Inside Look at American Newsrooms* (Cambridge: Polity, 2012).

17. Carlson, "Telling the Crisis Story of Journalism."

18. Mark Deuze, "What Is Journalism? Professional Identity and Ideology of Journalists Reconsidered," *Journalism* 6, no. 4 (2005): 442–64.

19. C. W. Anderson, Emily Bell, and Clay Shirky, *Post-Industrial Journalism: Adapting to the Present* (New York: Tow Center for Digital Journalism, 2012), http://towcenter.org/wp-content/uploads/2012/11/TOWCenter-Post_Industrial _Journalism.pdf /.

20. However, differentiation can also result from the purposive framing invoked by proponents of new forms of journalism—or advocates for the reinvigoration of alternative norms such as partisanship—who position the strictures of objective journalism as detrimental to news.

21. Carolyn Kitch, "Anniversary Journalism, Collective Memory, and the Cultural Authority to Tell the Story of the American Past," *Journal of Popular Culture* 36, no. 1 (2002): 44–67.

22. Hanna Rosin, "Hello, My Name Is Stephen Glass, and I'm Sorry," *New Republic*, November 10, 2014, http://www.newrepublic.com/article/120145/stephen-glass-new-republic-scandal-still-haunts-his-law-career.

23. Buzz Bissinger, "Shattered Glass," *Vanity Fair*, September 1998, http://www .vanityfair.com/magazine/archive/1998/09/bissinger199809.

24. W. Lance Bennett, Lynne A. Gressett, and William Haltom, "Repairing the News: A Case Study of the News Paradigm," *Journal of Communication* 35, no. 2 (1985): 50–68; Stephen D. Reese, "The News Paradigm and the Ideology of Objectivity: A Socialist at the *Wall Street Journal*," *Critical Studies in Media Communication* 7, no. 4 (1990): 390–409; Dan Berkowitz, "Doing Double Duty Paradigm Repair and the Princess Diana What-a-Story," *Journalism* 1, no. 2 (2000): 125–43; Thomas E. Ruggiero, "Paradigm Repair and Changing Journalistic Perceptions of the Internet as an Objective News Source," *Convergence* 10, no. 4 (2004): 92–106; Matthew Cecil, "Bad Apples: Paradigm Overhaul and the CNN/Time "Tailwind" Story," *Journal of Communication Inquiry* 26, no. 1 (2002): 46–58; Elizabeth Blanks Hindman, "Jayson Blair, The *New York Times*, and Paradigm Repair," *Journal of Communication* 55, no. 2 (2005): 225–41; Matt Carlson, "'Where Once Stood Titans'": 267–83; Matt Carlson, "The Reality of a Fake Image: News Norms, Photojournalistic Craft, and Brian Walski's Fabricated Photo," *Journalism Practice* 3, no. 2 (2009): 125–39.

25. Thomas S. Kuhn, *The Structure of Scientific Revolutions*, 50th anniversary ed. (Chicago: University of Chicago Press, 2012).

26. Matt Carlson and Dan Berkowitz, "'The Emperor Lost His Clothes': Rupert Murdoch, News of the World and Journalistic Boundary Work in the UK and USA," *Journalism* 15, no. 4 (2014): 389–406.

27. Matt Carlson, "Gone, but Not Forgotten: Memories of Journalistic Deviance as Metajournalistic Discourse," *Journalism Studies* 15, no. 1 (2014): 33–47.

28. Michèle Lamont, and Virág Molnár, "The Study of Boundaries in the Social Sciences," *Annual Review of Sociology* (2002): 167–95.

29. Thomas Gieryn, "Boundary-Work and the Demarcation of Science from Non-Science: Strains and Interests in Professional Ideologies of Scientists," *American Sociological Review* 48, no. 6 (1983): 781–95; Thomas Gieryn, "Boundaries of Science," in *Handbook of Science and Technology Studies*, ed. Sheila Jasanoff et al. (Thousand Oaks, CA: Sage, 1995), 393–443; Thomas Gieryn, *Cultural Boundaries of Science: Credibility on the Line* (Chicago: University of Chicago Press, 1999).

30. Already used in journalism studies by Samuel P. Winch, *Mapping the Cultural Space of Journalism: How Journalists Distinguish News from Entertainment* (Westport, CT: Praeger, 1997); Michael Schudson and C. W. Anderson, "Objectivity, Professionalism, and Truth Seeking in Journalism," in *Handbook of Journalism Studies*, ed. Karin Wahl-Jorgensen and Thomas Hanitzsch (New York, Routledge, 2008), 88–101; Seth C. Lewis, "The Tension Between Professional Control and Open Participation: Journalism and Its Boundaries," *Information, Communication & Society* 15, no. 6 (2012): 836–66.

31. Gieryn, *Cultural Boundaries of Science*, 1.

32. Andrew Abbott, *The System of Professions: An Essay on the Division of Expert Labor* (Chicago: University of Chicago Press, 1988).

33. Matt Carlson, "The Many Boundaries of Journalism," in *Boundaries of Journalism*, ed. Matt Carlson and Seth C. Lewis (New York: Routledge, 2015), 1–18.

34. These barriers have been reviewed more thoroughly in chapter 1 in their connection with professionalism.

35. Zvi Reich, "Journalism as Bipolar Interactional Expertise," *Communication Theory* 22, no. 4 (2012): 339–58.

36. Similarly, Gieryn points to scientists' belief in their social good.

37. Kimberly Meltzer argues that authority is hierarchical in Kimberly Meltzer, "The Hierarchy of Journalistic Cultural Authority: Journalists' Perspectives according to News Medium," *Journalism Practice* 3, no. 1 (2009): 59–74.

38. Dan Berkowitz, "Doing Double Duty Paradigm Repair and the Princess Diana What-a-Story," *Journalism* 1, no. 2 (2000): 125–43.

39. Brian Stelter and Bill Carter, "For Instant Ratings, Just Add Cash," *New York Times*, June 13, 2011.

40. Mark Deuze, "What Is Journalism?"; John Soloski, "News Reporting and Professionalism: Some Constraints on the Reporting of the News," *Media, Culture & Society* 11, no. 2 (1989): 207–28; Seth C. Lewis, "Tension Between Professional Control."

41. Barbie Zelizer, "Journalists as Interpretive Communities," *Critical Studies in Media Communication* 10, no. 3 (1993): 219–37.

42. Stanley Fish, *Is There a Text in This Class? The Authority of Interpretive Communities* (Cambridge, MA: Harvard University Press, 1980).

43. Barbie Zelizer, *Covering the Body.*

44. In Zelizer's view, "communities arise less through rigid indicators of training or education—as indicated by the frame of the profession—and more through the informal associations that build up around shared interpretations," Zelizer, "Journalists as Interpretive Communities," 223.

45. For an overview on this topic, see Barbie Zelizer and Keren Tenenboim-Weinblatt, eds. *Journalism and Memory* (London: Palgrave Macmillan, 2014).

46. Barbie Zelizer, "Reading the Past Against the Grain: The Shape of Memory Studies," *Critical Studies in Mass Communication* 12, no. 2 (1995): 214–39.

47. Matt Carlson and Dan Berkowitz, "Twilight of the Television Idols: Collective Memory, Network News, and the Death of Walter Cronkite," *Memory Studies* 5, no. 4 (2012): 408–22.

48. See Michael Schudson, *Watergate in American Memory: How We Remember, Forget, and Reconstruct the Past* (New York: Basic Books, 1992).

49. Nick Couldry, *Media Rituals: A Critical Approach* (London: Routledge, 2002). Couldry uses the terms to describe media rituals, but it is applicable here in the discussion of metajournalistic discourse.

50. Daniel Hallin captures this larger idea in his spheres-of-consensus model, in which journalists become arbiters of what topics may be considered as matters of consensus, legitimate controversy, or deviance. See Daniel C. Hallin, *The "Uncensored War": The Media and Vietnam* (New York: Oxford University Press, 1986).

51. Couldry, *Media Rituals*, 2.

52. Ibid., 28.

53. Abbott, *The System of Professions.*

4. RECOGNIZING JOURNALISTIC AUTHORITY: THE PUBLIC'S OPINION

1. Seth C. Lewis, "Journalism in an Era of Big Data: Cases, Concepts, and Critiques," *Digital Journalism* 3, no. 3 (2015): 321–30.

2. Matt Carlson and Nikki Usher, "News Startups as Agents of Innovation: For-Profit Digital News Startup Manifestos as Metajournalistic Discourse," *Digital Journalism* 4, no. 4 (2016): 563–81.

3. Pablo J. Boczkowski and Eugenia Mitchelstein, *The News Gap: When the Information Preferences of the Media and the Public Diverge* (Cambridge, MA: MIT Press, 2013).

4. David Leonhardt, "Navigate News with The Upshot," *New York Times*, April 22, 2014, http://www.nytimes.com/2014/04/23/upshot/navigate-news-with-the-upshot.html?rref=upshot.

5. This traffic statistic is from the *New York Times* media kit, available at http:// nytmediakit.com/digital.

6. The term *audience* is preferable as the simplest denotation of users of news media content, as opposed to other terms including the business-minded *consumers*, the medium-centric *readers* or *viewers*, or the normatively embalmed *citizens* or *public*.

7. C. W. Anderson, *Rebuilding the News: Metropolitan News in the Digital Age* (Philadelphia: Temple University Press, 2013).

8. Ernesto Laclau and Chantal Mouffe, *Hegemony and Socialist Strategy: Towards a Radical Democratic Politics*, 2nd ed. (London: Verso, 2001).

9. Nick Couldry, *Media Rituals: A Critical Approach* (London: Routledge, 2002).

10. Bertram H. Raven and John R. P. French Jr., "Group Support, Legitimate Power, and Social Influence," *Journal of Personality* 21 (1958): 400–409.

11. Tom R. Tyler and E. Allan Lind, "A Relational Model of Authority in Groups," in *Advances in Experimental Social Psychology*, ed. Mark P. Zanna (San Diego: Academic Press, 1992), 115–91.

12. Brett Caraway, "Audience Labor in the New Media Environment: A Marxian Revisiting of the Audience Commodity," *Media, Culture & Society* 33, no. 5 (2011): 693–708.

13. C. W. Anderson, "Between Creative and Quantified Audiences: Web Metrics and Changing Patterns of Newswork in Local US Newsrooms," *Journalism* 12, no. 5 (2011): 550–66.

14. For example, see Joseph Turow, *The Daily You: How the New Advertising Industry Is Defining Your Identity and Your Worth* (New Haven: Yale University Press, 2012).

15. Bernard Berelson, "What Missing the Newspaper Means," in *Communications Research 1948–1949*, ed. P. F. Lazarsfeld and F. N. Stanton (New York: Harper & Brothers, 1949), 111–29.

16. Ibid., 114. Italics in the original.

17. Anton J. Nederhof, "Methods of Coping with Social Desirability Bias: A Review," *European Journal of Social Psychology* 15, no. 3 (1985): 263–80.

18. Lester R. Wheeler and Viola D. Wheeler, "Newspapers in the Classroom," *The Elementary English Review* 22, no. 8 (1945): 324–29.

19. John J. Pauly, "Interesting the Public: A Brief History of the Newsreading Movement," *Communication* 12, no. 4 (1991): 285–97. See also Justin Lewis and Sut Jhally, "The Struggle over Media Literacy," *Journal of Communication* 48, no. 1 (1998): 109–20.

20. Markus Prior, "The Immensely Inflated News Audience: Assessing Bias in Self-Reported News Exposure," *Public Opinion Quarterly* 73, no. 1 (2009): 130–43.

21. This is also an issue in the role of news in education. See Pauly, "Interesting the Public."

22. Berelson, "What Missing the Newspaper Means," 125.

23. James W. Carey, *Communication as Culture: Essays on Media and Culture* (London: Routledge, 1992), 17.

24. Justin Lewis, *Constructing Public Opinion: How Political Elites Do What They Like and Why We Seem to Go Along with It* (New York: Columbia University Press, 2001).

25. Timothy E. Cook, *Governing with the News: The News Media as a Political Institution* (Chicago: University of Chicago Press, 1998).

26. Andrew Dugan, "Americans' Confidence in News Media Remains Low," Gallup, June 19, 2014, http://www.gallup.com/poll/171740/americans-confidence -news-media-remains-low.aspx.

27. Elizabeth Mendes, "In U.S., Trust in Media Recovers Slightly from All-Time Low," Gallup, September 19, 2013, http://www.gallup.com/poll/164459/trust -media-recovers-slightly-time-low.aspx. The wording of the question is: "In general, how much trust and confidence do you have in the mass media— such as newspapers, TV, and radio—when it comes to reporting the news fully, accurately, and fairly—a great deal, a fair amount, not very much, or none at all?"

28. "CNN Opinion Research Poll," CNN/Opinion Research Corporation, October 16–18, 2009, http://i2.cdn.turner.com/cnn/2010/images/03/09/top15.pdf.

29. Tom Jensen, "4th Annual TV News Trust Poll," *Public Policy Polling*, February 6, 2013, http://www.publicpolicypolling.com/main/2013/02/4th-annual-tv-news -trust-poll.html.

30. Again, this is only when speaking of being *an* authority rather than those *in* authority—governing bodies may lack credibility but easily exercise their coercive power.

31. This is taken up in chapter 7.

32. Dugan, "Americans' Confidence."

33. Arthur H. Miller, "Political Issues and Trust in Government: 1964–1970," *American Political Science Review* 68, no. 3 (1974): 951–72.

34. Timothy E. Cook and Paul Gronke, "The Skeptical American: Revisiting the Meanings of Trust in Government and Confidence in Institutions," *Journal of Politics* 67, no. 3 (2005): 784–803.

35. Frank Furedi, *Authority: A Sociological History* (Cambridge: Cambridge University Press, 2013), 153.

36. Rebecca Riffkin, "Public Faith in Congress Falls Again, Hits Historic Low," Gallup, June 19, 2014, http://www.gallup.com/poll/171710/public-faith-con gress-falls-again-hits-historic-low.aspx. The survey found only three public

institutions—the military, small businesses, and the police—garnered confidence from at least 50 percent of respondents

37. Hazel Erskine, "The Polls: Opinion of the News Media," *Public Opinion Quarterly* 34, no. 4 (1970): 630–43.

38. Barbie Zelizer, "When Facts, Truth, and Reality Are God-Terms: On Journalism's Uneasy Place in Cultural Studies," *Communication and Critical/Cultural Studies* 1, no. 1 (2004): 100–119; Jo Bogaerts and Nico Carpentier, "The Postmodern Challenge to Journalism," in *Rethinking Journalism: Trust and Participation in a Transformed News Landscape*, ed. Chris Peters and Marcel Broersma (London: Routledge, 2013), 60–71.

39. Yariv Tsfati and Joseph N. Cappella, "Why Do People Watch News They Do Not Trust? The Need for Cognition as a Moderator in the Association between News Media Skepticism and Exposure," *Media Psychology* 7, no. 3 (2005): 251–71.

40. Lewis, *Constructing Public Opinion*.

41. Pew Research Center, "Amid Criticism, Support for Media's 'Watchdog' Role Stands Out," August 8, 2013, http://www.people-press.org/2013/08/08/amid criticism-support-for-medias-watchdog-role-stands-out/.

42. Lewis, *Constructing Public Opinion*, 18.

43. Ibid., 9.

44. Its main polling arm, the Pew Research Center for the People and the Press, previously existed as the Times Mirror Center for the People and the Press, operated by the Times Mirror newspaper chain. For the sake of full disclosure, the author worked for the Pew-funded Project for Excellence in Journalism before it merged with the Pew Research Center.

45. The mission of the Pew Research Center can be found at http://www.pewresearch.org/about/.

46. Based on this description, one can imagine a relational theory of public opinion–survey authority.

47. Although many of the journalism-related questions were asked of only half the sample (n=740), with a margin of error of 4.2 percent.

48. Pew Research Center, "Amid Criticism."

49. Matt Carlson, "Journalistic Change in an Online Age: Disaggregating Visibility, Legitimacy, and Revenue," *JOMEC Journal* 3, (2013), https://publications.cardiffuniversitypress.org/index.php/JOMEC/article/view/308/316.

50. Matthew Hindman, *The Myth of Digital Democracy* (Princeton, NJ: Princeton University Press, 2008); Evgeny Morozov, *The Net Delusion: The Dark Side of Internet Freedom* (New York: PublicAffairs, 2012).

51. Axel Bruns, *Blogs, Wikipedia, Second Life, and Beyond: From Production to Produsage* (New York: Peter Lang, 2008).

52. Dan Gillmor, *We the Media: Grassroots Journalism by the People, for the People* (Sebastopol, CA: O'Reilly Media, 2004).

53. Clay Shirky, *Here Comes Everybody: The Power of Organizing without Organizations* (New York: Penguin Books, 2008); Yochai Benkler, *The Wealth of Networks: How Social Production Transforms Markets and Freedom* (New Haven: Yale University Press, 2006); Jeff Jarvis, *Public Parts: How Sharing in the Digital Age Improves the Way We Work and Live* (New York: Simon & Schuster, 2011).

54. Seth C. Lewis, "The Tension Between Professional Control and Open Participation: Journalism and Its Boundaries," *Information, Communication & Society* 15, no. 6 (2012): 836–66.

55. Sue Robinson, "Journalism as Process: The Organizational Implications of Participatory Online News," *Journalism & Communication Monographs* 13, no. 3 (2011): 137–210.

56. For a comprehensive overview, see Jane B. Singer et al., *Participatory Journalism: Guarding Open Gates at Online Newspapers* (Malden, MA: Wiley-Blackwell, 2011).

57. Andy Williams, Claire Wardle, and Karin Wahl-Jorgensen, "'Have They Got News for Us?' Audience Revolution or Business as Usual at the BBC?" *Journalism Practice* 5, no. 1 (2011): 85–99.

58. Jay Rosen, "Jay Rosen on Wikipedia's 10th Anniversary," *Atlantic*, January 13, 2011, http://www.theatlantic.com/technology/archive/2011/01/jay-rosen-on-wikipedias -10th-anniversary/69518/.

59. Hindman, *Myth of Digital Democracy.*

60. Richard Sennett, *Authority* (New York: Knopf, 1980), 10.

5. LEGITIMATING KNOWLEDGE THROUGH KNOWERS: NEWS SOURCES

1. Brian Stelter, "CNN and Fox Trip Up in Rush to Get the News on the Air," *New York Times*, June 28, 2012, http://www.nytimes.com/2012/06/29/us/cnn-and -foxs-supreme-court-mistake.html?_r=0.

2. Adrienne LaFrance, "Anatomy of a Spoke: How SCOTUS Blog Dealt with Its Biggest Traffic Day Ever," *Nieman Lab*, June 29, 2012, http://www.niemanlab.org /2012/06/anatomy-of-a-spike-how-scotus-blog-dealt-with-its-biggest -traffic-day-ever/.

3. *SCOTUSblog* was able to gain access through an early credential possessed by one of its staff members.

4. By the term *sources* this chapter refers to actors who provide material— information, quotations, opinions, documents, media—to journalists.

5. This is similar to Cottle's division between sociological and culturalist approaches to news access. Simon Cottle, "Rethinking News Access," *Journalism Studies* 1, no. 3 (2000): 427–48.

6. Herbert J. Gans, *Deciding What's News: A Study of CBS Evening News, NBC Nightly News, Newsweek, and Time* (New York: Pantheon, 1979), 128–31.

7. Zvi Reich, *Sourcing the News: Key Issues in Journalism—an Innovative Study of the Israeli Press* (Cresskill, NJ: Hampton Press, 2009).

8. For a classic example, see Steve Chibnall, *Law-and-Order News: An Analysis of Crime Reporting in the British Press* (London: Tavistock, 1977).

9. Mark Fishman, *Manufacturing the News* (Austin: University of Texas Press, 1980).

10. Oscar H. Gandy Jr., *Beyond Agenda Setting: Information Subsidies and Public Policy* (Norwood, NJ: Ablex Publishing, 1982).

11. Reich, *Sourcing the News.*

12. Alison Anderson, "Source Strategies and the Communication of Environmental Affairs," *Media, Culture & Society* 13, no. 4 (1991): 459–76.

13. Aeron Davis, *Public Relations Democracy* (Manchester: Manchester University Press, 2002).

14. Justin Lewis, Andrew Williams, and Bob Franklin, "A Compromised Fourth Estate? UK News Journalism, Public Relations and News Sources," *Journalism Studies* 9, no. 1 (2008): 1–20.

15. Leon V. Sigal, *Reporters and Officials: The Organization and Politics of Newsmaking* (Lexington, MA: D. C. Heath, 1973).

16. Leon V. Sigal, "Sources Make the News," in *Reading the News: A Pantheon Guide to Popular Culture*, ed. Robert K. Manoff and Michael Schudson (New York: Pantheon, 1986), 27–28.

17. Jane Delano Brown et al., "Invisible Power: Newspaper News Sources and the Limits of Diversity," *Journalism Quarterly* 64 (1987): 45–54.

18. Daniel C. Hallin, Robert Karl Manoff, and Judy K. Weddle, "Sourcing Patterns of National Security Reporters," *Journalism Quarterly* 70 (1993): 753–66.

19. Dan Berkowitz, "TV News Sources and News Channels: A Study in Agenda-Building," *Journalism Quarterly* 64 (1987): 508–13.

20. John Soloski, "Sources and Channels of Local News," *Journalism Quarterly* 66 (1989): 864–70.

21. Nick Couldry, *Why Voice Matters: Culture and Politics After Neoliberalism* (London: Sage, 2010).

22. Michael Schudson and C. W. Anderson, "Objectivity, Professionalism, and Truth Seeking in Journalism," in *Handbook of Journalism Studies*, ed. Karin Wahl-Jorgensen and Thomas Hanitzsch (New York: Routledge, 2008), 88–101.

23. Barbie Zelizer, "On 'Having Been There': 'Eyewitnessing' as a Journalistic Key Word," *Critical Studies in Media Communication* 24, no. 5 (2007): 408–28. See chapter 2 for more on news photographs and witnessing.

24. Richard V. Ericson, "How Journalists Visualize Fact," *Annals of the American Academy of Political and Social Science* 560, (1998): 83–95.

25. Gaye Tuchman, "Objectivity as Strategic Ritual," *American Journal of Sociology* 77, (1972): 660–79. Of course, with anonymous sources, journalists lose such protections: Matt Carlson, *On the Condition of Anonymity: Unnamed Sources and the Battle for Journalism* (Urbana: University of Illinois Press, 2011).

26. Daniel Hallin, *The 'Uncensored War': The Media and Vietnam* (New York: Oxford University Press, 1986).

27. W. Lance Bennett, "Toward a Theory of Press-State Relations in the United States," *Journal of Communication* 40, (1990): 103–25; W. Lance Bennett, Regina G. Lawrence, and Steven Livingston, *When the Press Fails: Politcal Power and the News Media from Iraq to Katrina* (Chicago: University of Chicago Press, 2007).

28. Soloski, "Sources and Channels of Local News," 864.

29. James W. Carey, *Communication as Culture: Essays on Media and Society* (London: Routledge, 1992).

30. Gans, *Deciding What's New*; Chibnall, *Law-and-Order News*; Gaye Tuchman, *Making News: A Study in the Construction of Reality* (New York: Free Press, 1978); Philip Schlesinger, *Putting "Reality" Together: BBC News* (London: Methuen, 1987).

31. For example, Glasgow University Media Group, *Bad News* (London: Routledge and Kegan Paul, 1976).

32. Stuart Hall et al., *Policing the Crisis: Mugging, the State, and Law and Order* (London: Macmillan, 1978).

33. Philip Schlesinger, "Rethinking the Sociology of Journalism: Source Strategies and the Limits of Media-Centrism," in *Public Communication: The New Imperatives: Future Directions for Media Research*, ed. Marjorie Ferguson (London: Sage Publications, 1990), 61–83; Philip Schlesinger and Howard Tumber, *Reporting Crime: The Media Politics of Criminal Justice* (Oxford: Clarendon Press, 1994).

34. Todd Gitlin, *The Whole World Is Watching: Mass Media in the Making and Unmaking of the New Left* (Berkeley: University of California Press, 1980).

35. See Todd Gitlin, *Occupy Nation: The Roots, The Spirit, and the Promise of Occupy Wall Street* (New York: It Books, 2012).

36. David Folkenflik, "Tracking the Media's Eye On Occupy Wall Street," *All Things Considered* (NPR), October 13, 2011, http://www.npr.org/2011/10/13/141320149/tracking-the-medias-eye-on-occupy-wall-street.

37. Jürgen Habermas, *The Structural Transformation of the Public Sphere: An Inquiry into a Category of Bourgeois Society* (Cambridge, MA: MIT press, 1991).

38. An excellent accounting of this period can be found in Bennett, Lawrence, and Livingston, *When the Press Fails*.

39. Carlson, *On the Condition of Anonymity*.

40. Matt Carlson, "Gone, But Not Forgotten: Memories of Journalistic Deviance as Metajournalistic Discourse," *Journalism Studies* 15, no. 1 (2014): 33–47.

41. Fishman, *Manufacturing the News*.

42. Richard V. Ericson, Patricia Baranek, and Janet B. L. Chan, *Negotiating Control: A Study of News Sources* (Toronto: University of Toronto Press, 1989).

43. C. W. Anderson, "Journalism: Expertise, Authority, and Power in Democratic Life," in *The Media and Social Theory*, ed. David Hesmondhalgh and Jason Toynbee (New York: Routledge, 2008), 248–64.

44. David L. Eason, "On Journalistic Authority: The Janet Cooke Scandal," in *Media, Myths, and Narratives: Television and the Press*, ed. James W. Carey (Beverly Hills, CA: Sage, 1988), 205–27.

45. Joseph N. Cappella and Kathleen Hall Jamieson, *Spiral of Cynicism: The Press and the Public Good* (New York: Oxford University Press, 1997).

46. Reich, *Sourcing the News*.

47. Carlson, *On the Condition of Anonymity*.

48. Jeffrey P. Hermes et al., "Who Gets a Press Pass? Media Credentialing Practices in the United States," *Berkman Center Research Publication* 11, (2014), http://papers.ssrn.com/sol3/papers.cfm?abstract_id=2451239.

49. Or at least credentialing became a topic among news media watchers.

50. The full rejection letter is available online at http://sblog.s3.amazonaws.com/wp-content/uploads/2014/06/Untitled.pdf.

51. The struggles of journalistic autonomy in non-Western nations has been analyzed in Adriana Amado and Silvio Waisbord, "Divided We Stand: Blurred Boundaries in Argentine Journalism," in *Boundaries of Journalism: Professionalism, Practices and Participation*, ed. Matt Carlson and Seth C. Lewis (New York: Routledge, 2015), 51–67.

52. Tom Goldstein, "The Walls Erected by Traditional Media," *SCOTUSblog*, June 23, 2014, http://www.scotusblog.com/2014/06/the-walls-erected-by-traditional-media/.

53. See Schudson and Anderson, "Objectivity, Professionalism, and Truth Seeking."

54. Although we should be careful not to dichotomize this distinction. After all, many journalists are called upon for their expertise through news analysis. Also, journalists often interview other journalists as part of delivering news. See

Kevin G. Barnhurst, "The Makers of Meaning: National Public Radio and the New Long Journalism, 1980–2000," *Political Communication* 20, no. 1 (2003): 1–22.

55. See chapter 3 for more background on boundary work.

56. Editorial, "Give Scotusblog a Seat in Court," *New York Times*, last modified July 1, 2014, http://www.nytimes.com/2014/07/02/opinion/give-scotusblog-a-seat-in-court.html.

57. The ideas in this section are more fully developed in Matt Carlson, "Sources as News Producers," in *The Sage Handbook of Digital Journalism*, ed. Tamara Witschge et al. (Thousand Oaks, CA: Sage, 2016), 236–49.

58. Of course, we don't know how many of these followers are actual supporters, as opposed to inactive accounts or international users.

59. Daniel Kreiss, *Taking Our Country Back: The Crafting of Networked Politics from Howard Dean to Barack Obama* (New York: Oxford University Press, 2012).

60. Maxwell E. McCombs and Donald L. Shaw, "The Agenda-Setting Function of Mass Media," *Public Opinion Quarterly* 36, no. 2 (1972): 176–87.

61. Bruce A. Williams and Michael X. Delli Carpini, "Unchained Reaction: The Collapse of Media Gatekeeping and the Clinton-Lewinsky Scandal," *Journalism* 1, no. 1 (2000): 61–85.

62. Kathleen Hall Jamieson, *Dirty Politics: Deception, Distraction and Democracy* (New York: Oxford University Press, 1993).

63. Matthew Hindman, *The Myth of Digital Democracy* (Princeton, NJ: Princeton University Press, 2008).

64. Jennifer Stromer-Galley, *Presidential Campaigning in the Internet Age* (New York: Oxford University Press, 2014).

65. Alfred Hermida, "#JOURNALISM: Reconfiguring Journalism Research about Twitter, One Tweet at a Time," *Digital Journalism* 1, no. 3 (2013): 295–313.

66. See also Dhiraj Murthy, "Twitter: Microphone for the Masses?" *Media, Culture & Society* 33, no. 5 (2011): 779–89.

67. Aeron Davis, *Public Relations Democracy: Politics, Public Relations and the Mass Media in Britain* (Manchester: Manchester University Press, 2002).

68. This topic is taken up in chapter 7.

69. Reich, *Sourcing the News*; David Ryfe, *Can Journalism Survive? An Inside Look at American Newsrooms* (Cambridge: Polity, 2012).

70. Although journalists are often news sources. This is also the case for journalistic metacoverage.

71. Eason, "On Journalistic Authority."

1. Bruno Latour captures this in his pseudonymous essay. Jim Johnson, "Mixing Humans and Nonhumans Together: The Sociology of a Door-Closer," *Social Problems* 35, no. 3 (1988): 298–310.

2. Lisa Gitelman, *Always Already New: Media, History, and the Data of Culture* (Cambridge, MA: MIT Press, 2006).

3. This included a repair and service apparatus. Julian Edgerton Orr, *Talking About Machines: An Ethnography of a Modern Job* (Ithaca: Cornell University Press, 1996).

4. The use of the word *typo* for *typographical error* dates to 1892: http://www.etymonline.com/index.php?term=typo.

5. Lisa Gitelman, *Paper Knowledge: Toward a Media History of Documents* (Durham, NC: Duke University Press, 2014).

6. Gitelman, *Paper Knowledge*, 92.

7. Daniel J. Boorstin, *The Americans: The Democratic Experience* (New York: Vintage, 1974).

8. See Gitelman, *Paper Knowledge*, chapter 3, for a detailed analysis of Ellsberg's photocopying practices.

9. David Rudenstine, *The Day the Presses Stopped: A History of the Pentagon Papers Case* (Berkeley: University of California Press, 1996).

10. Elsewhere, the technology made it easier for samizdat literature and the facilitation of an underground press.

11. James Reston, "Why So Many 'Leaks'?" *New York Times*, January 14, 1972.

12. Of course, documents too are challenged, as CBS famously learned after it retracted a story on George W. Bush's Texas Air National Guard service based on documents many considered to be forgeries. See Matt Carlson, *On the Condition of Anonymity: Unnamed Sources and the Battle for Journalism* (Urbana: University of Illinois Press, 2011), 52–70.

13. In some sense, the recording potentialities of the photocopier mimic the discourse around contemporary recording devices. See Mike Ananny, "Creating Proper Distance through Networked Infrastructure: Examining Google Glass for Evidence of Moral, Journalistic Witnessing," in *Boundaries of Journalism: Professionalism, Practices and Participation*, ed. Matt Carlson and Seth C. Lewis (New York: Routledge, 2015), 83–100.

14. C. W. Anderson, Emily Bell, and Clay Shirky, *Post-Industrial Journalism: Adapting to the Present* (New York: Tow Center for Digital Journalism, 2012), http://towcenter.org/wp-content/uploads/2012/11/TOWCenter-Post_Industrial _Journalism.pdf /.

15. See Alex Jones, *Losing the News: The Future of the News That Feeds Democracy* (New York: Oxford University Press, 2009).

16. Dan Gillmor, *We the Media: Grassroots Journalism by the People, for the People* (Sebastopol, CA: O'Reilly Media, 2004).

17. Mark Briggs, *Entrepreneurial Journalism: How to Build What's Next for News* (Los Angeles: Sage / CQ Press, 2011).

18. Claire Wardle and Andrew Williams, "Beyond User-Generated Content: A Production Study Examining the Ways in Which UGC is Used at the BBC," *Media, Culture & Society* 32, no. 5 (2010): 781.

19. Pew Research Center, "In Changing News Landscape, Even Television Is Vulnerable: Trends in News Consumption: 1991–2002," September 27, 2012, http://www.people-press.org/2012/09/27/in-changing-news-landscape-even -television-is-vulnerable/.

20. Matthew Powers, "'In Forms That Are Familiar and Yet-to-Be Invented:' American Journalism and the Discourse of Technologically Specific Work," *Journal of Communication Inquiry* 36, no. 1 (2012): 24–43.

21. Barbie Zelizer, "Journalism's 'Last' Stand: Wirephoto and the Discourse of Resistance," *Journal of Communication* 45, no. 2 (1995): 78–92.

22. James W. Carey, "Technology and Ideology: The Case of the Telegraph," in *Communication as Culture: Essays on Media and Society* (London: Routledge, 1992), 155–77.

23. Bryan Pfaffenberger, "Technological Dramas," *Science, Technology and Human Values* 17, no. 3 (1992): 282–312; Josh Braun, "Going Over the Top: Online Television Distribution as Sociotechnical System," *Communication, Culture & Critique* 6, no. 3 (2013): 432–58.

24. See chapter 3 and Juliette De Maeyer and Florence Le Cam, "The Material Traces of Journalism: A Socio-Historical Approach to Online Journalism," *Digital Journalism* 3, no. 1 (2015): 85–100.

25. Powers, "In Forms that Are Familiar."

26. David Ryfe, *Can Journalism Survive? An Inside Look at American Newsrooms* (Cambridge: Polity, 2012); C. W. Anderson, *Rebuilding the News: Metropolitan Journalism in the Digital Age* (Philadelphia: Temple University Press, 2013); Pablo J. Boczkowski, *Digitizing the News: Innovation in Online Newspapers* (Cambridge, MA: MIT Press, 2004); Nikki Usher, *Making News at the New York Times* (Ann Arbor: University of Michigan Press, 2014).

27. Jane B. Singer, "Who Are These Guys? The Online Challenge to the Notion of Journalistic Professionalism," *Journalism* 4, no. 2 (2003), 139–63.

28. The term *media* also refers to institutions, the content they produce, and their technology.

29. Josh A. Braun, "Transparent Intermediaries: Building the Infrastructures of Connected Viewing," in *Connected Viewing: Selling, Streaming, and Sharing Media in the Digital Era*, ed. Jennifer Holt and Kevin Sanson (New York: Routledge, 2014).

30. Anderson, *Rebuilding the News*.

31. See C. W. Anderson and Juliette De Maeyer, "Introduction: Objects of Journalism and the News," *Journalism* 16, no. 1 (2015): 3–9.

32. Ibid., 4.

33. Scott Rodgers, "Foreign Objects? Web Content Management Systems, Journalistic Cultures and the Ontology of Software," *Journalism* 16, no. 1 (2015): 10–26. See also Anderson, *Rebuilding the News*.

34. Boczkowski, *Digitizing the News*.

35. R. B. Friedman, "On the Concept of Authority in Political Philosophy," in *Authority*, ed. Joseph Raz (New York: New York University Press), 70.

36. Kevin G. Barnhurst and John C. Nerone, *The Form of News: A History* (New York: Guilford Press, 2001); Barbie Zelizer, "Where Is the Author in American TV News? On the Construction and Presentation of Proximity, Authorship, and Journalistic Authority," *Semiotica* 80, nos. 1–2 (1990): 37–48.

37. Barbie Zelizer, "On 'Having Been There': 'Eyewitnessing' as a Journalistic Key Word," *Critical Studies in Media Communication* 24, no. 5 (2007): 408–28.

38. For these last two incidents, see Aniko Bodroghkozy, *Equal Time: Television and the Civil Rights Movement* (Urbana: University of Illinois Press, 2013); Todd Gitlin, *The Whole World Is Watching: Mass Media in the Making and Unmaking of the New Left* (Berkeley: University of California Press, 1980).

39. Zelizer, "On 'Having Been There,'" 425.

40. Stuart Allan, *Citizen Witnessing: Revisioning Journalism in Times of Crisis* (Cambridge: Polity, 2013); Kari Andén-Papadopoulos and Mervi Pantti, "Reimagining Crisis Reporting: Professional Ideology of Journalists and Citizen Eyewitness Images," *Journalism* 14, no. 7 (2013): 960–77; Jane B. Singer, "Who Are These Guys?"; Wardle and Williams, "Beyond User-Generated Content"; Seth C. Lewis, "The Tension Between Professional Control and Open Participation: Journalism and Its Boundaries," *Information, Communication & Society* 15, no. 6 (2012): 836–66.

41. Stan Horaczek, "How Many Photos Are Uploaded to the Internet Every Minute?" *Popular Photography*, May 27, 2013, http://www.popphoto.com/news/2013/05/how-many-photos-are-uploaded-to-internet-every-minute.

42. Zeynep Tufekci and Christopher Wilson, "Social Media and the Decision to Participate in Political Protest: Observations from Tahrir Square," *Journal of Communication* 62, no. 2 (2012): 363–79.

43. Ananny, "Creating Proper Distance," 83–100.

44. This section is adapted from Matt Carlson, "The Robotic Reporter: Automated Journalism and the Redefinition of Labor, Compositional Forms, and Journalistic Authority," *Digital Journalism* 3, no. 3 (2015): 416–31.

45. Ibid.

46. Anderson, Bell, and Shirky, *Post-Industrial Journalism*.

47. Matt Carlson and Nikki Usher, "News Startups as Agents of Innovation: For-Profit Digital News Startup Manifestos as Metajournalistic Discourse," *Digital Journalism* 4, no. 4 (2016): 563–81.

48. See http://www.narrativescience.com/quill.

49. See http://automatedinsights.com/wordsmith/.

50. Gini Dietrich, "Can Computers Write a Better Story than Humans?" Ragan.com, last modified June 18, 2012, http://www.ragan.com/Main/Articles/Can_computers_write_a_better_story_than_humans_45050.aspx.

51. Mark Harris, "Give Us the Final Score at Old Trafford, Robo Motty," *Sunday Times* (London), May 12, 2012.

52. David Holmes, "Your Tweets Are Why the Next Walter Cronkite Will Be a Robot," *Fast Company*, http://www.fastcompany.com/1840644/your-tweets-are-why-next-walter-cronkite-will-be-robot.

53. Farhad Manjoo, "Will Robots Steal Your Job?" *Slate*, http://www.slate.com/articles/technology/robot_invasion/2011/09/will_robots_steal_your_job_4.html.

54. Steve Lohr, "In Case You Wondered, a Real Human Being Wrote This Column," *New York Times*, September 11, 2011. This prediction turned out to be incorrect.

55. Arjen van Dalen, "The Algorithms behind the Headlines: How Machine-Written News Redefines the Core Skills of Human Journalists," *Journalism Practice* 6, nos. 5–6 (2012): 648–58.

56. Nicholas Carr, *The Glass Cage: Automation and Us* (New York: Norton, 2014).

57. Hamish McKenzie, "Four Big Takeaways from Pew's 'State of the Media' Report," *Pando Daily*, March 18, 2013, http://pando.com/2013/03/18/four-big-takeaways-from-pews-state-of-the-media-report/.

58. Steven Levy, "Can an Algorithm Write a Better News Story than a Human Reporter?" *Wired*, April 24, 2012, https://www.wired.com/2012/04/can-an-algorithm-write-a-better-news-story-than-a-human-reporter/.

59. James W. Carey, "The Dark Continent of American Journalism," in *Reading the News: A Pantheon Guide to Popular Culture*, ed. Robert K. Manoff and Michael Schudson (New York: Pantheon, 1986), 146–96.

60. Michael Schudson, *Discovering the News: A Social History of American Newspapers* (New York: Basic Books, 1978).

61. This is true even as news stories have tended to shift to a more analytical style. See Katherine Fink and Michael Schudson. "The Rise of Contextual Journalism, 1950s–2000s," *Journalism* 15, no. 1 (2014): 3–20.

62. Elizabeth S. Bird and Robert W. Dardenne, "Myth, Chronicle, and Story," in *Media, Myths, and Narratives: Television and the Press*, ed. James W. Carey (Newbury Park, CA: Sage Publications, 1988), 67–86; Karin Wahl-Jorgensen, "The Strategic Ritual of Emotionality: A Case Study of Pulitzer Prize-winning Articles," *Journalism* 14, no. 1 (2013): 129–45.

63. Frank Pasquale, *The Black Box Society: The Secret Algorithms That Control Money and Information*. (Cambridge, MA: Harvard University Press, 2015).

64. Tarleton Gillespie, "The Relevance of Algorithms," in *Media Technologies: Essays on Communication, Materiality, and Society*, ed. Tarleton Gillespie, Pablo Boczkowski, and Kirsten Foot (Cambridge, MA: MIT Press, 2014), 167–94.

65. Langdon Winner, "Do Artifacts Have Politics?" *Daedalus* 109, no. 1 (1980), 121–36. For algorithms specifically, see Zeynep Tufekci, "What Happens to #Ferguson Affects Ferguson: Net Neutrality, Algorithmic Filtering and Ferguson," *Message*, August 14, 2014, https://medium.com/message/ferguson-is-also-a-net-neutrality-issue-6d2f3db51eb0.

66. C. W. Anderson, "Towards a Sociology of Computational and Algorithmic Journalism," *New Media & Society* 15, no. 7 (2013): 1005–21; Philip M. Napoli, "Automated Media: An Institutional Theory Perspective on Algorithmic Media Production and Consumption," *Communication Theory* 24, no. 3 (2014): 340–60.

67. Gillespie, "The Relevance of Algorithms," 168.

68. Eli Pariser, *The Filter Bubble: How the New Personalized Web Is Changing What We Read and How We Think* (New York: Penguin Books, 2011).

69. For the case of Google, see Siva Vaidhyanathan, *The Googlization of Everything (and Why We Should Worry)* (Berkeley: University of California Press, 2012).

70. Nicholas Diakopoulos, "Algorithmic Accountability: Journalistic Investigation of Computational Power Structures," *Digital Journalism* 3, no. 3 (2015): 398–415.

71. John Sepulvado, "Could a Computer Write This Story?" *CNN*, May 11, 2012, http://www.cnn.com/2012/05/11/tech/innovation/computer-assisted-writing/.

72. Samantha Goldberg, "Robot Writers and the Digital Age," *American Journalism Review*, November 25, 2013, http://ajr.org/2013/11/25/computer-might-replace-robot-journalism-digital-age/.

73. Manjoo, "Will Robots Steal Your Job?"

74. Wahl-Jorgensen, "The Strategic Ritual of Emotionality."

75. Matt Carlson, "Automated Journalism: A Posthuman Future for Digital News?" in *The Routledge Companion to Digital Journalism Studies*, ed. Bob Franklin and Scott Eldridge II (London: Routledge, forthcoming).

76. Patricia L. Dooley, *The Technology of Journalism: Cultural Agents, Cultural Icons* (Evanston, IL: Northwestern University Press, 2007).

7. CHALLENGING JOURNALISTIC AUTHORITY: THE ROLE OF MEDIA CRITICISM

1. Katherine Fung, "Obama to Barnard Graduates: Don't Listen to Media," *Huffington Post*, May 14, 2012, http://www.huffingtonpost.com/2012/05/14/obama -barnard-commencement-media_n_1515555.html.

2. This definition is meant to include a wide range of symbolic activities, in contrast with conceptualizations of media criticism that include only scholarly critique.

3. James W. Carey, "Journalism and Criticism: The Case of an Undeveloped Profession," *The Review of Politics* 36, no. 2 (1974): 227–49; Tanni Haas, "Mainstream News Media Self-Criticism: A Proposal for Future Research," *Critical Studies in Media Communication* 23, no. 4 (2006): 350–55.

4. Of course, journalists are not unified in their understandings of their practices; much media criticism emerges within the community through struggles over what journalists should or should not be doing.

5. C. W. Anderson, Emily Bell, and Clay Shirky, *Post-Industrial Journalism: Adapting to the Present* (New York: Tow Center for Digital Journalism, 2012), http://towcenter.org/wp-content/uploads/2012/11/TOWCenter-Post_Indus trial_Journalism.pdf /.

6. David Domingo, Pere Masip, and Irene Costera Meijer, "Tracing Digital News Networks: Towards an Integrated Framework of the Dynamics of News Production, Circulation and Use," *Digital Journalism* 3, no. 1 (2014): 1–15.

7. Daniel C. Hallin and Paolo Mancini: *Comparing Media Systems: Three Models of Media and Politics* (Cambridge: Cambridge University Press, 2004); Steven Maras, *Objectivity in Journalism* (Cambridge: Polity, 2013).

8. Matt Carlson, "Media Criticism as Competitive Discourse: Defining Reportage of the Abu Ghraib Scandal," *Journal of Communication Inquiry* 33 no. 3 (2009): 258–77; Robert L. Handley, "What Media Critics Reveal about Journalism: Palestine Media Watch and US News Media," *Journal of Communication Inquiry* 36, no. 2 (2012), 131–48.

9. Haas, "Mainstream News Media Self-Criticism."

10. See http://www.mrc.org/about.

11. Carlson, "Media Criticism as Competitive Discourse."

12. See http://honestreporting.com/about/.

13. See Simon Plosker, "NY Times Finally Covers Palestinian Incitement," *Honest-Reporting*, January 7, 2014, http://honestreporting.com/ny-times-finally-covers -palestinian-incitement/.

14. Matt Carlson, "Keeping Watch on the Gates: Media Criticism as Advocatory Pressure," in *Gatekeeping in Transition*, ed. Tim Vos and Francois Heinderyckx (New York: Routledge, 2015), 163–79.

15. Granted, media criticism certainly takes place interpersonally when people discuss the news.

16. Sarah Sobieraj and Jeffrey M. Berry, "From Incivility to Outrage: Political Discourse in Blogs, Talk Radio, and Cable News," *Political Communication* 28, no. 1 (2011): 19–41.

17. Michel Foucault, *Abnormal: Lectures at the Collège de France* (New York: Picador, 2003).

18. Peter Dahlgren, introduction to *Journalism and Popular Culture*, ed. Peter Dahlgren and Colin Sparks (London: Sage, 1992), 1–23.

19. See chapter 5 for how these critiques emerge around the subject of news sources.

20. Dahlgren, introduction to *Journalism and Popular Culture*.

21. Carlson, "Media Criticism as Competitive Discourse."

22. Kathleen Hall Jamieson and Joseph N. Cappella, *Echo Chamber: Rush Limbaugh and the Conservative Media Establishment* (New York: Oxford University Press, 2008).

23. Ibid., 161

24. Steven Maras, *Objectivity in Journalism* (Cambridge: Polity, 2013).

25. All quotations from the episode are taken from the transcript provided by the Lexis-Nexis database.

26. For McCarthyism and the press, see Barbie Zelizer, "Journalists as Interpretive Communities," *Critical Studies in Media Communication* 10, no. 3 (1993): 219–37. For Vietnam, see Daniel Hallin, *The 'Uncensored War': The Media and Vietnam* (New York: Oxford University Press, 1986).

27. Matt Carlson, *On the Condition of Anonymity: Unnamed Sources and the Battle for Journalism* (Urbana: University of Illinois Press, 2011).

28. Matthew Biedlingmaier, "Hannity vs. Hannity: Is He, or Is He Not, a 'Journalist'?" http://mediamatters.org/research/2008/10/09/hannity-vs-hannity-is-he-or-is-he-not-a-journal/145571.

29. See chapter 4.

30. Allen Salkin, "One Part Mr. Peanut, One Part Hipster Chic," *New York Times*, March 6, 2014.

31. Margaret Sullivan, "Trend-Spotting, with Wink at Mr. Peanut," *New York Times*, March 23, 2014.

32. Ben Yakas, "NY Times Gets Reflective about Their Ridiculous Trend Pieces," *Gothamist*, March 23, 2014, http://gothamist.com/2014/03/23/ny_times_gets_reflective_about_trends.php.

33. Karin Wahl-Jorgensen, "The Normative-Economic Justification for Public Discourse: Letters to the Editor as a 'Wide Open' Forum," *Journalism & Mass Communication Quarterly* 79, no. 1 (2002): 121–33.

34. Arjen Van Dalen and Mark Deuze, "Readers' Advocates or Newspapers' Ambassadors? Newspaper Ombudsmen in the Netherlands," *European Journal of Communication* 21, no. 4 (2006): 457–75; James S. Ettema and Theodore L. Glasser, "Public Accountability or Public Relations? Newspaper Ombudsmen Define Their Role," *Journalism & Mass Communication Quarterly* 64, no. 1 (1987): 3–12.

35. Axel Bruns, *Blogs, Wikipedia, Second Life, and Beyond: From Production to Produsage* (New York: Peter Lang, 2008).

36. For a review, see Eugenia Mitchelstein and Pablo J. Boczkowski, "Between Tradition and Change: A Review of Recent Research on Online News Production," *Journalism* 10, no. 5 (2009): 562–86.

37. Tim P. Vos, Stephanie Craft, and Seth Ashley, "New Media, Old Criticism: Bloggers' Press Criticism and the Journalistic Field," *Journalism* 13, no. 7 (2012): 850–68.

38. Susanne Fengler, "From Media Self-Regulation to 'Crowd-Criticism': Media Accountability in the Digital Age," *Central European Journal of Communication* 9, (2012): 175–89. See also Anne Kaun, "'I Really Don't Like Them!'—Exploring Citizens' Media Criticism," *European Journal of Cultural Studies* 17, no. 5 (2014): 489–506.

39. Henry Jenkins makes this argument in Henry Jenkins, *Convergence Culture: Where Old and New Media Collide* (New York: New York University Press, 2006).

40. Scott Rosenberg, *Say Everything: How Blogging Began, What It's Becoming, and Why It Matters* (New York: Three Rivers Press, 2010).

41. Vos, Craft, and Ashley, "New Media, Old Criticism."

42. Kevin G. Barnhurst and John C. Nerone, *The Form of News: A History* (New York: Guilford Press, 2001).

43. Carlson, "Keeping Watch on the Gates"; Handley, "What Media Critics Reveal about Journalism."

44. Matt Carlson, "Embedded Links, Embedded Meanings: Social Media Commentary and News Sharing as Mundane Media Criticism," *Journalism Studies* 17, no. 7 (2016), 915–24.

45. Sue Robinson, "Redrawing Borders from Within: Commenting on News Stories as Boundary Work," in *Boundaries of Journalism: Professionalism, Practices, and Participation*, ed. Matt Carlson and Seth C. Lewis (New York: Routledge, 2015), 152–68.

46. Annika Bergström and Ingela Wadbring, "Beneficial Yet Crappy: Journalists and Audiences on Obstacles and Opportunities in Reader Comments," *European Journal of Communication* 30, no. 2 (2015), 137–51; Bill Reader, "Free Press vs. Free Speech? The Rhetoric of 'Civility' in Regard to Anonymous Online

Comments," *Journalism & Mass Communication Quarterly* 89, no. 3 (2012): 495–513.

47. Robinson, "Redrawing Borders from Within."
48. See Vos, Craft, and Ashley, "New Media, Old Criticism."
49. This is the crux of media literacy. See William G. Christ and James W. Potter, "Media Literacy, Media Education, and the Academy," *Journal of Communication* 48, no. 1 (1998): 5–15.
50. Anderson, Bell, and Shirky, *Post-Industrial Journalism.*
51. Glen Feighery, "Conversation and Credibility: Broadening Journalism Criticism through Public Engagement," *Journal of Mass Media Ethics* 26, no. 2 (2011): 158–75.

CONCLUSION: THE POLITICS OF JOURNALISTIC AUTHORITY

1. In the 2014, PEJ was renamed the Pew Research Center's Journalism Project.
2. Project for Excellence in Journalism, *State of the News Media Executive Summary*, http://www.stateofthemedia.org/files/2011/01/execsum.pdf.
3. This murkiness also could be found within news organizations, as Pablo Boczkowski found in his study of early efforts by newspapers to go online. Pablo J. Boczkowski, *Digitizing the News: Innovation in Online Newspapers* (Cambridge, MA: MIT Press, 2004).
4. It is a wonderful coincidence that 2004 marked the first *State of the News Media* report and the publication of Boczkowski's *Digitizing the News.*
5. Meanwhile, during the same decade, digital advertising revenues increased from $1.5 billion to $3.5 billion for a gain of $1 for every $15 lost in print advertising. Pew Research Center, *State of the Media 2015*, April 29, 2015, http://www.journalism.org/2015/04/29/newspapers-fact-sheet/.
6. For a useful overview combining long- and short-term conditions, see David M. Ryfe, *Can Journalism Survive? An Inside Look at American Newsrooms* (Malden, MA: Polity, 2013).
7. Marcel Broersma, "Journalism as Performative Discourse: The Importance of Form and Style in Journalism," in *Journalism and Meaning-Making: Reading the Newspaper,* ed. Verica Rupar (Cresskill, NJ: Hampton Press, 2010), 15–35.
8. See Bruce Lincoln, *Authority: Construction and Corrosion* (Chicago: University of Chicago Press, 1995).
9. R. B. Friedman, "On the Concept of Authority in Political Philosophy," in *Authority,* ed. Joseph Raz (New York: New York University Press), 76.
10. Peter Dahlgren, introduction to *Journalism and Popular Culture,* ed. Peter Dahlgren and Colin Sparks (London: Sage, 1992), 1–23.

11. James T. Hamilton, *All the News That's Fit to Sell: How the Market Transforms Information into News* (Princeton, NJ: Princeton University Press, 2004); John H. McManus, *Market-Driven Journalism: Let the Citizen Beware?* (Thousand Oaks, CA: Sage, 1994).

12. Edson C. Tandoc Jr., "Journalism Is Twerking? How Web Analytics Is Changing the Process of Gatekeeping," *New Media & Society* 14, no. 4 (2014): 559–75.

13. Mark Briggs, *Entrepreneurial Journalism: How to Build What's Next for News* (Thousand Oaks, CA: Sage / CQ Press, 2011).

14. C. W. Anderson, *Rebuilding the News: Metropolitan Journalism in the Digital Age* (Philadelphia: Temple University, 2013); Andrew Chadwick, *The Hybrid Media System: Politics and Power* (Oxford: Oxford University Press, 2013); Sue Robinson, "Journalism as Process: The Organizational Implications of Participatory Online News," *Journalism & Communication Monographs* 13, no. 3 (2011): 137–210.

15. This is certainly true for journalism studies, with its particular modes of writing, argumentation, evidence, and interpretive communities.

16. This accounting is partly derived from Todd Gitlin, "A Surfeit of Crises: Circulation, Revenue, Attention, Authority, and Deference," in *Will the Last Reporter Please Turn Out the Lights: The Collapse of Journalism and What Can Be Done to Fix It*, ed. Robert W. McChesney and Victor Pickard (New York: New Press, 2011), 91–102.

17. Friedman, "On the Concept of Authority."

18. Pamela J. Shoemaker and Timothy Vos, *Gatekeeping Theory* (New York: Routledge, 2009).

19. Robert M. Entman, "Framing: Toward Clarification of a Fractured Paradigm," *Journal of Communication* 43, no. 4 (1993): 51–58.

20. Maxwell E. McCombs and Donald L. Shaw, "The Agenda-Setting Function of Mass Media," *Public Opinion Quarterly* 36, no. 2 (1972): 176–87.

21. Stuart Hall et al., *Policing the Crisis: Mugging, the State and Law and Order* (London: Macmillan, 1978).

22. Kevin G. Barnhurst and John C. Nerone, *The Form of News: A History* (New York: Guilford Press, 2001).

23. Nikki Usher, *Making News at the New York Times* (Ann Arbor: University of Michigan Press, 2014).

24. Mark Deuze, "What Is Journalism? Professional Identity and Ideology of Journalists Reconsidered," *Journalism* 6, no. 4 (2005): 442–64.

25. Jane B. Singer, "Out of Bounds: Professional Norms as Boundary Markers," in *Boundaries of Journalism: Professionalism, Practices and Participation*, ed. Matt Carlson and Seth C. Lewis (New York: Routledge, 2015), 21–36.

26. Matt Carlson, "The Many Boundaries of Journalism," in *Boundaries of Journalism*, ed. Carlson and Lewis, 1–18.

27. Matthew Hindman, *The Myth of Digital Democracy* (Princeton, NJ: Princeton University Press, 2008).

28. Matt Carlson, "When News Sites Go Native: Redefining the Advertising-Editorial Divide in Response to Native Advertising," *Journalism* 15, no. 7 (2015): 849–65.

29. Eli Pariser, *The Filter Bubble: How the New Personalized Web Is Changing What We Read and How We Think* (New York: Penguin Press, 2011).

30. C. W. Anderson, Emily Bell, and Clay Shirky, *Post-Industrial Journalism: Adapting to the Present* (New York: Tow Center for Digital Journalism, 2012), http://towcenter.org/wp-content/uploads/2012/11/TOWCenter-Post_Industrial_Journalism.pdf/.

31. The lack of a secure revenue model necessitates that new outlets—and existing ones as well—experiment with new forms. This scramble to build sustainable digital revenues serves as a reminder that journalistic models contain within them business models. Even journalism's detachment from the business side was itself a strategy of creating a market desirable for advertisers.

Index

Jarvis, Jeff, 117
Jefferson, Thomas, 35
Jenkins, Henry, 23
Jennings, Peter, 116
Jones, Alex S., 4
journalism: and coverage of grief,
71–72; as cultural production,
53–54, 69–72, 77; definition of, 6;
definitional control of, 76–77, 88,
167, 192; diversity of, 18–22; and
entrepreneurship, 146, 187;
expectations of, 7; narratives about,
77–79; norms of, 5, 16; objects of,
150–52, 162; as postindustrial, 20,
37; and the state, 187; technology
and, 145, 146–50; use of documents
in, 144
journalistic authority: as analytical
tool, 24; and autonomy, 38; and
boundary work, 85–88; and
collective emotions, 70–73; as
conceptual intervention, 23–24, 188;
definition of, 3–4, 13, 182–83; effect
of digital media on, 137, 149, 158–59;
and form, 51–67, 73–74, 184; of
images, 67–69; and journalist-
audience relationship, 99, 115–16,
118–19, 185–86; and media criticism,
178–79; as mediated, 52–53, 184; and
metajournalistic discourse, 78,
91–93, 164, 174, 177, 184–85, 186–87;
objects of, 151–52; politics of,
189–92; as privileged term, 4–9; and
professionalism, 30–33, 47–49;
recognition of, 99–101, 119–21;
relational approach to, 7, 13–22,
182–88; and reliance on sources,
124, 127–29, 131–33, 138, 141–42, 186;
research on, 3, 4; role of the
researcher in, 196–98; and

self-regulation, 84; and skepticism,
110, 120, 179; as stasis, 147–48; as
structured by survey questions,
112–16; and technology, 151–52, 160,
161–62, 186; and witnessing, 152–54
journalistic professionalism, 2, 14,
29–49, 149, 183–84, 192, 193; as
community making, 34–37;
contemporary challenges to, 46–47;
difficulties of, 31–32; as disciplining,
36–37; and objectivity, 40–42; and
relationship to storytelling, 56–57;
as separate from form, 53, 61, 69–73
journalists: and adoption of new
technologies, 148–49; as
authoritative chroniclers, 5; and
beats, 125–26; collective memory of,
89–90, 144; as deviant, 82–85; as an
interpretive community, 89; as
knowledge producers, 40–46;
performance of, 105–9, 110, 113–15,
120; and relationship with sources,
123–27, 131–33; as watchdogs, 106,
114–15, 119

Keller, Bill, 1–2, 20
Kennedy, John F., 4, 71, 89
Kissinger, Henry, 144
Kitch, Carolyn, 71
Klein, Ezra, 97
knowledge: control over, 11–12, 16–19,
183, 191; news sources' impact on,
124, 127–130; and professionalism,
40–46, 86; relationship to form, 51,
59. *See also* expertise
Kovach, Bill, 5
Kuhn, Thomas, 83

Lane, Charles, 83–84
Langdon, Loup, 67

Williams, Michael, 17
witnessing, 13–14, 69, 152–54, 162; by
    citizens, 20, 40
Witschge, Tamara, 46
Woodward, Bob, 90

Xerox, 143–44

YouTube, 139

Zelizer, Barbie, 4, 5, 79, 89, 148, 221n44